EXPATRIATE

James M. Minifie
EXPATRIATE

Introduction by Leland Stowe
L'Envoi by Hugh Keenleyside

Macmillan of Canada
Toronto

To my god-daughter,
Susan Margaret Lightbody

ISBN 0-7705-1323-9

Printed in Canada for
The Macmillan Company of Canada Limited
70 Bond Street, Toronto M5B 1X3

ACKNOWLEDGEMENTS

Expatriate, the second volume of James M. Minifie's memoirs, begun in *Homesteader,* was started early in 1973. Soon after the first draft of the manuscript was completed there was a decline in my husband's health, strength, and vitality. It soon became apparent that he would not be able to complete the rewriting of segments of the manuscript that required elaboration; so we agreed that I would take over this work. During a series of interviews, some taped, I obtained additional information and, under his supervision, began the editorial revisions. On June 13, 1974, James died; the manuscript was still unfinished, but after a lapse of six weeks, I returned to it.

In the months after my husband's death I received invaluable aid from many people — relatives, friends, colleagues, and others unknown to me personally. To my mother, Mrs. W. R. V. Wadsworth, I give my love for sustaining me through many weeks.

Special thanks are expressed to James M. Minifie, Jr., my stepson; to Eric A. Minifie, my brother-in-law, whose privately published memoir, *I Remember,* provided a picture of the Minifie family life during the Depression; and to my late husband's sister-in-law, Mrs. Richard Minifie.

Assistance was also received from Miss Denise Abbey, Maple Valley, Washington; Mr. and Mrs. Lawrence Fieldhouse and Albert W. Reid, Victoria, British Columbia; Whitelaw Reid, Purchase, New York; C. Knowlton Nash and William Hogg, both of the Canadian Broadcasting Corporation, Toronto. In addition, the editorial advice of Hugh Kane, vice-chairman, The Macmillan Company of Canada Limited, and of Kenneth A. McVey, executive editor, has been greatly valued.

A debt of gratitude is owed to Leland Stowe, Ann Arbor, Michigan; to Dr. and Mrs. Hugh L. Keenleyside and Mr. and Mrs. K. Ivor Worrall, all of Victoria, British Columbia; and to Dr. William Epstein, New York City. These friends provided encouragement and aid, without which this book would not have been completed.

Thanks are also due to officials of the Public Archives of Canada for allowing me to retain my husband's working papers for as long as they were needed.

Warmest appreciation is given to all these friends and to many others who made contributions.

GILLIAN WADSWORTH MINIFIE

FOREWORD

Near the end of my fourth year as Paris Correspondent of the *New York Herald Tribune* I was informed that a newsman from the cable desk would shortly be sent over to become my new assistant: his name, James MacDonald Minifie. In he strode one Parisian July day — a sturdily built incarnation of controlled energy, clean-cut and with the vice-like grip of the hand that immediately conveys forthrightness and sincerity. Two other things about him registered with equal force — the penetrating directness of his gray-blue eyes and the modulated resonance of his British-accented speech. He exuded an unquenchable zest for life, an innate gentility, and a kind of natural, outdoor heartiness (wafted directly, as I later discovered, from his boy-hood years on Saskatchewan's prairies). During the first day's shoptalk and swapping of ideas I quickly came to realize that we were indeed lucky; for in our intimate, three-person news bureau a misfit could create highly erosive irritations, disruptions, and problems. No fear of those from this prairie-reared gentleman.

Don, as friends all knew him, promptly proved to be remarkably modest and unassuming despite his exceptional breadth of knowledge. From the outset he displayed an unflagging zeal for hard work, backed by a driving compulsion for thorough investigation of any given event or topic. Tackling any subject—from the ideological tangles and contradictions of the dozen or more French political parties to the masked tentacles and financial complexities of Europe's Steel Cartel — he dug and dug like a frenetic gopher. His news despatches were buttressed with every relevant fact he could possibly unearth; and upon extracting stark evidence of some political or commercial chicanery Don would chortle with unrestrained glee. Yet he never flaunted personal achievements of any kind.

Nor did our equally industrious bureau-mate, Russian-born Sonia Tomara (who was virtually faultless in writing and speaking five languages), with whom we constituted the indisputably most congenial and, I firmly believe, most effective news-team trio of my journalistic observation. Almost miraculously, and for five wonderful years, we worked in the closest collaboration — equally zealous and utterly compatible, as firmly linked in friendship and mutual trust as by professional dedication. Those, indeed, were the golden years; and without Don they never could have been what they always remain in memory—of 24-carat quality.

Amidst epidemics of governmental crises, monetary devaluations, right-wing and left-wing plots, street riots, insurrections in Spain, and assorted challenges to the meeting of deadlines at top speed, Don remained imperturbable. Upon occasion the imbecilities of French bureaucracy provoked his imaginative invective; yet during these five years, while myopic European compromisers were heedlessly sowing the dragon's teeth of war, I cannot recall that he ever once truly lost his temper.

Perhaps those hard-grubbing, poverty-battling prairie years primarily accounted for Don's down-to-earth realism, especially in assessing people and cultures, issues and dogmas, false fronts and shibboleths — all of his consistently keen perceptions of mortals' characters and motivations, their charades and self-illusions. Yet he never took refuge in that corrosively numbing, self-deceiving cynicism that paralyzes the sensitivities and vision of too many reporters. He simply insisted upon seeing people's actions and artifices for the self-serving masquerades that they so often are.

Don's humor was entirely his own — low-keyed, slightly sardonic, sharply honed in expression, and barbed with verities. Philosophical by nature and blessed with perspective, he surveyed the human comedy with an appreciative glint in his eyes, secretly pleased at seeing through people's pretensions, and equally gratified at having accurately discerned what they really were and what they were up to. Politicians with axes to grind might fool others; but however affable and disarming, they rarely fooled him.

A combination of deft humor, uncompromising realism, and extreme conscientiousness are seldom found within a single person. But Don Minifie was endowed with these qualities in full measure; none greater than his commitment to personal and professional obligations. I am compelled to cite two incidents that you will encounter later on in these pages. When the sirens warned of another assault by the Luftwaffe on wartime London, Don, adhering to rigid rules, dashed down to the Savoy Hotel's subterranean shelter. Then he recalled that he had left the lights on in his room — a potential beacon for German pilots. Back he went, five stories up, with bombs already falling, and switched off the lights; as he turned, an explosion blasted him across the room. Blood gushed down his face; a shrapnel splinter had knifed deeply into one of his eyes, so destructively that the eye later had to be removed. Rather than leave the betraying lights gleaming until the raid was over, he had sacrificed a part of his vision — with never an uttered regret.

Some years later he was visiting a U.S. Navy aircraft carrier that was equipped with an innovative "short-run" plane-catapulting device. Short-run meant exactly that; as abbreviated a take-off as top-grade pilots could manage, and as tricky an operation as shoving a glider into a gale. The fact that no reporter had yet defied the laws of gravity in this maniacal fashion inevitably generated a determination in Don to do so. But the ship's reluctant top brass first had to be persuaded. Typically, Don reports what ensued with classic understatement: "So I smiled with my good eye, and stared the Chief Petty Officer down with my glass eye." And out he shot on a careening short-run take-off and a near crash landing, "to find myself something of a notoriety," he concluded (without elucidating the risks involved), "a cross between a hero and a fool, with the accent on the latter. However, I comforted myself with the reflection that the next time I wrote about carrier operations I would know what I was saying." These key words are the motivation of all top-ranking correspondents: "Next time…I would know what I was saying", as I know from personal experience.

Such a man is worth knowing; and Don Minifie's reportorial odyssey and his personal evolution, as recorded here, are richly worth knowing. You will participate in his adventures as an overseas reporter in peace and war, and in his adventures in perceiving and understanding—the inner growth and maturing of one of the true elite among English-speaking foreign correspondents. But you'll be wise to read thoughtfully and between the lines in order to learn some of the most important things about him—such as the qualities and the values that made both the outstanding reporter and the exceptional man.

Among one hundred or more of my multinational news-media colleagues Don was also the epitome of personal loyalty. Unshakably loyal to good friends, he unvaryingly maintained equal fidelity to the highest standards and ethics of our journalistic profession.

Similarly, loyalty to Canada, to its people, and to his Canadian background remained Don's magnetic needle to such a degree that in actual fact he never became, or could become, an expatriate in the dictionary definition of the word. He was quite incapable of abandoning or withdrawing from allegiance to the land that he deeply loved. Having been swept along by the experiences and perceptions in these pages, the reader finds that Don's essence emerges unmistakably: the ever-dependable, the questing explorer, and the discerner of men's deeds and follies—a man whose zest for living and whose loyalties remain as inerodable as the granite core of his Canadian Rockies. Surely many of those qualities and values were rooted in the prairies of his boyhood Saskatchewan. His maple leaf was lived in the earning.

LELAND STOWE
Ann Arbor, Mich.

CHAPTER
ONE

When I reached Oxford in the autumn (Michaelmas term) of 1923 to begin a three-year residence at the ancient university's Oriel College, my arrival crowned an academic career at the University of Saskatchewan cut short only by my selection as Saskatchewan's Rhodes Scholar for that year. Had I realized that almost half a century would pass before I returned to Canada as a permanent resident, the glow of satisfaction engendered by the event might have been diminished. Despite British birth, I had spent my formative years on the prairies where my mother, a younger brother, and I had emigrated in 1912 to join my father, who had been homesteading near Vanguard, Saskatchewan, for three years. Apart from a couple of years in the Canadian Army overseas, I had remained on the family farm, at Malvern Link School, and at Regina College, and I considered myself a Canadian. In the forty-five years I spent as an expatriate, roaming the world on both British and American passports, before I retired in 1968 to Victoria, Vancouver Island, where I became a fully-fledged Canadian citizen, Canada always remained my country.

At the time of my arrival in Oxford, Oriel College was warming itself in the glow of its approaching seicentenary. King Edward II had founded it as Saint Mary the Virgin's house in 1323. The founder's military activities were overshadowed by those of his father and of his son, while his civilian employments were chronicled by hostile quills. That did not deter his foundation from proudly incorporating the royal arms in its own blazon —

1

gules three leopards, or, in a border engrailed argent; and generation after generation of Oriel men incorporated in their routine devotions daily prayers for his soul, and for that of the College's co-founder, Adam de Brome, whose claims to divine forgiveness were possibly less pronounced, but more urgent.

Picture-postcards had made Oriel well-known outside its immediate circle of students, although its front quadrangle owed more to the tower of Merton College Chapel peeping over its roof than to its own crumbling Jacobean gables, or to the ornate hall entrance, proclaiming REGNANTE CAROLO in stone letters below what were believed to be effigies of Charles I, his queen, Henrietta Maria, and St. Mary the Virgin herself. The Second Quad reinforced its claims to the picturesque with the blazing autumnal colours of Virginia creeper, which covered the façade of its Augustan library until it was discovered that the vine was eating into the soft stone so fast that preservation of one or the other became an urgent alternative. Oriel chose to preserve the library, although removal of the creeper revealed an unsightly psoriasis of the walls, columns, and pilasters, distracting attention from their classic proportions and balance.

The Third Quad, to which I, as a newcomer, had been assigned, was an architectural hodge-podge. The High Street side was fully occupied by an architectural misdemeanour in local stone, committed by one alumnus and financed by another—no less than Cecil Rhodes himself, my benefactor. It housed, uncomfortably, a handful of undergraduates with no better claims to consideration, and two outstanding dons: W. D. Ross, who subsequently became a knight and Provost, and Marcus Niebuhr Tod, a gentle soul who remained an esquire but made a name in archeological transcriptions that reflected credit on the College at least equal to that of Beau Brummel, Queen Anne, or Sir Walter Raleigh, whose full-length portraits hung in the Hall.

An ornate Victorian-Gothic window marked the former rooms of Charles Oman, whose historical talents had endowed Oriel with a reputation as a haunt of Clio. Oman had left long before my time, but Oriel still basked in his glory. I enjoyed, or rather occupied, damp, ground-floor quarters below his, which had a quiet side-exit on to Oriel Street. This, however, was locked at six o'clock every evening, so that I was still subject to the exactions of Mr. Bishop, the Chief Porter, and Bough, his assistant, who collected their tuppences and sixpences at the main gate from night-owls who had missed the nine- and ten-o'clock bells pealed out by Big Tom in Christ Church, but were not bold or agile enough to climb over the wall, topped with broken glass, which guarded Oriel's sanctuary on the Magpie Lane side.

I left my battered portmanteau in charge of Bough as I set out to find my rooms, following Mr. Bishop's voluble but confusing directions. Bough provided me with a black fustian gown, of the standard pattern appropriate to Gentlemen Commoners (for Rhodes Scholars were not admitted by Oriel to the long gown and to other privileges enjoyed by its own Scholars). It was garnished with the cigarette burns and grease spots essential to its claims to authenticity. I wore it around my neck like a muffler, in what my first glance at the front quad assured me was the accepted fashion, and set out for "my rooms". The terms had romantic connotations which I associated with Sherlock Holmes's "rooms" in Baker Street. Some arcane principle had dictated that they should be numbered 16; half a century later the number was unchanged, although my name had been supplanted by a stranger's.

I opened the door of No. 16 with tense expectation, and entered a dark cavern with greenish wallpaper and pieces of heavy Victorian furniture which in a few years would be classed as "genuine, priceless antiques" but at that time were merely old-fashioned odds and ends assembled by my predecessor. They afforded a minimum of ease or comfort. The room smelled dank and the feeble fireplace made little impact on its Victorian chill. The adjoining bedroom had a simple iron bedstead and no fireplace, but a bath below the High Street front. This facility was a great mercy which put me far ahead of many freshmen who had no running water in their rooms, but had to dart, shuddering, across the quad and down to the baths in pajamas and slippers, whenever they could brave the elements.

3

As soon as I had taken off my trench coat I wandered back to the Second Quad to make my number with the Dean. He was a cherubic cleric in a dark suit and dog-collar, who looked as if he had just concluded a communion service with a sip of old tawny port from the chalice. His manner was cool; it implied regret that I was reading English Language and Literature, rather than History or *Literae Humaniores*. I might expiate that oversight by "attempting" Divinity, which he himself would tutor. For English he referred me to Percy Simpson, with a warning that Ben Jonson, although he was Mr. Simpson's speciality, was not necessarily the beginning and end of English writing. As a general guide, he referred me to G. N. Clark, who would be my "moral tutor". I gathered that I should approach him also with some scepticism, since his assessment of history enshrined the seventeenth century with a radiance which he might modify after he had completed his book on that period. In the meantime I would find "Nobby" Clark a trusty mentor for such problems as registering with the university, using the Bodleian Library, how to conduct myself during any encounter with the Proctors, and what to do about the Oxford Union: Join it, but avoid ostentation, the Dean thought, would be the message.

As soon as I could break away, I strolled down to the University Registrar, paid my guinea, and was given, as a receipt, a copy of *Excerpta E Statutis*, the regulations of the university done into Latin for universal understanding. Returning to Oriel, I parked my gown and *Excerpta* in my rooms for concentrated study, and set out for the Front Quad to consult Mr. Clark about what to do next. The only information I had extracted from *Excerpta* was that no females were allowed in my rooms, except a charwoman who should be *"senex et horrida"*.

I thought it would be well to check this rendering of the university's rules with my "moral tutor". He lived in the Front Quad, third floor. I knocked and entered, breathless, to find a plump gentleman in a blue shirt that made him look like a retired butcher, sitting in an easy chair by a glowing fire while he discussed their problems with four or five men in flowing Scholars' gowns. I had discarded my bedraggled relic shortly after leaving the Dean, thinking it too disreputable for an occasion like a first interview with my "moral tutor". Mr. Clark noticed its absence and declared he could not receive me improperly dressed. I slunk out while the scholarly sycophants tittered around the fire.

This unfortunate introduction prevented my relationship with Nobby Clark from ever maturing into the ideal communication between undergrad and don. I did not propose to risk another snub, while I thought a certain uneasiness of conscience hampered Nobby from making further advances. I paid a routine call, duly gowned, once a week, for a brief sketchy review of the essay I had ground out on some timeless topic set by Nobby. The only one I remember was "History Repeats Itself". It did not occur to me that history does not repeat itself; historians do. That epigram was reserved for some brighter quipster many years later.

My other mentor at Oriel, Percy Simpson, was mined from a different stratum. Eschewing Jacobean gables and furniture he had established himself in Rhodes Building, in a modern but practical room with good light and central heating, of a sort. The Americans sneered at it as installed merely to save the expense of a fireplace. This appealed to Percy, who had had a harrowing experience with open fires when a live coal popped out of his fireplace to set fire to the notes he had carelessly left on the hearth. They embodied years of work on Ben Jonson which had been his speciality from the first. He stamped out the flames, saving the room but not the manuscript. Nothing daunted, he started afresh, and by the time he reached Oriel as Instructor, his authoritative edition of Ben Jonson was in the ultimate prepublication stage, and soon to be added to Oriel's library shelves as the definitive text.

I found Percy in his bleak rooms smoking a cigarette that smouldered relentlessly towards his moustache, already stained to a rich nicotine hue. He welcomed me with an enthusiasm which I found positively disconcerting after my experience with my moral tutor. In a race with the glowing tip of his cigarette, Percy pointed out that the basic problem was to get me through

5

the Honour School of English Language and Literature with a satisfactory grade. To do this it was essential to propitiate Dr. H.C. Wylde, the authority as well as the examiner for the Growth and Structure of Early Middle English, by displaying some knowledge of the laws of linguistic development which he had formulated. Percy thought poorly of them, but as a practical man he advised me to buy Wylde's book and add to it Jespersen's study, which was both informed and readable—although it was somewhat presumptuous of a foreigner to formulate laws for English, despite the example of Grimm. As a further precaution, Percy recommended the services of a crammer and counselled against attending lectures, except possibly those given by Nichol Smith, who knew his topic and could convey knowledge in an interesting manner. For himself, Percy asked no more than a weekly essay or an analysis of an author or period, which would testify to a reading acquaintance with the topic. I added this to my weekly schedule and signed up with a frail elderly couple, who drilled me twice a week on the mechanics of English.

This ensured that I could extrude enough of my own reactions to English literature to satisfy the examiners that I was aware of its chief ornaments and could identify some of the sources of the light which they reflected. I worked through the program conscientiously for nearly three years to achieve Second Class Honours, which was all that either Percy or Nobby had forecast, or that Percy himself, in his day, had attained. I was not, however, consoled by this parallel, which I thought reflected rather on the examiners than the candidates.

My academic standing suffered from the amount of time and effort I had to dedicate to keeping warm at Oxford. My closest approach to comfort was in bed or huddled in a blanket in front of my fire. When it went out in the afternoon, I did too, to bake my back close to the roaring fire banked up in the Junior Common Room, while I gobbled up a mountain of hot, buttered toast spread with anchovy paste, of which the buttery had an apparently inexhaustible supply.

The J.C.R. was furnished with heavy leather armchairs and a long table, used for correspondence. On one wall a heavy portrait of Cecil Rhodes glared at us. There was no tribute to Newman, Clough, Gilbert White of Selbourne, Keble, or Matthew Arnold, all of whom had frequented this refuge from the Oxford chill, and, presumably, had consumed their plateful of anchovy toast while revising the Establishment to their liking. They left none of their books behind, either in type or in manuscript, and none was added between their day and mine, when undergrads used the facilities for afternoon naps, tea, and warmth, or for the Wine Club in the evening. An occasional conference was not excluded, although distasteful.

Oriel was bobbing along comfortably on a barely perceptible current, and I was content to bob along with it.

In my second year, I was permitted to move to a second-floor room in the Third Quad, which could with care and coal be warmed to sixty-five degrees. It was no less subject to the clamorous bells of St. Mary the Virgin which used to shake my bed with their hourly ran-ran-ran-rang . . . rang-ran-ran-ran, with, in addition, a quarterly jangle, diminished but insistent, which militated against sleep. No wonder we dozed before the J.C.R. fire.

Soon after my arrival, the Captain of Boats burst into my room to invite me to join the Oriel College Boat Club, and to go down to the river for instruction in handling an oar. I was so flattered by this recognition, which I rightly judged to be an exceptional honour for a newcomer from a non-rowing school, bespeaking acceptance by the undergraduate body, that I at once agreed, and from that moment made the river my career. I trotted beside Warner through Christ Church, using Peckwater and Tom Quads as a footpath, admiring the staircase, column, and fan roof built by a Mr. Smith of London for Cardinal Wolsey's Hall.

"The House make what they can of Wolsey," Warner confided, "but in fact they are 200 years younger than us, and even our Rhodes Building is not the fake Gothic monstrosity which Ruskin designed for them to face their Meadows and the Broad Walk."

After that favoured insight into academic pretensions and

reality I would have swum across the Thames had the Boat Club rules demanded it. On the contrary, Warner explained, this was frowned on, except at the conclusion of Eights Week, when conspicuous display might be overlooked.

The Oriel College barge was snugged up to the left bank, between Christ Church and Corpus Christi. It was a copy of a London waterman's barge, once used on state occasions to ferry the Lord Mayor on his official missions. We felt very superior to the Cambridge oarsmen who had to make do with boat-houses ashore; but the barge, though picturesque, was cold, cramped, dirty, and unsanitary, voiding its wastes directly into the Thames, known at that point as the Isis, a diminutive of *flumen Tamesis*. Just below the college barges, the Isis was joined by the Cherwell, a sluggish stream with a gravelly bottom, ideal for punting or for the instruction of tyro oarsmen in the rudiments of rowing. This was carried out in a heavy, two-oar, clinker-built tub with fixed rowlocks and seats, manned by two oarsmen and a cox. We soon learned that the rectangular rubber pad tied to the seat was no protection against calluses on the haunches. This lesson was driven home when I moved up to "Torpids", clinker-built eight-oar monsters, also with fixed seats and row-locks, which were supposed to be mandatory training for manning a racing, sliding-seat eight without putting a foot through the bottom. Torpids were, in fact, murderous brutes, more than justifying their name. They had to be thrashed along with a quick stroke, which was detrimental to sliding-seat style, tending to make novices bucket forward in a rhythm which neutralized the drive of their oars.

Candidates for tubbing and "toggers", the accepted variant of Torpids, were selected as much by weight as by any other rule. Heavies were needed for positions amidships, while stroke, seven, bow, two, and three should preferably be light but wiry.

I then turned the scale at 157 pounds, calculated as 11 stone 3 pounds, which was considered ideal for bow or two. Another youth, about the same build and weight, was selected as my fellow tub-man. Paul Norman Ellaway, like me a freshman from a non-rowing school, was a handsome creature with black hair, a

8

ruddy complexion, and a cheerful disposition. In his earlier school career he had been nicknamed "Spug", but nicknames tended to evaporate at Oriel, and his did not follow him from Oundle, to the great relief of his mother, whose Swiss upbringing had not fully adapted her to the English passion for slang. She had endowed her only son with an easy, familiar grasp of French and an un-English quality which Norman did his best to live down by cultivating a provincial Swiss accent and ignoring grammar and orthography. In this he was supported by his father, who had been an Alderman of Birmingham, where conversational French was not necessary for success. He had a much more substantial qualification, having made enough money in brass to retire on a comfortable income, which enabled him to send his son to a reputable but not ostentatious Oxford college, with an adequate but not plutocratic allowance. He was gratified that Norman had developed as a typical product, if there is such a thing, of the English public-school system. Neither of his parents realized that Norman's effortless grasp of oral French had encouraged him in a dangerous assumption that other essentials to success could be easily mastered. He balanced this in part, however, with a readiness to accept foreigners, colonials, and other off-beat characters which led to a close friendship with me that endured until his disappearance, years later, after one of the great air raids on Birmingham during the Second World War.

The irrelevant factors which had brought us into the same tub also determined that Ellaway, as the first name on the nominal roll, should be stroke, leaving me in the bow position, where I remained for the rest of my rowing career. It is the most uncomfortable seat in the boat, catching the wind and spray in winter, readily identifiable summer or winter to the cox for a shout of "Bow! You're late!"; more likely than most to "catch a crab", with more disastrous consequences. That is bow in any eight, fixed-seats or slides; if he is rowing in a coxless four or pair-oar, he is also responsible for steering, which is like driving along a speedway backwards, with a mobile road moving at speeds varying with the rainfall.

Rowing had its triumphs, however. Its prestige was enormous, and a crew which brought their college to the Head of the River, or even made a series of bumps, created an excuse for a Bump Supper and a gorgeous celebration with food, liquor, and a bonfire in Front Quad. In lively anticipation of these benefits, a table in Hall was reserved for the crew during training, where they could be provided with protein foods and beer in the interest of beefing them up to optimum weight and power. From time to time there would be a "portable", a social evening with port, held in the rooms of a crew member. The theory behind this was that port would deliver units of sunshine and energy into the crew members' frames, to be transferred to the oars by the thaumaturgy of the coach. All this preparation culminated in the splendour of Eights Week with its climactic swim across the river from the barges to the towing path.

Rowing preserved me from loneliness, and from nicotinosis. During training I gave up smoking and joined conscientious crew members in a morning jog around Christ Church Meadows. This was supposed to do wonders for our wind, but left me as breathless at the end as at the beginning of training, while my weight obstinately refused to rise until the end of term, when it shot up to twelve stone, demanding rigorous dietary discipline to bring it under control.

Rowing provided a psychological escape from nostalgia for the wide, cloudless skies of the prairies, and for the comfortable, academic routine to which I had adjusted at the University of Saskatchewan. I missed my comrades of the Class of '24, College of Arts and Science. Each day's mail delivery held the hope of news from home, and the sight of the postman making his rounds filled me with anticipation. The first copy of *The Sheaf* from Saskatoon was crammed with stories of the old gang returning to the university. Mother's letters told of my father's endeavours on the homestead and of their reward in the way of crops; she reported my younger brother Dick was "rushing" Hilda Hudson; Eric, the baby of the family, born when I was fifteen, was full of mischievous exploits. The biggest surprise I received by mail was an announcement from Vanguard of

10

Mary Pearson's marriage to Lawrence Fieldhouse, a sturdy Yorkshireman who had been working for her father. Mary, much sought after by local lads who admired her air of cheerful, attractive competence, her warmth and friendliness, had been my childhood sweetheart; now she had a husband and home of her own. I wrote the newlyweds my wishes for a long and happy life together, at the same time harbouring regrets that I could not be there in Vanguard to convey the greetings personally. My sense of remoteness from my parents, brothers, and friends on the prairie was tempered somewhat by visits from various relatives living near Burton-on-Trent, where I had been born. Aunt Myra, one of my father's sisters, invited me to spend Christmas 1923 with her; I renewed acquaintance with Aunt Netty and my cousin Doris at Bridgenorth, neither of whom I had seen since I was five; then, in January 1924, came my first expedition to Europe, when Aunt Clara, mother's sister, suggested I should join her and my cousin Dorothy at Caux, Switzerland.

The journey to Caux was uneventful, although I experienced my first brush with Paris traffic on a taxi ride from St. Lazare to the Gare de Lyon, a thrilling trip during which a brigand of a driver scraped the skin from three tramcars, going at everything else head-on. The Montreux train illustrated to me what I have known to be true ever since: that one meets Canadian friends unexpectedly all over the world; on this occasion, my fellow passenger was the mother of a Regina College friend.

Switzerland was a delight; I luged down mountainsides with Dorothy, both of us snow from head to foot and soaked to the skin but enjoying every second. Evenings were spent dancing, playing bridge, or attending concerts. When it came time to return to Oxford I was reluctant to leave Caux after such a wonderful vacation with my aunt and cousin, but the boating people at Oriel lost no time getting the togger out and I was soon back in the mainstream of university life.

Little by little I consolidated a group of kindred spirits in Oriel, with common interests in the river, surreptitious shove-ha'penny and darts at pubs infrequently dragged for delinquent gownsmen by the Proctors, and even studies. There was C. R.

(Bill) Oldham, Captain of Boats. There was P. G. Blandy, whose forebears had settled in the Canary Islands when they were a supply base for Wellington's Peninsular Campaign. He supervised my tubbing and periodically received, from home, cases of authentic sack, which he shared with me on the theory that if port was good for oarsmen, sack would be even better. Lester B. Pearson and Roland Michener were up at Oxford at the time. They identified with their colleges, St. John's and Hertford, and did not congregate in clots with other Canadians as the Americans did — to their disadvantage, we believed. On another level there was A. K. McIlwraith, of Toronto, whose intellectual superiority was effectively concealed by a cultivated enthusiasm for skittles and beer at The Trout Inn. He later edited with distinction a volume of Restoration plays, but at my time he was best known for his collection of Scriptorum Classicorum Bibliotheca Oxoniensis, and his affection for rowing, and for a very old pair of sponge-bag trousers.

This group, with a couple of satellites, foregathered for skittles at The Trout, shove-ha'penny at the Lamb and Flag, and warmth at the J.C.R. Two of them entered the Indian Civil Service, which was then dragging the university grounds for promising minnows. I was fortunate enough to elude its net, but Hugh Lambrick and David Symington, the two best minds in our group, were pulled aboard and whisked out of English public life, which they would have served with distinction. Lambrick produced a *History of Sind*, but Symington was absorbed by the Indian Establishment and I never heard of him again. Their rooms in Oriel's Front Quad were a rendezvous for compatible neighbours with a taste for mulled wine and for ghosts, whose rappings on the staircase could be heard distinctly after the second canister of mulled wine had begun to simmer on the hob.

Oriel in those days was a witches' kitchen of real or reputed supernatural visitants or hants. The Front Quad, in addition to the poltergeist on the Lambrick-Symington staircase, had a portly spectre which was alleged by sceptics to be no more than an emanation of Nobby Clark, drowsing by the fire. The Library was endowed with another ghostly personality which guarded the Muniment Room, a tiny antechamber with richly carved cedar panelling and a heavy chest, reputed to contain the documents endowing Oriel with such worldly goods as the college possessed; but since the chest was always locked, this could neither be proven nor dismissed.

I contributed unwittingly to the Library's eerie reputation. One afternoon in winter I sat reading in a comfortable window seat. I was too relaxed to turn on the lights when dusk fell, but sat there drowsing until I heard someone coming up the winding iron staircase which served as a hidden entrance to the Library from the J.C.R. I knew the whereabouts of the celestial globe, the display case of manuscripts, and other obstacles so well that I could walk through them unerringly in the dark, silently following the strip of matting. I heard the hidden door open; someone entered while I continued my silent advance, but as my bulk crossed the fading light of the window where I had been sitting, I heard a gasp of terror from the intruder, who scrambled pellmell for the door and tumbled down the iron stairway. The intruder obviously mistook my dark shape for some unearthly presence advancing upon him; too terrified to speak, he turned tail, stumbling over obstacles which seemed to be tripping him up in his flight.

I made no attempt to find out who he was, but noticed with amusement an intensification of reports of a ghostly presence in the Old Library. They became so insistent that one of the philosophical societies felt justified in engaging a professional diviner to inspect for possible hyperphysical attributes a battered, two-handed sword, hanging on the wall above the High Table in the Hall. It had a vague aura of evil about it which encouraged legendary associations with King Edward II, or his friend, and co-founder of Oriel, Archbishop Arundel, who had fought alongside him. The diviner reported matter-of-factly that the sword was a fake antique, not more than fifty years out of Birmingham, without a glimmer of mystery or romance about it. That verdict reduced interest in the Library legends, too, and Oriel settled back into its timeless tranquillity, to the relief of both Dean and Provost. The Dean made plain his disapproval of spectral research when I asked for permission to stay up for a few days after the end of term to watch for shadowy manifestations.

He said coldly that the Church of England did not recognize ghosts; and that was that. I decided to let the matter rest there rather than take it up with the Provost, who would probably have dealt with ghosts in Latin, if at all. The Reverend Lancelot Ridley Phelps used to ejaculate snippets of Latin whenever he came within range, but the English pronunciation which he used varied so widely from the synthetic German reconstruction of classical pronunciation which I had been taught that I could not identify, much less understand, the words.

Phelps was a tradition Oriel men were proud of, and he knew it. His long white beard and black straw boater were objects of veneration whenever they appeared. Indoors he replaced the boater with a mortarboard; it was worth the encounter with dinner in Hall to witness the ceremony of grace-before-meat conducted between the Provost at High Table and the Head Scholar at the Scholars' Long Table, below the salt. The High Table was resplendent with choice pieces of such plate as Oriel possessed, which was not very much. Only some 291 pounds of gilt and 521 pounds of "white" plate remained, for the College had responded loyally to the call for help from King Charles I, and had melted down its plate to subsidize the Royalist forces engaged in the struggle against egalitarianism, the proletariat, Parliament, levellers, and whoever else epitomized for that generation what later became socialists, left-wingers, or Reds. Oriel's contribution did little to sway the issue, and Oriel got little thanks and less return for it. However, such as it was, the remaining college plate glittered in the discreet glow of electric candelabra, as the Provost raised his mortarboard to the Head Scholar, who advanced two paces, bowed, and intoned in synthetic Teutonic Latin accents:

> Benedicte deus, qui pascis nos a juventute nostra, et praebes cibum omni carni; repli gaudia et laetitia coram nostram; Ut nos, quod satis est habentes, abondemus in omne opus

14

bonum; per Jesum Christum, Dominum nostrum, qui Tecum et Spiritu Sancto, Sit omes honos, laus et imperium, In saeclo saeclorum, Amen.

Provost and Head Scholar bowed to each other again, and we all sat down to what it pleased the buttery to offer us, plus up to a quart of purchased beer in silver tankards donated and suitably inscribed by former collegians. I often received a pint-pot with a whistle in the handle, that it might be fulfilled which was spoken by the prophet, saying: "Let him have wherewith to wet his whistle." My colleagues were loud in their condemnation of the food; I was not, for I compared it favourably with the grub on a threshing gang, not that it was any better, but I preferred eating in Hall under the soft glow of the electric candles, with the hammer-beam timbers of the roof looming dimly above us, to gobbling skilly on enamel plates in the cook-car.

Observed at a distance, the High Table did not appear to be any symposium of wits; the dons tucked into their victuals and ignored everything else, except when the Provost, who of course sat at one end of the long table, sent a remark rocketing down the board. I doubt whether it could be comprehended more than two places away, for he used to cover up a nervous stammer by interlarding his remarks with an explosive monosyllable best rendered as "Cha!", so that an extended conversation would go like this: "My dear boy! Cha! I do hope, Cha! that you will read Greats, Cha! English Language and Literature? Cha! It won't last like *Literae Humaniores,* Cha! And I hope you allow yourself plenty of time for diversion! Cha! *Nunc est bibendum*, as I'm sure you don't need to be reminded. Well, good-day! Come to tea with me some time, Cha!"

I took up his invitation, but it was a painful effort in which I tried to formulate apt replies to what I thought he was saying to me, so far as I could disentangle his remarks from his ejaculations.

Phelps's idiosyncrasy was so notorious that Oriel men used to flock to morning chapel on the thirteenth of each month to hear the Provost intone: "Extol Him, that rideth upon the heavens, as

15

it were upon a horse; praise Him in His Name CHA, and rejoice before Him."

We saw him on the towpath, but that was no occasion for quiet chat; he appeared briefly at Boat Club bonfires in the Front Quad, but only to deliver a routine exhortation to avoid excess, before retiring to his lodgings muttering *metron beltion*, "moderation is better". If not converted, we were nonetheless moved by the sight of his venerable figure anxiously following the sparks from the bonfire. But he was no more capable than Nobby Clark of establishing a solid rapport with the undergraduate members of his college who did not spring from the nobility or landed gentry. The Provost, in short, was a snob, with less to be snobbish about than the President of Magdalen or the Dean of Christ Church, both aristocratic refugees from the world.

My intellectual advancement after three years at Oriel was modest, although the college might retort that sow's ears were unsuitable for silk purses. At that time Oriel was so crowded that third-year men had to find outside lodgings. These had to be approved by the Proctors who gave little thought to anything but the exclusion of pubs and brothels. Convenience for studies did not enter their criteria, and my diggings, duly approved by the Proctors, were distant from Oriel, but uncomfortably close to the Lamb and Flag and to a roost of nightowls from Balliol.

Their activities shattered my sleep for the week before my final "Schools", leaving me so dazed that I could hardly read my examination paper, much less respond convincingly to it. This accident, added to what I still consider to have been a singularly unimaginative Board of Examiners, who conducted my *viva voce* interrogation in the manner of a continental *juge d'instruction*, consigned me to Second Class Honours. The fact that neither Nathaniel Curzon, the distinguished British Secretary of State for Foreign Affairs, later Viceroy of India, nor my brilliant Canadian scholar friend, Charles Wayland Lightbody, who became a well-known professor of history, did any better did nothing to reconcile me to what I felt, and still feel, to have been a miscarriage of justice. Failure to detect an incipient viceroy or a

16

budding professor reflected, I felt, much less on the candidates than the examiners.

How I felt about it made no difference. In 1926 Oriel duly presented me with five guineas' worth of books, appropriately ornamented with the college crest embossed in gilt, and I set out to take the world by storm with no qualifications but my B.A.(Oxon.). The question of primary importance was how I would make a living for myself, and I was forced to recall the objection to university education frequently voiced in the West: "Just a waste of time because it leaves you unskilled for any profession," the critics said. "Better spend the four years and the money making a start in business." Their criticism was valid in the case of some students whom I had observed appropriating blocks of other people's thoughts, which they regurgitated undigested at suitable intervals. University training had taught me that in modern democracies the great need is for men who can and will think for themselves. I left Oxford resolute in my aims to do just that.

CHAPTER
TWO

Financially I was at the end of my rope; I listed the alternatives which would put me on a sounder footing. Teaching was possible, so I wrote to Regina College asking whether there would be a place for me on staff, only to receive a negative answer. Posts in British preparatory schools were always filled by the time my application arrived. My other alternatives, writing and farming, I rated respectively as improbable and impossible. My mother, who had spent several months in Britain earlier in 1926, knew of my predicament. In her youth she had been sent to a "finishing" school in Stuttgart where, along with the social graces so necessary to a young Victorian lady, she learned conversational and written German. After the First World War, knowledge of the German tongue was not considered to be such an asset; French once again became the language for those with aspirations to the diplomatic service and, for that matter, teaching. Mother knew that I had no proficiency in it; mulling the matter over in her mind after returning to Canada, she decided that some time at the Sorbonne in Paris would certainly do me no harm, and might improve my chances of obtaining a job. About the time I was packing my bags to return home in despair, a letter arrived from Vanguard advising me that, if I wished to study at the French university for a year, Father would make the necessary funds available. I leapt at the chance.

The academic discipline I had experienced at Oxford had built up an attachment to the English, and thus to the European, way of life more powerful than I suspected until the time approached either to return to the western hemisphere or to slip into an expatriate role with no firm footing in either the Old World or the New.

Oxford's central position put it within easy reach of the Continent. While at Oriel, I took care to follow the recommendation of the Rhodes trustees that I broaden my mind by travel. At the end of my first term I went through the ritual of an interview with the Provost and a panel of dons, who assured him that I had a responsible attitude and would shed, if not lustre, at least no discredit on Oriel if allowed to return for the Trinity term; my life style was creditable although my literary style left something to be desired. The Provost then delivered his academic recommendation: "Cha, my boy, Cha! Ha! A useful exercise would be to translate the third editorial of *The Times* into Latin, and turn it back, after three days, into what *The Times* regards as English. Cha!" I bowed, the Provost bowed, the dons nodded, and I shuffled to the door. This ceremony completed, I packed my bags and headed for the station, en route for Paris.

Eddy Mims, who roomed on a neighbouring staircase, had directed me to a clean, discreet, and inexpensive pension in the Latin Quarter, on a street picturesquely named rue de l'Arbalète, although there were neither records nor tradition of a crossbow having been used in the area. On the fifth floor of a building at the end of a courtyard with plane trees, the Pension Mollet accommodated students, civil servants, a bank clerk, and musicians whose instruments were too bulky or noisy for hotel rooms.

Peeping over the chimney-pots, the Val-de-Grâce dominated the eaves and gutters of the Quarter, which was marked off on the opposite flank by the Pantheon, where the great, fortunate, or worthy citizens of France, whether Kingdom, Empire, or Republic, were entombed in a majesty considered appropriate to civilian cadavers. It was flashy, but fell notably short of the imperial grandeur of Napoleon's Hôtel des Invalides, whose spiked dome produced a breathtaking enlargement of a Prussian helmet — a reminder, too often unheeded, of the basic kinship of the military psyche, internationally simpatico.

19

During the rest of my stay at Oxford, I made various trips to Europe; Strasbourg, Antwerp, Florence, Venice, and Rome were all on my itinerary, but it was to the pleasant ambience of Pension Mollet that I always returned when feelings of homesickness overcame me. Mlle Germaine Mollet, the proprietress, and her niece Anne gave the place the air of warmth and welcome so longed for by the foreign students who resided there, most of them Canadian or American. The same faces congregated chez Mollet each vacation, to the extent that we began to think of ourselves as a family. It was in this familiar haven that I made my home for the months I remained in Paris.

Registration at the Sorbonne was a simple procedure requiring only that applicants should have the patience to stand in line for several hours before their names were called. It was agreed that my prospective thesis should be on the French antecedents of Chaucer, and that the preliminary research should be completed by Christmas 1926. With that aim in mind, I obtained from the British Embassy in Paris a permit which enabled me, as a foreign student, to use rare sources in the Bibliothèque Nationale. While that library, with its huge collection of medieval manuscripts, is undoubtedly one of the finest in the world, I was hampered in my research there because the catalogues at that time were complete only to the letter K. Hours were wasted foraging for volumes hidden in dark recesses of virtually unlit rooms.

Paris in those days boasted a large North American colony which enjoyed a gay life on each stratum; the inhabitants of Pension Mollet were no exception. Together we attended dances and social events of all kinds. The city offered much more too: the Louvre had a fascination, for we recognized not only the quality of the works hung there, but their excellent condition, which compared favourably with art in Italian and Belgian collections I had seen. For those of us with a penchant for music, Paris had opera, light musicals which were French versions of Broadway hits, and concerts given by the notable singers and instrumentalists of the period. Some evenings we spent quietly at Mlle Mollet's fireside playing cards, reading, or writing letters home, but more frequently bright lights lured us to observe and share Parisian café life. Friendships with Canadians I had met at Oxford and earlier at the University of Saskatchewan I maintained by joining the Cercle des Etudiants Canadiens, which met frequently for dances and lectures.

But soon after New Year 1927, several factors combined to mar what had been a delightful existence: news from home indicated that my parents were on the verge of separation, my financial position was deplorable, and worrying about both circumstances had reduced to nil my ability to work on the thesis I had been preparing. I determined that my best course of action would be to return to England where I might be able to find work teaching. If that strategy failed, then I would return to Canada.

News of my decision was greeted with regret by my friends at Pension Mollet, who produced, as a farewell salute on the day of my departure from Paris, a "birthday" fête with presents from everybody. Then all of us trooped off to the station, exchanged embraces and melancholy good-byes, and I embarked on the lonely rail-and-boat journey to England.

Money problems continued to plague me in London; there seemed to be no jobs for which I qualified, and I was forced to pawn my watch, camera, and a highly prized gold chain to pay for rent and food. At a point when the future appeared blackest an avenue of escape from my miseries opened when a travel agency, Franco-Belgique Tours, advertised for a guide-conductor. I applied and was accepted on the strength of being able to locate on the map of Europe a series of place-names rattled off by a burly interviewer with an authoritative manner, a heavy American accent, and a square backside. He gave me a handful of cut-rate railroad tickets of extended mileage, as well as cash, travellers' cheques, and a summary of his company's promises, which struck me as lavish. However, my share in fulfilling them would be to move my group and their luggage from point to point on schedule, and see them installed in such comfort as second-class hotels afforded. Acquainting them with local points of interest would be a responsibility of the company's local agent.

I remarked that while there would be thirty in my group I had been given only twenty-five railroad tickets. The executive with the square backside explained that this was where the profit lay. It would be my problem discreetly to tip or bribe train conductors in each country to make their passenger-count tally with the number of tickets. Five dollars, particularly if paid in U.S. currency, would take care of a short-fall of sixteen or seventeen per cent. A smaller but graciously offered tip-bribe to customs officers who examined ladies' baggage on the trains would ensure that nobody was embarrassed by over-zealous searches of intimate containers. The square backside tipped me a sly wink and outlined another problem I would be expected to solve.

Americans coming overseas, he explained, left more than their socks and handkerchiefs behind; they threw overboard their entire heritage of Puritan morality, and the New Englanders were the worst, particularly the women. Since most of the members of these tour groups were nubile women, it was important that they should conclude their intinerary if not *virgines intactae*, said the square backside juicily, at least not pregnant. I asked if I was supposed to issue contraceptives? No, I was not; good advice, he thought, would be enough. Disregarding his own assessment, he detailed a recent group's unhappy experience with maternity.

"They all want to get screwed without getting caught," he said, "and usually they are only fifty per cent successful."

Telling the square-bottomed man that I would bear this in mind, I took the money and the tickets, left the cheap rooming-house, and returned to Paris, looking the model "Oxford man" —grey flannel "bags", "sensible" brogues, Fair-Isle jumper and a blazer with the Oriel crest. The effect was authoritative and, in its way, impressive, even to me!

I found twenty-nine women and two men, all Americans, jammed uncomfortably in a second-rate hotel near Les Halles that was full of the smells of a wholesale market with poor drains. The tourists were in good heart, however, and pretended that it was "so romantic" to find pyramids of cabbages and cauliflowers piled on the sidewalk overnight. Their ages ranged from twenty to sixty-plus. The young ones had extracted the price of a month's tour of Europe from fathers, brothers, or lovers; the elderly had saved nickels and dimes for years for this final splurge; all were dominated by a determination to get their money's worth and to see all the wonders of the world that a lifetime's reading had brought to their notice. I soon found that statistics impressed and satisfied them, and that if I boned up on the population and manufacturers of the cities and areas through which we were passing, I could meet every legitimate expectation. I combined the *Guides Bleues* and Arthur Young's *Travels in France and Italy* to such purpose that I was considered an infallible and universal authority. An elderly lady from the middle West nearly stumped me by wanting to know if the cauliflowers piled on the sidewalk came from the famous experimental vegetable gardens near Naples, and if so, would the tour visit them, for she wanted some seed.

I had been awakened long before dawn by workmen unloading the cabbages shouting to each other in what sounded like Italian, but was incomprehensible to me. After chatting with a few of them in a neighbouring bistro, I mastered their Midi accent sufficiently to learn, to my astonishment, that the finest cauliflowers did indeed come from Naples, where the experimental gardens were one of the wonders of the world. They added that the strain was closely guarded, for the seed was not generally available and could only be purchased in person and in retail quantities by vegetable-growers, not by seedsmen.

Our tour was not scheduled to visit Naples, but modest excursions to points of particular interest were permitted at my discretion, so I was able to include the vegetable gardens, along with Vesuvius, Pompeii, and Lady Hamilton's villa, without question or dispute from management. When I informed the elderly cauliflower fancier of this, she wept a little for joy, and for the rest of the tour lived for that precious moment. She did not want to speed along the Corniche Road. She could not care less about Columbus's house at Genoa. The marble quarries at Carrara left her cold, and so did the beach at Viareggio where Keats's body was cremated. She did not want extra baths, she never complained about her room, or the food, or the heat. She wanted to take things easy until she was safely home, with her cauliflower seeds safely buried in the rich Indiana soil. She became an invaluable buffer between me and the inevitable irreconcilables who wanted more of everything than the prospectus had promised, and she passed on to management such glowing accounts of my omniscience that I had some difficulty severing my connection with the tourist industry at the end of the season.

My happy experience with the elderly lady and her cauliflower seeds partly offset unpleasant episodes with one of the two male members of the tour. A greasy man with a furtive air came up to me in Paris asking to be directed to "those shows— you know!" He was not interested in the Moulin Rouge or the Folies Bergères, he wanted an entrée to private pornography peepshows. I took this amiss. In the first place, I did not know where to find them myself; secondly, even had I known, I did not propose to act as pimp for any of these establishments. So I told him roughly that he would find juicier joints right in Chicago, and that the touring company would have nothing to do with perversion. My mention of Chicago was based on recollection of some of the stories retailed by Joe Labrique in the Canadian Forestry Corps camp at Loch Morlich about his alleged adventures in sin in the Windy City, but it hit the nail right on the thumb, and the greasy man withdrew, wondering audibly: "Why did I come abroad when I could have been on vacation?" The next day the tour moved on to Nice, out of season, hot, uncomfortable, the stones of the beach too hot to be trodden barefoot.

Consequently, I was horrified but not surprised to receive a telephone call just as I was about to take an afternoon nap behind drawn blinds. An agitated female voice explained that one of the men in our party had suffered a heat stroke and gone mad.

"What do you mean, mad?" I asked.

"Well, he's half-naked and has attacked one of the girls. He's just outside in the corridor now, and I'm scared to death."

I hurried to the floor below, and sure enough, just as I feared, there was the greasy man, hair and clothing dishevelled, cowering in a corner and mumbling something that sounded like "Place Pigalle". I found this reassuring, first because he was not half-naked, just a bit mussed-up, and secondly, he remembered where he had been a couple of nights before. I was quite alarmed, just the same, for he was a big man, and had he become violent, he would have taken some overpowering. That would have created a commotion, with the hotel and the tour alike upset and the schedule disrupted before it had really got under way. That would also have meant the end of my job. So I spoke soothingly to him and led him to a room where he lay on the bed, moaning a little but otherwise normal. I urged him to take it easy, and went to another room to find a doctor. The resident physician had gone to the hills to escape the heat. Then I got through to the U.S. Consul, who fortunately had not gone to the hills. He responded efficiently and soon had the consular physician on his way to the hotel. After a brief inspection, he announced that our man had suffered a cerebral accident, probably brought on by overstrain, excitement, and heat; he prescribed bed-rest and a return to the United States as soon as possible. The Consul agreed to supervise this.

I assembled my group, told them what had happened to head off scare-stories and bussed them down to the station, where we caught the evening train to Genoa. Dropping off one individual gave me more leeway with train tickets and room allocations; I passed the time until we reached Genoa going to each compartment to deliver a little homily on the urgency of keeping suitcases always ready to move at short notice. I combined this with paternal advice to the women to take sceptically the claims to nobility professed by such natives as they might meet, no matter how attractive; and, when we reached Rome, I reinforced my ban on visits to the Colosseum by moonlight by noting that it was not only dangerous, but was made unromantic by the local custom of using the monuments of antiquity as latrines, thus enjoying physical and aesthetic catharsis simultaneously. This had the desired effect; Rome was taken without loss or damage. We viewed with appreciation the panorama of the Bay of Naples; the little old lady received her package of cauliflower seeds as if they had been pearls. Nobody wanted side-trips to Capri or Vesuvius, so I thankfully entrained them and we returned to Paris exhausted but content.

The touring company received such enthusiastic reports of my handling of the expedition that it offered to renew my contract next season and to assign me to the special luxury tour of Berlin, with lush expense account and instructions to gratify every whim of the customers, regardless of cost. I could foresee monumental headaches in such an assignment, for my German was quite shaky and Heaven knew what scrapes these barbarians would get into and expect to be rescued from without mischance. Above all, I was exhausted, and wanted release from nominal rolls, baggage counts, porters, and hotels, so I shrugged off Berlin and the tourist industry generally, and returned to London once again, having decided that I would attempt to make a living as a writer, an endeavour that I had rated as improbable before.

Predictably, my effort failed, along with my cash, although I stretched it to the utmost by dossing at the Duchess of Connaught's Memorial Hostel, which afforded low-cost housing and breakfast to deserving Canadians, and by dining on the Bedford Head's one-shilling special. I developed an acquaintance with Mabel, the barmaid at the Bedford Head. which netted me surreptitious pints of bitter, ordered but forgotten by absent-minded patrons.

It was a career without a future, and I was glad when my money ran out, forcing me to do the same. I spent most of my days on the Thames Embankment, gloomily sketching out plots for short stories that would never be written, until I was recognized by Robin Clark, our former toggers coach, who, with great insight and generosity, realized that I was dangerously morbid and needed rousing out of my apathy.

He ran me up in his car to his quiet country farm near Oxford, where he and his wife and dog led a bucolic existence in which he tempered farming with coaching college crews, and cultivated hay and local rustics as a counterpoise to too many undergraduates. Robin's hospitality was whole-souled, but I realized

26

that I could not sponge on it forever, so I accepted the first opening turned up by an employment agency, and started work in the spring of 1928 as an assistant master in a minor prep school in Sussex.

The school was in an old house on the fringe of Haywards Heath, a small market-town on the Southern Railway, as it then was, about halfway between London and Brighton. Its residents commuted to London until they retired, after which they sat in their front bay windows and watched the "up" trains take their juniors to the same routine. The school accommodated some seventy or eighty boys between ten and fifteen years of age, engaging to prepare them to pass the entrance hurdles to the public schools from which they could hope to pass into Oxford, Cambridge, or the Services. This called for a solid grounding in Latin, some French, a pinch of history and geography, a smattering of mathematics, and sports, sports, and more sports.

My schedule called for academic subjects in the morning and a jolly afternoon refereeing cricket, which my charges were required to play as soon as the soccer season concluded. I also presided over table and maintained some sort of order in the evening study period. For diversion between classes, meals, and study periods, I used to drop down to the Liverpool Arms, a dreary second-class pub facing the station, devoid of amenities or grace, existing by and for the guzzling of beer.

One could, of course, spend an evening in Brighton, but I saw no profit worth the expense of a return ticket, so I stayed at the Liverpool Arms, lingering over a pint of bitter as long as I decently could, finding entertainment in darts and shove-ha'penny on such evenings as I did not devote to writing. But neither these pursuits, nor the fact that we were served treacle pudding for dinner twice a week, could blind me to the dreariness of such routine. I started saving my salary until I had the £100 fare demanded by a small American line for the voyage from Tilbury to New York, whence I hoped to make my way back to Canada.

When the time came to leave, to my great surprise, the headmaster begged me to stay on for another semester. The school

27

was just finding its feet, he said; my students had all done well, and since two other masters were also leaving, a complete change of staff would not look good on the prospectus. I do not recall that these arguments were emphasized by any raise in salary; nor did I demand or expect one, for I knew how precarious the school's finances were, but I preferred the certain discomforts of the known to the uncertainties of the unknown. I stayed on for another semester, then resolved to break away from the Old World before my ties to it became any firmer. The problem of saving enough to pay the fare from New York to Regina, Saskatchewan, where I could be reasonably sure of finding a job, remained unsolved. The solution appeared to be to go as far as my funds allowed and work westwards from that point.

CHAPTER
THREE

Before leaving England, I had dashed off, almost as an after-thought, a note to F. J. Wylie, whom I had known as Oxford Secretary of the Rhodes Trust, telling him of my plans to head for New York as a first step to returning to the prairies if and when my finances permitted. Blessed by intuition and experience in handling Rhodes Scholars' affairs, Mr. Wylie suspected rightly that I should need guidance; so he passed the word to Elmer Davis and Christopher Morley, American authors living in New York and both former Rhodes Scholars who had gone up to Queen's and New College long before my time, asking them to keep an eye on me. It was well he did so, for I was down to my last few dollars when I received a call from Davis suggesting that I drop around for a drink. Elmer Davis at that time had made something of a name for himself as a free-lance writer. He had been one of the last Rhodes men to go up to Oxford in "the good old days" just before the outbreak of the First World War, and his subsequent career in journalism and, later, in radio endorsed the judgment of the scholarship selection committee of Franklin College, Indiana. Davis demonstrated his practical outlook by recommending that I get a job on a newspaper, which would ensure that I had food, lodging, and the writing discipline of a deadline. I could go on from there to the more remunerative field of magazine writing.

Aware that it was not easy to crash the fortresses of the press without experience or credentials, Davis generously wrote notes of introduction to George Birchall of the *New York Times*, to

Stanley Walker of the *Herald Tribune*, and to friendly pundits of the *Sun* and the *New York Post*, who might offer the less-exacting hours of an afternoon paper.

I went to the *Post*, where they apologized for having nothing to offer but the "lobster pot", which involved rewriting other people's copy or stories already in print, from 2:00 to 10:00 in the morning. The *Post* did not seem surprised when I bowed out of that one, a decision I have never regretted. The *Sun* was not interested. I went on to the *New York Times*, where Mr. Birchall was out of town and not expected back until Monday. His assistant counselled me to go across the river to Jersey and get a job on some paper there; after a few years I might come back to the *Times* with enough experience to make it worth while to hire me. I went around the block to the *New York Herald Tribune*, the last shot in my locker. It took all my resolution to undertake this fourth assault. I was within a hairbreadth of throwing up this whole project, but I had nowhere to go and no money to get there. So, despite my cold feet, I took the elevator up to the fifth floor of the *Tribune* building and inquired for Stanley Walker. The presses were rolling, and their steady drumming sounded like artillery fire softening up the fortress for imminent attack.

I was not kept waiting long. After a few minutes a bustling copy-boy took me into an enormous room, cluttered with desks and newspapers. A swarm of young men were reading, tearing out pages, snipping at them with giant scissors, and doing something mysterious with a paste-pot; a few were typing fitfully. At one side of the room, a vast desk was laden with telephones—the upright, independent-earphone type which was already on its way out—clipboards, scissors, and paste-pots, as well as copies of the newspapers whose offices I had just left. A thin, youngish man with a green eyeshade was prodding this clutter with a heavy, black, paper-wrapped pencil. He laid a half-smoked cigar on the edge of the desk, pushed up his eyeshade, and told me to sit down.

I perched on the business-end of the cigar on the edge of the desk and jumped up with a shout as I felt the sting. I figured my interview with the *Herald Tribune*'s city editor was over, but to my amazement, Stanley Walker apologized for the mishap, pulled up a chair, and said: "There's an empty desk over there which was occupied by a compatriot of yours; he has left, so if you want $25 a week, it's yours. Here's the style sheet. Take it home and look it over; come back tomorrow and start work."

I staggered out, scarcely believing my ears, and hurried back to my lodging, where I spent the evening reading and rereading the style sheet. It featured advice on the importance of correct initials, the infallibility of the telephone book in that respect, and a warning that the Burlingames considered any variant spelling of their name to be actionable. "Commit murder if you like, but don't get the paper into a libel action. It is no defence to say an item is accurate and factual, and was printed without malice; if there is any doubt, read it over to our lawyer. Get the significant data on who did what, when, and where, in the opening sentence or lead." It offered a sample lead which contained, within thirty-four words, the essential elements of time, place, and action:

> Mayor James J. Walker told the Manhattan Borough Council meeting in the Goldfish Room of the Waldorf Hotel today that he would not tolerate the Aquarium being used as a rendezvous for man-eating sharks.

Early next afternoon on a January day in 1929 I strolled into the city room prepared to accept $25 a week and any assignment the *Herald Tribune* cared to give me. I was welcomed by a brisk reminder from Stanley Walker that my day started at 10:00 a.m. I pointed out that the style sheet said nothing about hours of work, neither had he himself set a time.

He smiled bleakly at this evidence that I had read the sheet, and explained that $25 would not go far in New York, so he would see that I got plenty of night assignments, which would ensure one good meal a day, free, except for a tip to the cloakroom attendant, which he advised me not to overlook. He expressed more confidence than I felt that I could supplement my salary with items for the Sunday paper, which ran a page of think-pieces contributed by reporters. He then handed me a

31

black paper-wound pencil similar to his own, and I went to my seat. For the next few months I covered such events as an Esperanto dinner at which hosts and guests would have quarrelled bitterly over pronunciation if they had been able to understand each other. I covered a conjurers' banquet where the rabbit got into the salad bowl and then the conjurer got into the sauce. I covered water-power conferences that damned ecologists and ecologists who damned dams. I stayed conscientiously at every assignment.

My predecessor at the *Herald Tribune* had been Richard Law, son of a former prime minister of the United Kingdom, who had performed well enough to justify Stanley in making another exception to the rule "Only Texans need apply." The city room was jumping with Texans, like Stanley himself. Some of them, like "Tex" O'Reilly, advertised the fact; others let their presence tell the story.

By contrast, the reportorial staff of the *New York Times*, which might have been expected to proclaim Tennessee, where Adolph Ochs hailed from, was composed mostly of New Englanders, as was the front-office staff of the *Herald Tribune*. It was no handicap in the *Trib*'s bull-pen to have come up through St. Paul's School and Yale, but a dash of in-breeding had not prevented the *Herald Tribune* from becoming a sprightly newspaper, willing and able to give the *New York Times* some tough competition. At least until the publisher began hiring management experts, who nearly put the paper out of business in their zeal to manage what had better been left alone to jog along as a newspaper should. Our experts delayed building up reserves of newsprint on the grounds that it would soon be cheaper. Consequently, when the tug-boat strike began, we ran out of paper; the *Times*, not having experts, did not.

One reason the "experts" had been called in was to alleviate the financial burden under which the paper staggered. Its former owner, Mrs. Whitelaw Reid, had died at the peak of the Great Bull Market; her estate had been appraised at current levels and death duties had to be paid on that scale at a time when all values had collapsed with the 1929 market crash. It took years to pay off this burden, although staff salaries were far below those of the *New York Times*, and side-benefits which *Times* men enjoyed, like pensions, bonuses, expense accounts, and similar gulps of Ochs-blood, were not available to reporters on the *Trib*, who carried the ball against three times their rivals' numbers with the instruction: "Always be the last to leave."

My desk chanced to be placed between two of the most original minds the paper could produce. "They're crazy," Stanley Walker warned me. "Just nuts! But they're not dangerous, except maybe to themselves. Make what you can of them."

Edward Pendray spent his spare time, and any loose cash he could muster, on rockets. He used to take the rockets across the Hudson River to the Jersey Meadows for experiments with the Interplanetary Travel Society, which was planning rockets powerful enough to carry a cargo and crew to the moon, or even farther—Mars, perhaps. Nothing crazy about them, of course. Apprehensively, I shifted my chair a little farther away, as my neighbour's idiosyncrasy shifted ever closer to lunacy. His beard bristled, and I seemed to discern electric sparks flowing from it into interstellar space. I was intrigued to find that the Society's members actually believed that sooner or later, and probably sooner than we imagined, space travel would be a reality. In this faith they dedicated their bodies to the ferocious mosquitoes of the Jersey Meadows, and their souls to the ferocious incredulity of their colleagues. To justify his retention on staff (which at that time had no slot for spacemen), Stanley Walker passed on to Pendray a request from Ogden Reid, the owner of the *Trib*, to mark every typographical error or imperfection — broken letters, "unjustified" lines, misplaced commas, brackets, etc.—on a full page of type over the past week, in order to check on the linotypes and casting mats in the pressroom. This meant scrutinizing some 300,000 symbols, a desperately boring task, but one which gave the proto-spaceman time to plan his next stage in planetary propulsion. During this exercise, Pendray grew a short black beard; when an assignment was complete, he shaved it off.

On my other side sat Robert Shaplen, no less far-out in his

thinking than the interplanetary planner, for his dream was a truly *liberal* weekly, in which he proposed that I should participate. I thought interplanetary travel should have priority, as being less speculative, for in my evening assignments to banquets, I had listened to scores of after-dinner speeches without discerning the least trace of liberalism, either original or reflected; there was nothing but hard-shell materialism, glazed with standard political platitudes.

However, I kept my opinions to myself and listened to Ed Pendray planning moon landings and Bob Shaplen projecting liberal weeklies while I banged out obituary columns for those worthies whose demise might justify an enthusiastic biography of 500 words if it were ready set-up to slam into the obit page. I worked on Poincaré, Diamond Lil Brady, one of the Sitwells, and James J. Walker, mayor of New York, developing a guardedly sardonic style in keeping with my instant epitaphs, until Stanley decided to give my talents wider scope.

The opportunity arose when the English Madrigal Singers gave a program sponsored by the Canadian Pacific Railway, at the Royal York Hotel in Toronto. Stanley gave me a railway pass, a sheet of instructions on how to file press despatches, and an order on the cashier for an advance on expenses. It was not a story of any great significance, but on the other hand it cost the *Trib* nothing but wire tolls and my expenses. If I loused up the assignment, nobody would notice but the C.P.R. publicity office. It was worth what was known as a "half-B head" on Page 15, and that was what it received. But compared with the normal evening-banquet stories I had been covering, it was exciting, hot news, and I overwrote it so voluminously that the telegraph editor ordered me to cut down the file. On my return I clipped every precious by-line, pasted everything into a scrapbook, and lost it.

Meanwhile, Stanley promoted me to the day rewrite desk as the best method of teaching me to summarize; he urged me to acquire speed by learning to type by touch, instead of by scrutiny. I was so conscientious about this, however, that I slowed down disastrously and Stanley, in despair, moved me over to the night rewrite desk, where the pressure of deadlines would be so intense that I would be forced into speed, regardless of method.

The night rewrite shift lasted from 6:00 p.m. to 2:00 a.m. It was devoted to writing up items phoned in from district reporters or clipped from the early editions of the *Times* and the late afternoon finals. The result was fed into the "lobster-pot" of next day's early afternoon papers, which thus appeared with a remasticated smear of what had been news three days before, but was now ground into a newspaste spread to be gulped down by diners at an automat as they gobbled their meatloaf spread made from the leavings of three-day-old banquets.

My task was to introduce some spice of real news into this smear, by telephoning some hapless victim at midnight and reproducing as much of his comment as could be purged of libellous and obscene matter. I soon got to know who could be pressured into confirmation or denial of late-breaking stories. My resolution to intrude mainly by telephone was bolstered by the report going the rounds that one victim had refuted a rumour that he was sick, nigh unto death, by hurling a thunder-mug at a reporter who had followed up his telephone inquiries with a personal visit. Payson Terhune "had been a reporter once himself" and appreciated the value of direct action in preference to a City News Association denial. I came to respect CNA denials as affording valuable leads into stories which could be followed up with great advantage if carried out discreetly. I learned in this rough school that denials were issued only if there was something disadvantageous which could not be concealed any longer. In later years I found that this principle had universal application; its corollary laid it down that the only antidote to irritating rumours was to counter them with others or to supply a new and vivid incident, the equivalent of a flying thunder-mug, which would divert the inquiring reporter's interest and attention. Years later when I had become a minor oracle worth quoting myself, I obtained much mileage out of this principle, besides acquiring some repute as "a good news source".

35

While I was in New York, however, the minor oracles reported in to the night rewrite desk; I mangled their copy, noted what I could understand over a noisy telephone, and ground out enough to provide a half-B head and perhaps even give my opposite number on the *Times* a headache. Then I relaxed until the next edition of the *Times* was flung on my desk.

Even under these circumstances I retained some independence. On one occasion, the assistant night city editor tore a story out of the *Daily Mirror*, a miserable scandal sheet with a high nuisance value that made it obligatory reading. He tossed the item to me with a request that I check it and write a story about it. The item played up a report that the Lindberghs had reserved a private room in the maternity wing of the Presbyterian Hospital. I threw the item back to the assistant night city editor, saying I was a reporter, not a midwife. The editor looked hard at me over his spectacles, adjusted his flaming red tie, and let the matter drop. I had expected to be fired on the spot, but even though I escaped, I thought it advisable to avoid further incidents. For years afterwards, as the Lindbergh baby tragedy ran its implacable course, I congratulated myself for rejecting any part in the tornado of journalistic impertinence which was so obviously going to sweep through the Lindbergh household, and would ultimately shatter it.

But the press was as relentless as the presses; there was nothing I could do to change its attitude that there should be no restraint on the publication of whatever an overworked, overtired, harassed rewrite editor considered either as news or as something that would make the opposition sit up. If papers like the *Times* and the *Trib* had no compunction, what could be expected of others?

With this in mind I took the first opportunity of a vacancy to move over to the cable desk, and from that vantage put in a bid for the first opening overseas. This came up when Number Two in Paris was transferred to Rome as part of an extensive reshuffle whereby correspondents who had been in their post long enough to know both it and the language reasonably well were moved to countries where both would be strange to them. This policy dictated that our Rome correspondent, who knew no German, should be moved to Berlin, while our Berlin man went to Moscow, where he could not even read, much less speak, Russian, and had to hire someone to translate the newspapers for him. Following this principle to its illogical conclusion, our Albany man, who knew the New York State can-of-worms, was sent to London, where the language was as strange as it could be and remain English, while the background and significance of what was said, done, or sometimes even thought in Albany, had no possible relationship to anything in his new post.

However, all this was in fulfilment of the *Herald Tribune*'s theory that a new man would find news in everything, since he would see it with a fresh eye, sharpened by recent information on what the home office wanted and what it thought newsworthy. The *New York Times* worked on the opposite principle; it feared that a correspondent could not evaluate events, or report them in perspective, until he had had years of experience in a post while he built up connections and news sources which would enable him to winnow grain from chaff. Our material was indeed more vivid but much of it was so overplayed that occasionally even the State Department complained.

My appointment to Paris, which was not long delayed, occasioned some caustic comment about sending to Paris a man who was suspected of an acquaintance with French which would be bound to corrupt his all-American outlook, already tainted by British nationality and passport, to which I clung firmly, despite broad hints that I was an anomaly in the *Trib*'s current nationalistic stand against the *Times*' polyglot representation.

Until now, the demands of my job had left little time or energy for my home — a typical American situation at the time. In February 1929, I had married Helen Gordon, an American artist whom I had met during my months at the Sorbonne in Paris, where she was a student also. We gave up our noisy, cramped quarters in New York without a qualm, sawing off the lease of our apartment. We arrived in Paris in July 1930.

Helen's delight at leaving the pressure, clamour, and dirt of New York was reinforced by her desire to resume art studies with one of the masters in the Colorossi or Le Duc studios. At the time of our marriage neither of us had any money of our own, nor could we count on financial support from our families who had also been finding survival difficult since the collapse of the stock market. Out West, homesteaders like my father were hard pressed to make ends meet; in addition, the Minifie family had now dispersed, for my brother Dick had married Hilda Hudson, had sired two daughters, and was farming land of his own. Mother, to whom the prairie had always been alien land, separated from my father, and leaving Eric, my youngest brother, on the homestead, had made a new home for herself in the milder, pleasant, old-country atmosphere of Victoria, British Columbia.

While I was working at the *Trib*, Helen had managed to eke out a slender living as a mail-order salesman for the Gotham Silk Hosiery Company. Her job was to stimulate sales in "the sticks" by informing retail outlets of the latest fashions, designs, and colour fads in ladies' hosiery, and plying them with early samples. It was a deadly type of pressure cooking, but it kept her in silk stockings and pin money.

My return to Paris took me back years; I could see no changes, even the call of the *marchand d'habits* in the courtyard below was the same. We reoccupied my old quarters in the Pension Mollet, 39 rue de l'Arbalète. They were inexpensive and afforded easy access by autobus to the *Herald Tribune* bureau, which was then in rue des Halles, alongside the Central Market. Vegetables trucked in overnight were piled high on the sidewalk — pyramids of cauliflowers, mountains of carrots, fennel, celery, potatoes, red cabbage, green cabbage, curly greens, kohlrabi, sea kale, turnips, rutabagas, beetroot, lettuce, radishes, mushrooms and fungi, truffles in boxes, spinach, salsify, artichokes looking like hand-grenades, green peppers, red peppers, chicory, horseradish, beans, and tomatoes disputed the sidewalks with pedestrians and their dogs.

After threading my way through this labyrinth, I walked up a flight of decrepit stairs to the *Herald Tribune* office and a boisterous welcome from Leland Stowe, our man in Paris. A shock of prematurely white hair belied his youthful figure and spirit.

They had done him no good with the dull boys on the cable desk, I suspected. Neither had the financial juggling which enabled the bureau to maintain, on call but not on staff, without objection from the front office, an official of Havas Agency, then almost a wing of the French government. Léon Bassée knew what was going on, and how to winnow the facts out of official communiqués. In other offices such services might have been covered by the ignoble title of tipster; but Bassée was more than this. He was counsellor and friend as well, and a devoted, patriotic Frenchman, whose analysis of the political philosophy of the Third Republic would not have disgraced Voltaire. He also had a comprehensive file on the love-life of Parisian politicians, and its impact on events in bed and out. He knew where Geneviève Tabouis got her ideas and where Edouard Herriot got his. He was aware of the connection of *Le Matin* with the Comité des Forges, and through them with Krupp. He recognized the dangers of this secret power infrastructure, and warned us not to be misled by surface glitter. He deeply disliked and distrusted Pierre Laval, who was just beginning his long rise to power and, ultimately, execution as a traitor. Bassée, long before others, suspected "the little man with the white tie and the black teeth" of questionable relations with France's enemies through the Comité des Forges, with which he also associated François-Poncet, whose dandified elegance contrasted sharply with the studied proletarian dowdiness of the Radicaux-Socialistes generally. By the time I arrived in Paris, Stowe had already established an affectionate collaboration with Léon Bassée, which endured as long as the Third Republic, whose demise during the Second World War preceded Bassée's by only a short time.

When France collapsed, Bassée returned to his farm rather than endure Paris under the hated Boches; but he was a city man, plump and vulnerable as a partridge, and the country damp, combined with despair at the collapse of the Ligne Maginot, brought on a pulmonary congestion that killed him. He did not live to see the liberation.

The third desk in the *Herald Tribune*'s Bureau was occupied by Sonia Tomara. Sonia was a very special case, although of a category overrepresented in Paris at that time — the emigré White Russian, living on the family jewels and hopes of returning to Holy Russia when the unholy Bolshevists had been thrown out. When the family jewels and hope had both vanished, Sonia taught herself shorthand (of a sort) and learned to type (after a fashion). With that equipment, fluent French, Italian, and Spanish, and a persuasive personality, she had no difficulty getting a job with Stowe as office factotum. Her English was strong enough to enable her to grind out a daily technical piece on the stock market, noting trends on the Bourse and appending a list of standard stock prices — Suez Canal, Pechinay, Dollfus-Meig, Nord, Ceinture, P.L.M., and the like. Sonia had persistence, which she needed to battle through the French telephone system to obtain long-distance appointments for Stowe. She had a practical sense more developed than it was in most Russian emigrés and she did not mind what hours she worked. Under her influence our bureau flouted American business routine by setting up an electric kettle on the radiator, and giving ourselves a tea break whenever we felt like a relaxing half-hour's analysis of the latest political gossip. Bassée often joined us, and emptied a new cup of scandal with each pot of tea, interpreting the innuendoes of *Le Canard Enchaîné*, and the slanders of *Action Française*.

Sonia welcomed me with enthusiasm when I wandered into the shoddy offices in the rue des Halles. I tried to give her a picture of how the *Herald Tribune* operated, who was doing what to whom, and what the future might hold for the foreign service. This depended to a large extent on how much copy the cable desk could sell to the syndicate and thus show a bookkeeping profit; this in turn meant selecting stories which had wide appeal in various sections of the United States.

My explanations were interrupted by shouts from a back room, followed by a long, high-pitched flow of criticism. "Mr. Hills," Sonia confided *sotto voce*, "hauling Eric Hawkins over the coals. He makes life miserable for everyone, but he keeps the Paris *Herald* in the black."

The story current on the copy desk was that old Mrs. Whitelaw

Reid, publisher of the New York *Tribune*, became so exasperated by Gordon Bennett's endless offers to buy her paper, and merge it with his own New York *Herald*, that one day she snapped back at him, "Don't talk to me about selling the *Trib*, it's not in the market, except to buy your *Herald* rag!"

"Done!" retorted Bennett. "Sold." When Mrs. Reid came to she found she had bought not only the New York *Herald*, but with it a foundling in Paris which everyone had forgotten. Years later the Paris *Herald* was still a going concern, making money, and enjoying a golden after-glow of authority from the days of Stanley Livingstone and the Brothers Goncourt, when the *Herald* was not only the fount of news but the arbiter in art, dress, taste, manners, and literature. Its critics were the joy and terror of society and artists. They could be influenced, but they could not be bought, which made them unique for the era, and for Paris.

There was nothing of the Mauve Decade about Lawrence Hills, but his exaggerated Americanism endeared him to the expatriate colony where noise was often mistaken for authority and truculence for patriotism. The American Club elected Hills its president, and were happy in their choice, for he scared the timid and bluffed the arrogant until membership reached record height and enthusiasm, and the club's views were eagerly sought by politicians anxious to swim with the current, if only they could find it.

Hills' political convictions were simple but fervent. He had no use for aesthetes, "radicals", the English, or the Russians, and Amurrica would come to no good by aping either their manners or their morals. Hills could sing "My Country 'Tis of Thee", off-key but on request, and believe it. He was a strong physician who infused some of his exuberant life-force into the clogged arteries of his patient. The American colony and the Paris *Herald* could not have made the mark they did without Lawrence Hills, but this realization did not induce undying affection. They would have liked to dump him, but they did not dare to, for who, after all, could replace his harsh mid-Western accent and his instinct for what would appeal to his brash but unsure mid-

Western audience. Executives of this stamp were supported, if not in fact created, by devoted female secretaries, who filled the voids in their bosses' education, social graces, and ability by an intuitive grasp of affairs, ruthless ambition for their bosses, and sacrificial abnegation. Such was Renée Brasier, a female Cerberus who guarded all access to Hills' sanctum and took dictation in English or French, mutely correcting solecisms in either language. She fervently disliked most of the Paris *Herald*'s editorial staff and all of the *Herald Tribune*'s correspondents' bureau, whom she suspected of secretly despising Hills but lacking the guts to openly defy him. She had unlimited resourcefulness, which was never so taxed as in the episode of the Favourite Daughter.

The Paris *Herald* was a haven for little old gentlemen who had known better days and needed to supplement their reduced income with regular, if small, accretions. To ensure these they accepted, in order to remain in Paris, posts which younger, more affluent men would have rejected scornfully as offering neither adequate reward for the present, nor hope for the future.

One of these little old gentlemen solicited Mlle Brasier's help in bringing his daughter to join him in Paris. Mlle Brasier agreed. She was a marvel of efficiency. She obtained sacrifice fares on the French Line, and suborned Eric Hawkins into creating a job for the girl on his editorial staff.

As so many Americans did in those days, and quite possibly still do, the young woman threw Puritan conventions overboard as she stepped on deck, and had a wonderful time all the way across. However, being young and inexperienced, she overlooked prophylaxis, and arrived in Paris in much poorer condition than she realized, but full of enthusiasm for the boundless freedoms offered by French social mores. The editorial staff of the Paris *Herald* encouraged this ardour, until Mlle Brasier was compelled to use her utmost persuasive powers to obtain emergency accommodations at the American Hospital for almost half the editorial staff of the Paris *Herald*, and to supervise operation of a jury-rig to keep the paper in production until the staff recovered. The paper never missed an issue.

An anchor of enduring strength in all this hubbub was Vincent Bugeja, a Maltese of encyclopaedic knowledge, who had somehow found a good anchorage on the Paris *Herald* where he could use his omniscience to flesh out the dry bones of agency copy from Havas, U.P.I., I.N.S., and Universal to make readable items to fill any space available. He was a fresh-air fiend, forever displaying to the *Herald* staff a hairy, scarlet chest as the health ideal. Unfortunately he was more prone to heavy colds than anyone else in the office, which detracted from the authority of his nudist views. He smoked a dirty, stinking pipe with strong plug tobacco that made the city room more unsavoury than burning rubber itself, as was demonstrated when his colleagues shredded a rubber pouch which Buge absent-mindedly stuffed into his pipe and lit up. Buge disappeared periodically to revisit his native Malta, where he was a mainspring of the Labour Party. Sober and sedate, he avoided the affliction with which the sins of his juniors were visited, and his reliable expansions of Havas copy carried the Paris *Herald* through foreign and domestic crises without a falter.

FOUR

As least member of the bureau I devoted myself to financial matters, carefully studying the profusion of figures issued by the Bank of International Settlement, and occasionally poking around the Banque de France, which was still selling gold bars over the counter. They were eagerly gathered up by elderly gentlemen with spade beards who wrapped them in a copy of *Le Journal des Débats* or *L'Intransigéant* as if they had been so much French bread, to be carried off under the arm. Each bar had a smaller nugget tied to it for purposes of test and assay, the whole package weighing at least ten kilos, or 22½ pounds, worth, at normal rates, over $500. This brought it within the range of the thrifty French bourgeois who preferred to hide gold in his own home and bedstead, sacrificing interest and comfort to security, after having been swindled by a series of National Defence bonds whose guarantees had reduced to worthless paper the dowries of a generation of hopeful brides.

The Pension Mollet epitomized the outlook of the *petite bourgeoisie* of the Twenties; suspicious to a degree of all that the Third Republic said or did, they nevertheless bought its bonds while hoping for its demise. This demise they forwarded as far as they could by supporting Colonel François de La Roque, leader of the Croix de Feu, a paramilitary organization, Paul Reynaud, Edouard Daladier, Joseph Paul-Boncour, and even Léon Blum, leader of the Socialists, and Louis Marin, boss of the extreme Right. They still quivered over "L'Affaire" which had sent Colonel Alfred Dreyfus to Devil's Island thirty years before. The revelations of treachery, treason in high places, and corruption in the army and civil services which the trial disclosed still dominated French thinking, as Negro slavery dominated American background thinking in Washington, D.C., at the same time.

Guests at the Pension Mollet heard a daily rehash of "L'Affaire" and regarded with suspicion the "gnomes of Zurich" who were believed to be as busily engaged in inflating the French franc as their peers had been in deflating the French army. Obviously, the Third Republic could not stand the strain of another "Affaire" but this was precisely the prospect opened up by the Bayonne municipal-bonds scandal, better known as the Stavisky affair, which gobbled up much of what was left of the bourgeoisie's savings, along with its faith in the Third Republic, and precipitated the ultimate disaster. I covered the story from the outset, and came up against the inevitable dilemma — the consequences of the disaster to the government and to the regime could not be fully broadcast without precipitating the disaster.

It was only one of too many financial scandals that undermined the Third Republic. The city of Paris had tried to lure investors, or rather gamblers, by issuing lottery bonds, but I never heard of anybody drawing a lucky number; the general scepticism did not deter *les poires* (a popular term which could be translated "suckers") from seeking fortune in the Derby, the Irish Sweepstakes, or the Bayonne pawnshop lottery. The gambling fever produced psychological and financial disaster comparable to the South Sea Bubble of 1720, or Law's Mississippi Bubble the same year. The Third Republic was approaching the stage signalled by the croupier's chant *"Rien ne va plus"* — the bets had been placed, the wheel was spinning, and the money would soon be raked in.

Vincent Bugeja was an invaluable source of help to me in my daily struggle to obtain accurate information on all these occurrences from the Paris press. More than thirty newspapers published daily; it was impossible to read them all, but two publications were priorities.

Le Canard Enchaîné was a joy, in both script and illustration, but needed abundant interpretation and glosses to explain the backstairs gossip and allusions which were its stock-in-trade.

L'Action Française was a dangerous promoter of violence, with strong royalist sympathies. Bassée warned us against putting any stock in the Comte de Paris's chances of recovering the throne of France. These chances were not improved by support from *L'Action Française*, or from Les Camelots du roi, or from Colonel de La Roque's *sbires*; Charles Maurras was too vitriolic, Léon Daudet too restrained, to be effective. Most of all, the royalist cause was wounded by the satirical shafts of *Le Canard*, for the Duck always appeared decked in the trappings and suits of royalty and quacked through brilliantly written political comment that sent me to the newspaper kiosk early every Wednesday morning to pick it up before the issue was exhausted. I took it to the nearest café which announced *dégustation d'huitres*, and sat down to enjoy *Le Canard* with a dozen *portugaises*, a litre of Pouilly Fuissé, and a plate of brown bread and butter. These were pleasant stimulants to meditation or to watching the *midinettes*, with their gay hatboxes, tripping down the Champs-Elysées.

In Paris you absorbed politics and sex with the air you breathed. It was as important to know who was Herriot's mistress in 1930 as it was to be informed of Louis xv's in 1730. It was important to know whom Maurras meant when he referred to Paul-Boncour as *ce Don Juan de lavabo*, for if a prominent cabinet minister was open to blackmail, you might be sure the Germans would use this weapon, as they did; it was important to know how brittle the French infrastructure had become, as the Germans also knew.

For many objects of his scorn, Maurrus invented entirely new epithets, always referring to Monsieur Pierre-Etienne Flandin, a capable minister in the Tardieu cabinet, as *ce flandrin de Flandin*. The word *flandrin* does not occur in any standard French dictionary, and it is certainly not recognized by the Académie; it was created by Maurras as a sort of abusive echo.

Maurras and Daudet made the most of the easy-going laws of libel which considered that anything could be expiated if a retraction were printed the following day in the same position, type, and length, as the original slur. All that did however was to draw attention to the libel, which might have passed relatively harmlessly but for this emphatic reiteration.

Besides *Le Canard* and *L'Action Française*, I also relied heavily on the back pages of the *Journal des Débats* and *Le Temps*, where *Dernières Nouvelles* snuggled away, and also read *Oeuvre* because it reflected Geneviève Tabouis's views; she was not only a well-informed writer, but received her information, along with other benefits, from Edouard Herriot, whose mistress she was. Herriot was one of the most attractive political leaders of his day, and a power in the Radical-Socialist Party. He was honest, which perhaps put him at a disadvantage among a gang of crooks. Too candid for his own good, he was enthusiastic about principles and ideas; but he loved his victuals, and was forever going to Vichy to lose weight, and to Dijon to regain it.

Knowledge of the amiable weaknesses of French ministers was particularly important in view of the skilful use by the Germans of female informers, just at a time when the great defensive chain of the Maginot Line was being constructed. However, these little strumpets may have received more than their share of credit—or discredit. For there was very little that any competent military man could not find out by a cursory reading of the papers, particularly of their advertisements. Indeed, one big contractor called for tenders for subcontractors through advertisements in the press which revealed structural details of the Maginot Line with astounding precision. With this information on file, a flight from Paris to Frankfurt or Berlin was all that was needed to fill out the blueprint of the topmost secrets of French defence.

Another valuable source of news was the Wednesday luncheons of the Anglo-American Press Club. These were held in quiet rooms near the Palais Royal, where cuisine was rated above security. No cocktails were permitted, but sound white and red wines, *en carafe*, appealed to palates sensitive to the chef's *chef-d'oeuvre* and often inspired ministers to float trial balloons in the guise of unpremeditated indiscretions.

Strolling back under the chestnut trees while these explosive materials fermented, it was hard for diners, whether newsmen or ministers, to ignore the lithe limbs and clinging satins of the young women parading their charms before the *flaneurs* in the sidewalk cafés, who were topping off a good luncheon with a *fine maison* which lifted you out of your boots and a *café filtre* which brought you back to earth. Long before Christine Keeler and Mandy Rice-Davies rocked London back on its heels, we used to drop confidential information into ministerial ears at the Press Club luncheons and time its reappearance at Le Select or La Rotonde.

This practice was well known, but once the napkin was tied around his neck, the average French minister threw discretion to the winds. Herriot kneaded the crumbs of his *petit pain* as he dilated in depth on the importance of defence and foresaw withdrawal to the Pyrénées if need be; Paul Reynaud, racked by his nervous tic, took a pessimistic view of French finances under the impact of war, while Edouard Daladier, a cigarette drooping from the side of his mouth, outlined cabinets of all the talents, which would never hold together through two votes of confidence in the Chambre des Deputés. On the corner of the Champs-Elysées and rue de Berri, Le Select welcomed foreign correspondents who liked to spend the afternoon reading newspapers or writing powerful pieces which would give Sunday readers in Washington, New York, or Boston the lowdown on French politics. Percy Philip, of the *New York Times*, Arnold Dosch-Fleurot, of the New York *World*, and Leland Stowe and I for the *Herald Tribune*, drafted our punditry for the Sunday section in these comfortable surroundings, which we compared favourably with the din and clatter of our home offices, where such thinking as was done competed with the threatening growl of presses reeling out the Sunday supplements. We were aware of the fragile nature of the political dispensation in France and of the corrosive effect of satire on French institutions. It was as caustic in the twentieth century with Maurras as it had been in the eighteenth with Voltaire, and we correctly anticipated that any exceptional strain would bring the institutions crashing down.

To watch the legislature in action, as well as to preserve the memory of times passing, we looked in at the Chambre des Deputés, although it offered the poorest facilities for journalists I ever encountered until I became acquainted long afterwards with the Legislative Assembly of British Columbia. We had a cage much like the "musicians' box" at the Opéra, high up under the roof, where the acoustics were wonderful and the ventilation terrible. From that height the House looked like a puppet show, where little figures bobbed and bowed with stiff gestures, and climbed to the rostrum like customers going upstairs in a *maison de joie*; they struck their attitudes and said their pieces to the accompaniment of an impassioned fantasia on a great silver bell by the President of the Assembly and a rattling drum-fire of his ivory baton against the desk. It was not uncommon for two deputies to leave their seats in the hemicycle and jump into the well of the Chambre to exchange fisticuffs and challenges.

The list of prime ministers (which was our standard translation for Présidents du Conseil) was long, but as unimpressive as their persons.

Edouard Daladier's lips were always stained with nicotine (but from cigarettes, not chewing). Camille Chautemps, timid and vague, rarely held office long enough to make more than his maiden speech. Paul Reynaud bobbed and nodded in perpetual motion of *tic douloureux*. Paul-Boncour padded up to the rostrum like Donald Duck, to quack assurances of defence readiness "to the last button"; and the press in the musicians' box sniffed the *esprit de corps* and wished themselves well out of it.

The hemicycle seating of the Chambre des Deputés permits gradations of political colouring that the opposing benches of the House of Commons do not encourage; in the House of Commons you are black or white and well advised not to change your colouration; in the Chambre, a slight adjustment of a place or two, the better to reflect ideologies, developing or receding, might pass unnoticed except by specialists. Louis Marin sat over with the Right and was faithfully reported by the *Echo de Paris*; Léon Blum, mournfully dolichocephalic, sat in the middle of the *bancs des gauches*, just to the right, however, of the communist right-wing, but to the left of the non-communist socialists

S.F.I.O.; he could rely on *Le Populaire* to print the address he was never allowed to complete; André Tardieu, contemptuous of the hurly-burly, surveyed both wings with disfavour from the seat just to the right of the centre *fauteuils*; he always appeared to be on the point of sticking a cigarette (Players or Chesterfield, of course, as a protest against the French tobacco monopoly) into his long black holder, his sign-manual for the cartoonists.

The cartoonists and the caricaturists both took extreme liberties with the Palais-Bourbon and its cast; one humorous periodical devoted an entire issue to a description of the establishment as a brothel. Illustrated by the devastating pen of Jean Penés, the widely-admired cartoonist Senep, of the *Echo de Paris*, this *tour de force* presented Tardieu climbing the steps of the rostrum, while an usher with a towel over his arm intones: "Un monsieur qui monte" (gentleman coming up). Léon Blum, embraced by the editor of the communist *L'Humanité* on a Louis xv couch, exclaims with woebegone face: "Mon Dieu! That hurts!" Louis Marin, sitting on a *pot de chambre*, promises: "I will either defecate or get off the pot." Vain boast. A backside protruding from a rumpled bed is labelled "Front Populaire". Many shook their heads over this issue, but the day after it appeared copies could only be obtained as a favour from the lady at the newspaper kiosk. Everybody agreed that Penés and Pertinax had gone much beyond the bounds of acceptable satire, but they all bought copies if only to prove their judgment sound.

In this Bartholomew Fair hurly-burly, ominous warnings of deep-seated political malaise could be detected. On the night of February 6, 1934, I noticed the sinister array of police personnel-carriers parked in the little side streets leading into the Champs-Elysées, between the Rond-Point and the Arc de Triomphe de l'Etoile. There must have been thirty or forty of them, all packed with black-helmeted *gardes mobiles*, the tough auxiliary police whose appearance always meant that violent demonstrations were anticipated. We believed that the *gardes mobiles* sometimes instigated the violence they were supposed to control; at all events towards nine o'clock I heard gunfire and shouts lower down the avenue; our building employees warned me that the Champs-Elysées was not a healthy spot that evening. I stayed in the Paris *Herald* building, a solid structure which had been designed with defence in mind; the elevators could be put out of action without difficulty, after which the upper storeys could be reached only by a narrow, winding staircase of stone, easily defensible against a mob. Soon after midnight the uproar died down and I reconnoitred cautiously to assess the chances of getting home safely. Both the *gardes mobiles* and the rioters had gone home to bed, and the street was littered with caps, berets, an occasional priest's skimmer, and canes; but there were no bodies, no blood, and no empty shell-cases. At that time I had insufficient experience of the suppression of peaceful assembly to notice the absence of the sharp, sweet stench of tear gas. Since I had heard firing, there must have been some empty shell-cases, but I found none that night, and by next morning the débris had been cleaned up. I concluded that much of the firing I had heard must have come from the *gardes mobiles* parked in the side streets, firing warning shots to scare off all but the dedicated activists. I deduced from this that the encounter would be blown up by propaganda far beyond its actual significance. So it was, but this did not prevent its becoming of great consequence, igniting the combustible materials with which the stage of the Third Republic was always littered.

Stowe had the misfortune to be absent, covering a hotly disputed election in Spain, at the time of the riot. This gave me a clear field and I made full use of it, firing off lead stories, side-bars, follows, interpretives, and editorial material, regardless of instructions to hold down the file for economy's sake. By the time Stowe returned we had wildly exceeded our month's word-ration, and my by-line was all over the paper. Since I had written early with the needs of the make-up editor in mind, the cable desk was happy that deadlines had not been squeezed and thus overlooked the extravagant use of space and words. Stowe generously credited me with a first-rate achievement, and ensured that the front office knew that he appreciated my work.

After this, it became standard procedure to send me out of town on feature stories hitherto considered out of my field. All sorts of delightful oddments came my way: the *Micheline*, a railroad coach on rubber tires; a revival of Mozart performances at Louis XVI's private theatre at Versailles; ceremonies at Fontainebleau and Chantilly. Ultimately, later in 1934, I was sent to Spain to investigate the Basques' separatist desires and their demonstrations in favour of home rule. This portentous story, of special interest to the Paris *Herald* which was sensitive to the motivations of English iron-masters with close relations to the iron-export trade out of Bilbao, foreshadowed the Spanish Civil War, which I was eventually to cover off and on for about fifteen months between its outbreak in 1936 and May 1937.

Stowe was reluctant to return to Spain, in view of the spectacular French stories he had missed during his last incursion into the Peninsula, so I did not feel that I was poaching on his preserves. I was, in fact, a little reluctant myself to take on such an assignment, since I did not speak Spanish, and had only a limited reading capacity in the language. However, ignorance of local dialects had never been a disqualification for American reporters, who were thus the less likely to have their Simon Pure American integrity sullied by close contact with barbarian ideas. The fact that I was, or claimed to be, a Canadian was not held against me, since most of my editors cherished the simple-Simon notion that Canadians were only Americans in embryo who would qualify as Plymouth Rocks as soon as their pinfeathers had fallen.

In theory, the Paris bureau obtained permission from New York before going on any assignment which might be expensive; but this involved so much delay that when events crowded us we covered the story independently, on the theory that once we were on the spot, New York would never get around to recalling us as long as the copy flowed in. This put the onus on us if the assignment did not pan out in terms of front-page material. This was awkward, for the first week of an assignment had to be dedicated to catching up with the *New York Times*, whose man by then had the situation well in hand, the sources lined up, and the rat-holes catalogued.

However, no objection was made to my taking on the Spanish

assignment for a brief period, not long enough to be contaminated by too close a contact with Spanish or Spaniards. As was then the practice of British subjects embarking on journeys to which some element of risk was attached, I obtained, from the British Consul-General in Paris, an addition to my British passport — a safe conduct for a three-month visit to Spain. My passport, good for ten years and renewable, had been issued under the authority of a former Oriel man, George Nathaniel, Marquess Curzon of Kedleston, Earl of Kedleston, Viscount Scarsdale, Baron Ravensdale, K.G., P.C., K.G.C.S.I., etc., etc., His Majesty's Principal Secretary of State for Foreign Affairs, and it requested and required all concerned to allow me to pass without let or hindrance and afford me every assistance and protection of which I might stand in need. It was a document that breathed authority in every line and I never lost confidence in its capacity to assist and protect me, no matter what wicked foreigners might design to molest me. I flashed it in some pretty ticklish situations and it never failed in its mission. In an illegal second passport, I obtained from the Basque representative a long screed, rubber-stamped in green ink, which I took on faith since it was in Euskadi, and which I never had translated but used with assurance on the Basque front prior to the fall of Bilbao. All other Spanish documents I shunned.

I arrived in Bilbao with New York's injunction ringing in my ears: "Report what you see; what you don't see, don't take anybody's word for." The cable desk had sent word that they were going crazy trying to make sense out of wire services' contradictory reports, left-wing "propaganda", and fulminations from "the Power-House" — the Roman Catholic hierarchy in St. Patrick's Cathedral, which was putting the heat on advertisers to insist that only "reliable" news of Spain be printed. I had become acquainted with the "St. Patrick's porcupine" on the rewrite desk, and I knew what an unprincipled creature it was. So I felt that if I reported the facts as I saw them, I was laying my head on the block, and that the *Herald Tribune* would not be able to protect me, but would rather dislike me for being a nuisance. These fears did both the New York management and its Paris offshoot an injustice. They printed my copy without tampering and supported me and the Spanish Republican Government editorially. The metropolitan parent paper did this at some risk, for it was scanned painstakingly by the powerful Roman Catholic organization in New York, whose headquarters were only a few blocks away. It worked by indirection, rarely telephoning the management, but making it clear to advertisers that they should not imperil their immortal souls or their pocketbooks by dealings with supporters of leftists, pinkos, and radicals. The Power-House found these terms of abuse and commination very useful, since they could not be defined but had a general application and carried an implied threat of boycott to which advertisers were exquisitely sensitive. There was also the unadmitted but very practical alliance with the discredited but still-powerful Tammany organization which had to be handled with kid gloves, for in the nature of things every newspaper broke so many arbitrary rules and regulations that City Hall could have closed down every press in the borough had it chosen to enforce them all. The *New York Times* was not subject to this discipline, but it, too, could not afford to alienate the formidable support of the Jewish community which, as usual, was far more open-minded than St. Patrick's, although no less ruthless.

In France, the Paris *Herald* had to tread circumspectly between the American Legion and the French labour unions while competing with the Paris edition of the *Chicago Tribune* for the favour of the expatriate colony and of the far-flung British refugees from high taxes and low revenues in the United Kingdom. The management of the Paris *Herald*, however, took their cue from the home paper and gave my despatches prominence which often embarrassed me when I saw my revelations spread in bold type on the neighbouring kiosk. As the Spanish cauldron showed no sign of simmering down, on my return to Paris I suggested to New York that it would be well to have somebody on the spot when it boiled over instead of awaiting the event before sending somebody to clean up after the *New York Times* had covered the story like a blanket.

New York, however, shuffled their feet while we waited with

what patience we could muster as the Spanish Republic's time ran out. Early in 1936 President Azaña introduced a program designed to placate the liberals, but which failed to do that although it infuriated the conservatives. The liberals also were incensed at having been betrayed, as they saw it, by one of their own, for Azaña claimed their support on the basis of his liberal principles. It was a typically Spanish situation, in which everyone suspected everyone else, and justified his lowest sentiments by the highest principles.

When New York's permission finally arrived I fell into the middle of this muddle, spent two or three weeks trying to straighten out my impressions, and returned once again to Paris convinced that a fearful upheaval was in the making and that very little news coming out of Spain could be relied on. The views, even of experienced observers, were equally suspect. For instance, I was very graciously allowed to read the despatches being fired off to Washington by the American Embassy in Madrid. I was astounded to discover that in January 1936, only seven months before the cataclysm burst in full force over the Peninsula, the State Department was being assured that the current episodes should not be mistaken for preludes to an approaching storm, but rather recognized as the after-effects of a political hurricane which had, so to speak, blown itself out. Little wonder if officials in Washington made some curious decisions about the Spanish Civil War. However, they were not alone; neither Downing Street nor the Quai d'Orsay was much better served.

It was not surprising, then, that State Department specialists had quaint ideas about what was going on in Spain when they had to rely on what found its way from "the pouch" to the Spanish desk, plus what could be strained out of despatches from special correspondents of the *New York Times* and the *Herald Tribune*, combined with demands for action sent in by what few business corporations survived. Among these were the International Telephone and Telegraph, which had close connections and interests in Scandinavia and the Caribbean (on the surface an odd combination, but with historical and personal

55

justification); Rio Tinto, a vast conglomerate which boasted its origin in demands for copper and cannon arising from the Napoleonic Wars, but which had branched out into complementary power, transport, and mining enterprises; textile mills in Catalonia; fruit growers, vintners, and olive-oil processors in the fertile flatlands of the Levant; ranchers from Estramadura who raised the brave bulls for the corridas in Madrid; iron-masters of Viscaya and Bilbao who still enjoyed preferential treatment from the English Black Country magnates who had set up a farsighted relationship in the days of George III between their ravenous blast furnaces and supplies of iron ore secure from the whims of juntas, emperors, brigands, or leaders of any other stripe or spot.

French coverage was highly partisan. Horrendous stories of rape, arson, and mayhem filled the popular press; the wire services rewrote the lead for the day-file. In Paris, the conservative *Echo de Paris* thundered against "the Reds", while the socialist *Populaire* inveighed against "les fascistes"; nobody bothered much about the facts. But in the summer of 1936, it became evident that the revolution, which centred in the great industrial area around Barcelona, deserved closer observation when both the Ford and General Motors works were seized by the Republicans. Protests by the American government netted the companies some compensation, but what would happen in the cases of the other foreign-owned concerns remained questionable.

Stowe wanted to send me to Catalonia, but was uncertain whether such a prickly assignment would be a favour or a penance. He shelved the problem by putting it up to New York for solution, but to our surprise he received an immediate "Go ahead".

FIVE

I prepared to leave for Barcelona by the overnight train; air travel was still uncertain and perilous. I should have been elated; instead, being still unfamiliar with the language, I was full of misgivings. Stowe reminded me that my lack of Spanish was no loss. Catalonians don't have it either, he said: "Just spik Ingleesh, they'll catch on; or get yourself a bed-mate; it's the natural way to learn a language." He summed up, "Look under every stone, and write what you find there."

After an uncomfortable night in a wagon-lit couchette, I found myself floundering in darkness through the railroad tunnel that runs beneath the Franco-Spanish frontier at the eastern end of the Pyrénées. Stumbling owl-eyed into the glaring sunlight, we passengers were herded into a shed by a blue-jowled man in a "mono", the blue overalls which became adopted as a kind of uniform in the Republican armies. A revolver barrel poked out of his hip pocket. He glanced cursorily at a salvo-conducto I'd taken the precaution to obtain from the Spanish Embassy in Paris, straightened it out carefully, and then pressed onto it a rubber stamp with a huge five-pointed star, crossed rifles, and the motto "Lucha contra Analfabetismo". He cautioned: "Take care of this. It will get you anywhere in our territory, but don't let the U.G.T. see it." I asked who the U.G.T. were. He replied with snarling disdain: "Communists! Reactionaries! Traitors to the People!"

I pointed to the letters F.A.I. on his cap and raised my eyebrows in interrogation.

"Federacion Anarquista Iberica," he explained. It seemed, and was, a contradiction in terms, but the Anarchists had been reduced to organizing in order to survive. I gathered that the F.A.I. and the U.G.T. were not on friendly terms, so I stowed away my salvo-conducto in an inside pocket and decided to entrust my safety to my stolid British passport. In Barcelona I hopped into a taxi, telling the driver to take me to the best hotel in town. This was always sound practice, particularly when supported by expense accounts.

Its soundness was immediately demonstrated, for I found a note for me at the desk from the correspondent we shared with the *Morning Post*. He was a sound man with long experience in Spain and a reputation for generous guidance to visiting specials. I had been instructed to make what use of him I could, at the same time assuring him that I was not about to poach on his territory, so I made an appointment with him for the evening at nine o'clock. "Spanish time or English time?" he asked.

"What's the difference?"

"About three hours. Nobody in Spain comes to an appointment at the stated time; it would be an outrageous breach of manners, for nobody would be ready for them. Three hours is about the standard differential with Madrileños. It's rather less with Catalans or the Basques, who are inclined to be punctual as well as factual, which Castilians think is very dull of them—sort of a Sancho Panza approach to life."

I found Catalan officials very gracious about giving interviews; they damned the Communists as little better than enemy agents, and blamed nightly murders and executions on them. I heard reports of mass graves, looted monasteries, raped nuns, and the whole deck of cards; but I never found what I would accept as irrefutable evidence in support of these charges, although I made a special trip up the coast to Mataró to examine a reported mass grave, which was not there. I did come across a group of CNT (Anarchist) *milicianos* who had looted an apiary, and were stumbling along the road munching honeycomb and licking their fingers like children at a Sunday-school picnic. I hired a car, and a driver who knew enough English to understand what I wanted. The "cork ports" along the Costa Brava were picturesque and friendly, but I wanted to get away from them. Everybody seemed to be telling me only what I wanted to hear, so far as their antennae could discern it, rather than what they themselves believed to be the truth. Truth in Catalonia at that time depended on what political faith you subscribed to. On one occasion I surprised a rustic into saying "They'll be back again!" — meaning the Anarchists, who had already paid his farm one devastating visit. He was pathetically eager to cover up his blooper. I read him a laudatory article about a local Anarchist worthy in a Barcelona paper. He shrugged and accompanied me to the nearest automobile dealer whose shop window, normally displaying the chrome and leather of sumptuous Hispano-Suizas, was bare as a florist's in winter.

The dealer, as anticipated, spoke fluent English and French. He studied the article; my companion discreetly returned to the sidewalk; the dealer then said that the Anarchist worthy was the worst robber in the local group, who had stolen all the dealer's stock, driven them off without bothering to service them, and then raced them over difficult highways until they ended in the ditch, where they might now be viewed. Destruction seemed to be an end in itself, and the dealer, not unnaturally, would have welcomed any alternative which would impose some sort of civil control and order. I asked about the road to Huesca, which was variously reported to be in Catalan, Communist, or rebel hands. The dealer strongly advised against trying to reach the city, as an Anarchist column had set out for it a few days ago.

The dealer pointed to a long story purporting to be an eye-witness account of the storming of Huesca, featuring the sacrificial heroism of an Anarchist *miliciano* who had strapped explosives to his body, rushed under heavy fire to the city gates, and there detonated them.

"I doubt if there's a word of truth in that rigmarole," the dealer said. "They more likely drove a stolen truck into the gates, then fired it, and blew up everything while they made a getaway, to do some looting before everything burned up. But it's the sort of drivel these fellows print, then the wires pick it up, and it goes all over the world, doing us no good at all. I don't know what's happened to the city, or to my agent, or to my stock. And I guess it's like that all over the Generalidad. I'll sure be glad when someone who isn't an outright bandit takes over and straightens things out."

Another story, also front-paged, reported the capture of Teruel by a Spanish army column, and anticipated its early recapture by Catalonian forces. If true, the dealer hoped that the capture of Teruel would permit army columns to cut through to the coast, thus bisecting Catalonia, crippling its military effort, and taking it out of the Civil War. But had Teruel fallen?

"There's no way of knowing," the dealer concluded, "short of going up there to see, and it's a difficult road at the best of times, and these are not the best." The dealer advised against visiting Teruel. If it was in the hands of *milicianos*, some nervous mechanic with a rifle, doing sentry duty, would be firing at footsteps or shadows, under the impression that his post was being ambushed. If the army held Teruel, the sentry would wait until he could see you before firing. Better keep away.

It was simply a question of by whom you would rather be shot, the dealer argued: *milicianos* or military. Since he hoped to die in his bed much later, he proposed to get the hell back to Barcelona while he still had a car under him. I was only too glad to turn back with him, for I was not fulfilling a useful purpose by risking my life for a story I could not report, or for a cause, like Catalan independence, which was none of my business, except as a reporter; and a reporter without a cable-head was not likely to move much copy.

However, the development of the revolt in Catalonia would determine whether Spain survived or crumbled into bits and pieces, returning again to the situation before the monarchs of Castile and Aragon had compressed them into a single peninsular unit. The divisive tendency was developing fast under the stresses of the Civil War, which added social and political solvents to the existing geological and ecological diversity. Failure to consider these factors would mean dismissing the Civil War as an isolated phenomenon without identifiable cause or predictable effect; its lessons would be lost, its history distorted by headlines, and its consequences misinterpreted in the partial light of current bias. It was essential to find out what the "proletariat", the small mechanic or farm labourer, was feeling and doing in the interior. To do that meant taking a wide sweep into the countryside, which meant time and expense that I was not prepared to undertake without authorization. However, the difficulty of getting through by telephone to Leland Stowe in Paris, and the complexity of my explanation when I did get through, understandably raised doubts in Stowe's mind, and he deprecated further assays into danger and expense.

It was a sound decision; Stowe could not have ruled otherwise without consulting New York, and they would not have determined policy offhand, but only after agonizing hesitation and conferences that would probably end with throwing it all back to Stowe. So I accepted his ruling and came back to Paris where I found myself something of an oracle among members of the Anglo-American Press Club, whose views happened to coincide with mine, and something of a pinko to the rest.

It was about this time that political disputes became inflamed by the application of derogatory colour. It was not a new feature; Samuel Butler, in 1662, had mocked Hudibras as "Presbyterian true blue", but the derogatory stain had crossed the spectrum from blue to various tints of red, from purple to pinko. Mindful of the madness which had hastened the ruin of Byzantium, when partisans of the Blue or the Green slew each other in the streets for no more reason than their party colour, I deprecated the use of such terms as "Red" or "Black" as meaningless provocations. The arguments of sanity had little impact in a political society which was reorganizing peninsular transportation by painting all its rolling-stock red and black, the Anarchist colours.

They varied this waste of time and materials — both in short supply — by painting railroad passenger coaches with colourful vistas of the landscape through which the coaches would roll, if the railroads ever resumed normal traffic operations.

The colour neurosis spread over Europe, becoming more

sinister with each remove. Mussolini's Black-shirts evolved into Hitler's Brown-shirts. The choice of a tie to match or to disguise one's political affiliation became a life-or-death matter, as agonizing as and even more serious than an Oxford undergrad's hesitation between ordering a Second-Eight blazer, which he was then entitled to wear, or a First-Eight glorification to which he might aspire by the end of Eights Week.

Early in the autumn of 1936, I found myself once again in the Iberian Peninsula, this time in Madrid, attempting to prove or to disprove the contradictory claims that were sending the *Herald*'s cable desk crazy. One of the disagreeable aspects of life in this city was that the raw recruits in the government forces were obsessed with rifle-fire. Movement after dark was, for this reason, quite dangerous. If you walked quietly along the street, the *miliciano* stationed at any corner fired because he thought you were trying to jump him by surprise; if, on the other hand, you marched noisily down the middle of the street, he fired for fear a column might be approaching. It was well to stay safely within the grounds of the U.S. Embassy, where the military attaché, Colonel Fuqua, a soldier with an alert sense of humour, was instructing the inmates on how to use cover in defending the Embassy from the roof. Even the roof, however, was not entirely safe for there was a continuous rattle of musketry from the trenches not half a mile away; it began at dusk and grew in volume like a hailstorm until about midnight. What went up had to come down. A small-calibre A.A. shell was lodged in the roof outside my bedroom for months. Nobody tried to remove it, and it was still there when I left Madrid.

The term "Fifth Columnist" was invented about this time as the result of a foolish speech by General Mola, an incompetent whom General Franco had put in command of his forces in the north. He announced in a radio broadcast from Burgos that the fall of Madrid was imminent, for he was advancing with four columns, while a Fifth Column was waiting inside the city to seize control and open the gates when he gave the word. This stupidity ensured the arrest and probable execution of every Madrileño who had money, property, or position, which might render him indisposed to the Republic. The Republic took no chances: the Fifth Column had to be wiped out. On this excuse thousands were jammed into the incongruously named Carcel Modelo for no better reason than for being prosperous, fashionable, or clean.

In the neighbourhood of the prison, screams could be heard every night as the inmates were loaded into trucks and borne away to the city dump to be shot. There was reported to be a vast common grave at Alcalá de Henares, some twenty miles east of Madrid, where imperfectly buried bodies could be seen for months afterwards. I made several attempts to nail down this report, but without success, for my *miliciano* driver could not or would not find the spot, and the peasants he questioned were surly, and either too frightened or otherwise indisposed to reply. However, I found a sandstone ledge heavily pitted by bullets which was said to have been the place of execution; it looked like the town dump; I asked a scavenging boy whether he had found any cold cuts that morning. He shrugged and replied without emotion: "Nada!" "Nothing!"

Spain in those days was a veritable Tower of Babel, for every interested party had its own version of what was going on. Even two generals guarding the same front disagreed on whether or not General Franco's troops opposing them were equipped with tanks, and if so, what type; or whether Franco himself was using Arab levies, and if so, what tribes were they—tall Ghoums from Morocco, Berbers from the Jebel, or Negro warriors from the Sahara or Rio di Oro. Nobody knew "where ignorant armies clash by night". Nobody knew whether Nava del Rey, to the north, had fallen; nobody knew whether Franco had cut the main roads to Cadiz and the south at Aranjuez; nobody really knew if there had been Italian troops at Guadalajara, where the government was loudly proclaiming a victory over Fascist forces. The only answer was to see for oneself; so I obtained authority to ramble around in the outlying areas around Madrid to pin down the facts. Armed with this permission I obtained from the Spanish Army Ministry the services of an army vehicle, complete with driver and armed *miliciano*, to conduct me safely to critical areas, and back through the lines to Madrid. The only stipulation was that I remained within a day's drive of the capital, and did not try to "escape" to the Franco columns, which had reached the crest of the Guadarrama Mountains, and were, so to speak, looking down the throat of Madrid.

I drove northwards through the mountains, enjoying the beautiful forest scenery; there was no trace of rebel presence in the vicinity of Nava del Rey, which meant that they had not reached the Guadarrama passes from the north. My driver peered nervously into the thickets, expecting Moors at every corner. His fears infected me, but he was so nervous that, when I told him to return to Madrid, he stalled the car in the middle of the road while turning around. It gave me a chill to imagine what would have happened if there had been a line of Moors barricading the road. Fortunately there was nobody in sight. The outlook on the main road from the north was less reassuring. From an observation post set up by the Loyalist Army, I could see shells bursting, apparently at random, but effectively denying the highway to traffic.

The railway from the north was also under fire. We spent hours watching a little engine shuttling between two tunnels only a hundred yards or so apart. With a defiant peep-peep of his whistle the driver opened up the throttle and hurtled his engine across the open space like a rabbit, just gaining the haven of the second tunnel before shells popped onto the tracks. They burst with a deceptively innocent puff of smoke and a genial report like an opened pop bottle, so much less intimidating than the aggressive explosions I heard in Madrid, but no less deadly. The scene had a strange quality of playfulness; the contest between the engine and artillery was like a children's game; but it was deadly serious, for it meant that Madrid was cut off from bulk supplies from the north and east by rail, leaving only the southern approaches free, and the rebels were already strongly established in the fortress of Toledo by the occupation of Alcazar. They were claiming to have cut the eastern roads to Valencia and Barcelona. If that were true, the fall of Madrid was only a matter of time, and all the slogans in the Loyalist arsenal could not prevent it. It was essential to find out the facts and, since neither side's version could be trusted, I determined to probe as far as Aranjuez, an important road-and-rail junction thirty miles south of Madrid. If the rebels held Aranjuez, Madrid was surrounded and its fall could not be long delayed.

Next day, I arranged with the War Ministry for a car, and set off with Dennis Weaver of the *News-Chronicle*, a non-competitor, on the first of a series of forays to test the southwestern road in case reinforcements or supplies were coming in from Portugal. I'd first teamed up with Weaver some time before. He was a cheerful companion for excursions up to the fronts; it was good to have a responsible colleague to exchange ideas with, and from whom I could pick up the latest rumours that were current in the Western European capitals; we wanted to investigate reports that tanks had appeared on the Toledo front and that Moors, the historic enemies of Spain, were being used along with tanks in Franco's columns. If there were tanks, we wanted to find out who was supplying them, and if there were Moors, how they were being used by that fervid arch-nationalist, Franco — *El Caudillo*, as he was beginning to call himself in imitation of Mussolini's self-designation of *Il Duce*. In pursuit of these ends, we bowled along endless Spanish highways, seeking somebody who could give authoritative answers to our questions, and at the same time trying out the temper of non-combatants behind the lines.

One of the first small towns Weaver and I hit on our sortie was Illescas, about twenty-five miles southwest of Madrid, the usual Spanish mix of an imposing church around which huddled a multitude of hovels. Illescas had something more, however, for it had been host in 1525 to King Francis I of France after his capture at the Battle of Pavia. The house where he had been immured was still the best in town, and probably not much changed since the sixteenth century. What fascinated me about Illescas, however, was a sign on the city walls which read JARDIN DARWIN; not the sort of thing you expected in a little town in Castile, so I asked some loiterer about it. He was laconic: "The apothecary," he said, indicating with his thumb the biggest house in town. I headed there at once; there were huge flagons in the window, full of coloured fluid. The walls were lined to the ceiling with little drawers inscribed with gilt-Gothic lettering: SAL HEPAT, TILIA, NUX VOMICA, etc. The flooring was of red tiles, freshly scrubbed. I introduced myself to a buxom lady behind the counter, and asked about the JARDIN DARWIN. I was astonished at the reaction. It was, she said, a fantastic idea of her husband's, who spent much more time looking after it than he gave to the business. I asked if I could talk to him myself. This provoked another reaction: "Alas!" she said. "He went with the *milicianos*, who needed medical help. You will find him with the column on the road to Madrid." The poor lady began wringing her hands as she dilated on the irresponsibility of leaving his business to follow a column of *milicianos*, loading onto her shoulders the burden both of the business and of keeping up the JARDIN.

This was the topic I wanted to get back to, so I asked her to show it to me, if she would be so kind. She was reluctant but I pressed hard, until, volubly excusing the untidiness of the house, she brought me to a garret where the sunshine poured in on bunches of grapes laid out to dry, and on a bushel basket full of stones. She pointed to these with a contemptuous gesture: "He gave the children a candy for each stone they brought in from the arroyo [river-bed]." She shook her head. "Three bushels of them!"

I looked at the stones. Some were entire, some were chipped, still others were finely worked neolithic artifacts—knives, scrapers, points, and arrowheads — a superb collection. I was so enthusiastic over this discovery of the lonely archeologist working in the very shadow of the church that his wife abated some of her hostility, explaining some of her husband's idiosyncrasies by his addiction to irreligious books, like those on his desk. I went over to the shelf, and there found Darwin's *Origin of Species* in translation, *Drake's Voyages* in Spanish translation (*Viajes del Drago*), and the *Journal of Friar Odoricus* in Latin, all neatly bound in leather, with gilt tooling on their spines. The good lady began to puff a little with pride at my obvious reverence for her husband's erudition; then she congratulated herself on faithfully tending his treasures in his absence and volunteered to show me his garden.

Behind a sheltering wall he had laid out a closely packed botanical garden. In the centre was a greenhouse. She explained that her husband had been particularly fascinated by American plants, and had made a considerable collection of cactuses, which he raised in the greenhouse. Proudly she announced: "I cared for these ungodly plants myself, watering them daily." This seemed ominous; we went to the greenhouse, and there were the poor man's prized cactuses, watered daily, and covered with mildew and other parasitic fungi. I could have wept at the thought of his collection being destroyed by kindness while the poor little apothecary did his part for liberty of mind and thought in this medieval Spanish town.

And that is the story of the Apothecary of Illescas. Weaver and I looked for him on the road back to Madrid; we found a *miliciano* column roasting an ox for dinner; the apothecary was pointed out to me as a treasured intellectual who had thrown in his lot with the Popular Front. I cherished the romantic memory of the roadside bivouac, with the Apothecary of Illescas standing by the fire watching a *miliciano* basting the huge carcass, while a comrade cleaned the offal in a bucket; that night he would eat well. We did not stay for dinner; we wanted to get back through the lines, before the *miliciano* sentries began to get sleepy and took to firing at shadows to keep themselves awake.

Weaver and I returned to Illescas only a short time after. Murder was not the only atrocity alleged against the Loyalists; every crime on the calendar was charged to them, on the theory, perhaps, that some were bound to stick. Many did, some deservedly, but the diversity of charges made investigation of them all impossible. For instance, Franco's radio put out that the famous El Greco paintings in the church at Illescas were being removed for sale to the Russians, or perhaps to the Americans—they were rich. A good lie was never allowed to die for lack of supporting detail. Emissaries from Petrograd and the Metropolitan Museum in New York were invented to buy up, crate, and cart away Spanish art treasures. Witnesses were produced who had seen them being boxed up. Knowing that such charges were often diversions to cover rebel operations of a nature that could then be blamed on the Loyalists, Weaver and I drove to the little town to see for ourselves what went on. It was more than we could have dreamed up.

We found the square full of activity, which at first glance bore out the stories of wholesale art-looting. The square was crowded with trucks and workmen busily crating pictures worth a fortune: El Greco's *Crucifixion*, another which I thought I recognized as *The Burial of Count Orgaz*, by the same artist, and a variety of smaller works. It looked at first sight as if Franco's charges, for once, were true, but when we looked more closely we found that the carefully packed crates were all addressed to the Art Museum at Valencia. The *miliciano* in charge of the operation swore that these very scarce trucks and the gasoline for them had been commandeered to move the treasures of Illescas out of the claws of the rebels, lest Franco seize them for sale to the Americans, who, he assured me, would pay handsomely for such masterpieces, and no questions asked.

I accepted this as a reasonable assumption. When, much later, I went to Valencia after the government had moved there, I made a point of inquiring after the El Grecos. They had arrived and were safely housed in Valencia. That was one contradiction solved, but at much personal fatigue and some risk.

Another sally I shared with Weaver brought us to the headquarters of General Miaja, who was in nominal command of an ill-organized and worse-equipped gaggle of trade-union levies, maintained by the Communist U.G.T. (Union General Trabajadores) column, which was holding, after a fashion, the centre segment of the southern front.

General Miaja was a squat little man, wearing a combination of "mono" and uniform which detracted from his quality either as a worker or as a soldier. He smoked incessantly, but explained in a husky whisper that he had lost his voice trying to explain his military orders to the leader of an Anarchist column which had just come from Catalonia to take up positions on his right. The effort had exhausted his patience, his cigarettes, and his voice, leaving him still unsure of where the Sangue y Ierro column was and what it proposed to do.

I checked with the Anarchists who complained that, if they had not been there to keep an eye on him, General Miaja would have retreated all the way back to Madrid. They added the usual charge that he was a disguised Franco agent, only looking for a chance to betray the Republic. Obeying his orders, therefore, could be abetting the betrayal of the Republican Army, and, as such, be punishable by death.

These sentiments were passed on to me by Compañera Belun, a physically solid but spiritually tempestuous young woman, who had moved up from Huesca with the Anarchist column. Her ardent enthusiasm had been transformed into passionate distaste by the incompetence, brutality, and callousness she had witnessed. The Anarchists had sought to motorize their column by looting the automobile agencies in Barcelona of their stocks of Rolls Royces, Hispano-Suizas, and Cadillacs; she herself had commandeered an Austin Seven, a miniature bug which she preferred as more proletarian than the flashy Talbot-Darracqs favoured by many comrades whose minds had been imperfectly indoctrinated with proletarian principles. Tagging along with her was the homeliest woman I had ever seen; she had a muddy skin, poor teeth, unkempt black hair, and a bumpy figure. Compañera Belun recognized that the girl had made a poor impression me. She hastened to correct it.

"Don't underestimate Milly Bennett," she said. "She may not look like much, but she has a powerful attraction for men. She has charm."

According to Compañera Belun, Milly had held up an Anarchist offensive on the Huesca front for weeks by her intrigue with the commander of the column, and it was a moot question whether the commander or Milly more deserved to be shot. Milly was an American, which may have saved her. Some romantic appeal of the International Brigade had lured her from her home to Spain, where she soon fell victim to the prevailing infection of disillusionment and suspicion. She denounced the International Brigade as incompetent, or worse, and threw in her lot with the Anarchists, as the only Simon Pure revolutionaries to be found. All the rest, she said, were Fifth Columnists.

CHAPTER
SIX

It was not child's play probing into remote areas to establish who controlled them. I found this out in a tragic encounter only a short time after, while I was still trying to test Franco's claim that he had cut off Madrid from the rest of the country by straddling the road to Toledo at Aranjuez.

Weaver had no mind to go on another long probing mission so I set off alone with a *miliciano* and the same driver who had taken me north to Nava del Rey a week or so before. I was not too happy with the driver, remembering how he had panicked and stalled the car in the wild, wooded foothills of the Guadarrama Mountains; however, the War Ministry had no other personnel available, so I swallowed my misgivings and set out.

Faced with the open wheatlands of Castile, my driver gave full rein to his craving for speed. He never dropped below 100 kilometres an hour, which is roughly 62$\frac{1}{2}$ m.p.h. We roared through clusters of houses so fast that I had difficulty recognizing landmarks, but felt that we were getting farther from Madrid than might be healthy. There were no peasants working in the fields, no *milicianos* drilling beside the road; there was an eerie quiet over everything which made me nervous. I leant forward to tell my driver to turn around and go back to Madrid, and was horrified to see ahead of us, about a quarter of a mile away, a line of men strung across the road. They had rifles, all pointed at us. I shouted to the driver to turn fast. He slowed down and stalled. The armed men made threatening gestures with their rifles. I got out in haste, put my hands on my lapels to indicate that I was not armed, and walked with deliberate speed towards the riflemen.

Their appearance did not improve on closer acquaintance. Most of them wore riding-breeches, puttees, and grey sweaters, looking like down-at-heels versions of a D. H. Lawrence gamekeeper. Most of them brandished revolvers. One of them played with a light machine-gun from which he fired a burst in the direction of our car. A man in what looked like a Loyalist Army uniform sat beside the road, with his hands to his head, which was bleeding freely. I cautiously slid one hand down to my side pocket, from which I fished my blue British passport. Holding it well in front of me, I advanced to the head gamekeeper, incongruously intoning: "Periodista American. No tira," which I took to mean, "Don't fire." It was so understood, although the head gamekeeper kept an automatic pressed against my chest, while an underling shot my driver, who had crept up beside me for protection. He fell dead on the road. I looked away to the right, where a deep coulee sheltered a group of horses, among which flitted little dusky men with dirty turbans; with a sinking heart I identified them as Franco's Moorish auxiliaries, among whom I did not wish to be thrown. My captors were jabbering noisily around me, edging me towards the coulee, when their ranks parted before a fat white horse mounted by an Othello-figure with a bushy black beard, who ordered me in Spanish to accompany him as he turned away.

"Where to?" I asked.

"Talavera."

I thought my best ploy would be to pitch my ante high, so I boldly answered, "As an American journalist, I request to see General Franco." I made the request as a policy tactic, figuring that if I got into trouble, no matter how bloody-minded the underlings, they might think twice about manhandling someone who wanted to see the boss — he might indeed be a friend or be potentially useful to the boss, in which case any impeder of his mission would soon find his nuts in the cracker.

His reply astonished and delighted me. "There is another Americano journalist who makes the same request. Perhaps he will identify you."

"What is his name?"

"It sounds like Horrell."

I laughed cautiously. If it was really Hank Gorrell of the United Press, then I was safe, for he would soon have the story on the wires, and the vast apparatus of American diplomacy would be alerted. Colonel Fuqua would want to see me for what intelligence I could give him of Franco's strength and of conditions behind the lines. "Be pleased to take me to Señor Horrell," I requested, "and then to General Franco in Burgos. Meantime, please ask this gentleman to take his pistol out of my stomach." I thought giving Gorrell's name the Spanish pronunciation might help identification.

Blackbeard spurred his horse into the crowd, and I stuck close beside him as we pushed through the brittle stubble, glistening in the evening sunshine. I was obsessed by the thought that the cable desk in New York would be quite upset if they did not get my customary despatch round-up on the rebels' advance on Madrid. They would be even more upset if I got myself killed or wounded. They wanted a live correspondent whose copy would fill half a column in good time for the first edition; they emphatically would not want to be loaded with a front-page obit just as they were locking up the forms, while the *Times* was leading the paper with Herbert Matthews' story on the front page and a full-column jump inside.

My relief at getting through the lines was chilled by the recollection of the salvo-conducto which the Anarchists had stamped with a huge red star, the Anarchist symbol, when I passed through Barcelona in July. It required all loyal brethren of the C.N.T.-F.A.I. (dread initials of the Anarchist activists, as they would be called today) to give aid and comfort to "an honoured friend, known for his enthusiasm for Anarchists . . ." and so on with more tributes to my supposed pro-Anarchist fervour and activity that could hardly fail to be my death-warrant if the document fell into the hands of either the Communists, who hated the Anarchists bitterly, or the rebels, who hated everybody, and particularly the press. My problem was how to get rid of that incriminating piece of paper without being observed. The material was too tough to permit the classic expedient of mastication; it was too big and too conspicuous to be used as toilet paper, except in a lavatory fitted with a water-closet into which it could be torn up and washed away.

My kindly guide took me to an abandoned auto, dismounted from his fat white nag, and invited me to enter the car, which I did reluctantly, having no wish to repeat the experience with the roadblock. However, he got in beside me, explaining that he had instructions not to let me out of his sight until I was turned over to the regional commander in Talavera de las Reinas. When I let him know that I was in urgent need of easement, he nodded understandingly and turned aside into a stubble field. I tumbled out, prepared to defecate prairie-extemporaneous style, but my captor leapt out after me, so I quickly substituted plan Piss-pot for plan Thunder-mug, and urinated copiously. I explained to my admiring captor that, being an effete urbanite, I was conditioned to comfortable seating, flowing water, and privacy, before I could defecate. Being a *caballero* himself, he nodded understandingly, and observed that the nearest facility of that importance was the Hotel Inghilterra at Avila on the other side of the Sierra de Gredos. I suggested that we drive to this haven at all convenient speed, but my guide demurred at crossing the Sierra de Gredos at night; he suggested Talavera de las Reinas, where we could eat a good dinner and get a quiet night's sleep. I agreed on Talavera, but the inn looked unpromising; its performance matched its appearance. There was no "Water", only thunder-mugs under the bed. There was a further formality. Before we could even settle in there we would have to be questioned by the Intelligence Service. My guide cheered me mightily by telling me that Señor Horrell of the United Press had also been brought to Talavera, and was at that very moment being interrogated. My guide escorted me to a grim two-storey building, by appearance either a barracks or a prison. At one end of a long gallery on the second floor was a large desk, dimly lighted;

on one side was a rebel officer; opposite him was Hank Gorrell. I wanted to rush up and embrace Hank, but my guide warned me not to go near him, lest we seize the opportunity to adjust our stories to the detriment of the facts.

I got the pitch and sat down on a case of hand-grenades. I was fascinated by a painting hanging on the wall opposite me. It was a three-quarter-length representation of a monk, wielding a cross, butt against belly; the shaft of the cross gradually merged into an arquebus which the monk was brandishing. I was so fascinated by this personification of the church militant that I made no effort to listen to Hank's interrogation, which I could not have heard anyway, and was apparently so uninterested that when the interrogation was over, the guards made no effort to prevent Hank exchanging a few words with me.

"The bastards tried to find out what field defences there were around Madrid," he muttered. "But I didn't give them anything. Don't you either!"

I shook my head. "Not me!" I did not dare hand my Anarchist salvo-conducto over to Gorrell before the very eyes of the guard; it would have been asking for trouble, besides ensuring plenty for Hank to explain away, so I took the seat he had just occupied and waited for the rebel officer to open fire. He was a fresh-faced young fellow, like an English public-school senior. His accent suggested that that might have been so, in which case even he was probably rabidly "anti-red" as most of the well-to-do were. He was a Crusader! However, he was not likely to order me to be executed, so I replied pleasantly to his questions about barbed wire and trenches between here and Madrid, saying that I had seen nothing of military significance, but on the other hand as a matter of principle I had refrained from looking too closely in order to preserve a journalistic neutrality.

He fired up at the word, making it clear that he did not believe there was a neutral journalist in the entire press corps; they all gave the "red" version, he said. I replied mildly that we gave what we could get, and the Loyalists were much freer in their treatment of the press. In that connection, I added boldly, I would be happy to give General Franco's version, so please let me have a salvo-conducto and transport to Burgos, with a letter of recommendation to General Franco. This sally was successful beyond my hopes. A general salvo-conducto was handed to me, and a car and driver were authorized to convey me to the border by whatever route I preferred. I could spend the night here in Talavera and leave first thing in the morning for the north and France. I went to bed happily, but still without destroying that infernal Anarchist pass. Toilet facilities were the usual *pot de chambre* under the bed. I slept well, and was up early next morning, taking time to admire the morning star and the eastern constellations before dawn. I did this inconspicuously, for I did not want my departure to be delayed by an official inquiry into my documentation on account of my eccentricities. We roared out of Talavera and across the Sierra de Gredos. My driver was the usual Spanish speed-demon who drove at a flock of mountain sheep as if he were Don Quixote reincarnated. We raced around the medieval red-brick crenellated walls of Avila until we came to the Puerto del Norte. Through its majestic arch I was thrilled to see the façade of the Hotel Inghilterra. I explained my urgent need to defecate, to which my driver responded by dashing through the city gate to draw up at the hotel entrance in style. Securing a promise that I would not try to escape, he waited for me with the engine running, not wishing to leave the car untended lest it be stolen.

I raced to the spacious washroom. I never heard more gratifying music than the trickle of that flush tank. I tore my incriminating salvo-conducto to shreds as if I had been preparing for a school paper-chase, threw them into the bowl, and pulled the chain. I watched until the last scrap had been carried away, then I strode back to the car. My driver had a pleasant sense of humour. "You didn't take long," he joked. "But you certainly look as if you dropped a load off your mind!"

"I did!" I replied as I jumped in. He trod on the accelerator and we drove back through the gate. I turned around for a last look at that lovely city, its walls glowing rosy red in the setting sun.

"Nice hotel!" my driver commented proudly.

"First class!" I agreed.

It was good to be going north again. We touched Burgos, but found no sign of Franco. This was no disappointment to me; I was merely gratified that my stratagem had succeeded and that I would be returning to Paris before long. At St. Jean Pied de Port, on the frontier, I was amused to hear a correspondent of one of the London newspapers telephoning an "eye-witness" account of the entry of rebel forces into one of the Basque citadels. His account was full of vivid detail, uninhibited by the fact that he had not been there at the time, but had been snugly ensconced at Hendaye, Biarritz, or St. Jean. It was typical of Spanish Civil War reporting, and caused me to wonder how much of the epic of the American Civil War had been of like authenticity; this struck home, because the legendary heroes of my own paper had battened on the myth of their presence in the campaigns of General Ulysses S. Grant, in which the original Whitelaw Reid had distinguished himself by carrying despatches on the battlefield and reporting them in the New York *Tribune*. However, that was no skin off my nose, although my competition on the *New York Times* was indulging in absentee "eye-witness" reports of Spanish Civil War episodes so blatantly as to enable me to ignore New York's queries, inspired by his accounts, by cabling "Another Carney exclusive." Herbert Matthews, however, found the situation very trying; he was conscientious enough to check every wide-eyed Carney story that his paper had printed. He was then faced with the problem of straightening out the facts, without too obviously undercutting his colleague.

Physically and emotionally fatigued after the ordeal on the road to Aranjuez, I was happy to return to my family in Paris, which now included a small son, and to enjoy the generous enthusiasm of Leland Stowe. I looked forward to a pleasant winter of uneventful assignments from which there would be little risk of any physical danger. In Spain, the war continued its chaotic course and I had no desire to become enmeshed in it again until the spring of 1937 when, after months of reporting Parisian political ploys, I felt drawn once again to the Iberian Peninsula.

In view of the Spaniards' indifference to their destiny, it seemed unreasonable to expect me to risk my life on their behalf, but I had no hesitation in accepting an assignment to the Basque provinces where fighting against a common external foe was not complicated by an internal struggle within the province itself, or so I thought.

However, my assignment was glorified by the fall of the ancient Basque capital, Guernica, on April 26, 1937, and the consequent threat to Bilbao, the port through which iron ore was shipped to Britain. The English iron-masters, who had been left cold by the defence of the Alcazar at Toledo, were at white heat over the threat to their ore supplies. Sensing their interest, the *Morning Post* syndication, for which I also worked, was anxious to obtain reliable coverage of the Basque situation as it developed.

With this incentive, I soon found myself aboard a light plane, making an adventurous flight out of Pau, skimming the wave-crests to avoid detection by possible rebel aircraft until we put down safely amid filled-in bomb craters on the field at Bilbao.

Everything contrasted strikingly with the Madrid I had left in the autumn of 1936. The streets were clean and tidy, with bomb damage neatly and expeditiously repaired in populated areas. Press communications were rapid and uncensored. I had no trouble hiring a car which would enable me to circulate safely; but I found that my harrowing experience on the road to Aranjuez had made me so nervous that every blind corner caused me an agony of apprehension which made it unendurable to probe closely into the front line. In this quandary I sought the companionship of Gerda Grep, a Norwegian girl who was covering the Basque front for *Arbeiderbladed* of Oslo and happened to be staying at the same hotel and using the same pressroom.

She was cool, collected, and thorough, anxious to investigate personally every rumour as well as every official statement. Her paper's expense allowance was less flexible than mine, so I exchanged a seat in my car for her company and comforting knowledge of Guipuzcoa and Viscaya provinces, the heart of Basque defences.

Bilbao contrasted pitifully with Barcelona, which was still packed with consumer goods. Bilbao was stripped clean. I cannot forget the bleakness of a small stationery store whose shelves were cleaned out: no pens, no pencils, no paper. I could buy only a tiny notebook as a great favour, but it was an inadequate substitute for my fat, opulent French *carnet* into which I had poured such lush notes and clippings in Madrid.

Fortunately, there were still empty pages left in this *carnet* into which I copied an item dated April 28, 1937, from Agence Espagne, Bayonne. I reproduce it, for it deals authoritatively with many controversial events in the Basque campaign. This item states:

> The insurgent radio [in Burgos] announces that last night General Mola, C-in-C rebel troops on the Basque Front, declared in a public speech that Bilbao would suffer the fate of Guernica, the former Basque capital, of Eibar and of Durango, which were entirely destroyed by the incendiary bombs of the German aviation in the service of the Spanish rebels. We shall raze Bilbao, and its site, naked and desolate, will change the desire of the English to support the Basque Bolshevists. The capital of a perverse people which dares oppose the irresistible cause of the national idea, must be destroyed.

Delenda est Carthago!

This frank admission by Agence Espagne that Guernica was "entirely destroyed by German incendiary bombs" cut the ground from under the feet of interested political commentators who advanced the theory that Guernica was destroyed by Anarchists from the northwestern provinces of Santander and Oviedo, or by the Viscayans themselves to arouse international indignation. Apart from the inherent absurdity of these postulates, Basque forces actually received the surrender of one German pilot whose plane was brought down in the foothills. He was a tall, spare young man in his late twenties; he was quite frank and willing to talk. I took notes of the interview with Georg Kohl, whose Dornier 17 was brought down near Brunete, north of Madrid. A mechanic by trade, Georg Kohl was born in the Palatinate, near Amberg, May 25, 1909. How he came to be shot down in a Dornier 17 over Brunete when he was twenty-eight years old is worth relating in detail, for it documents incontrovertibly German and Italian intervention in the Spanish Civil War, which was a very lively issue at the time.

His German military service began at Amberg when he was twenty-five in Regiment No. 16. He signed a four-and-one-half-year contract on a promise of being trained as Pilot, first class; he had done glider flying, in which the Germans were proficient, since he was eighteen. He entered an aviation school in April 1935, and was later sent to Kottbus where he received B-2 and C-2 certificates as a pilot.

But he wanted to see action, so, he told me, "I spoke to the commander of my company about the possibility of enlisting for Spain. He replied that he would send the request on to the proper authorities."

A few weeks later he was given seventy marks, with which he set out by boat from Hamburg, for Spain; but the ship returned to port after two weeks at sea, and he was sent on to the Ministry of War, Berlin, where he was assigned to a special section which sent him and two other "civilians" by Lufthansa to Rome. He stayed the night in a hotel there, then was flown, in a single hop, to Seville, where he stayed in Hotel Regina. "There were German officers there without uniforms," he told me. "I met a German army friend there." From Seville he flew in a Junker to Salamanca, where he was incorporated in a unit in which the only Spaniards were a few mechanics; the officers were all Germans under Commander Neudorfer.

Ten Dornier 17's had just been sent to Spain for tests. These were two-motored jobs, capable of about 250 m.p.h., which was not fast, even for those days, but they could carry ten bombs of 50 kilos each, three machine-guns, and a crew of three. They flew at 15,000 feet for precision work against artillery batteries. At the same airfield there were Heinkel III's, also being tested in Spain, and used later against London. Our captive first saw the Dornier 17 that spring at Ansbach. He had been in Spain only two weeks when he was brought down on his second flight.

"We set out with other bombers of the same class [Dornier or

Heinkel] for the Sierra," he went on. "In my plane were Lieutenant Seidel and radio-telegraphist Schmidt, both Germans. Over Avila we picked up our escort of Italian chasers ["fighters"], Fiats. We were attacked by four government chasers. When they saw them the Italians fled, and we never saw them again. My machine was brought down and we took to parachutes. My two companions were wounded."

There was not much more that Commander Kohl could tell me. He received 400 pesetas (about $80 at that time) while he was in Seville, but did not know what the monthly rate was because he had not filled out the month before he was shot down.

As military aviation these Heinkels and Dorniers were quite primitive machines; the Russian "Chatos" could handle them easily. But their appearance in Spain gave the French and British military aviation experts much too optimistic an idea of what they would have to deal with in the next war, for which these were obviously trial runs. The French, feeling secure of future air control, relaxed; but, fortunately, the British continued work on the Hurricanes and Spitfires without disclosing them to the Germans in Spain.

These aircraft made the difference between victory and defeat in the Second World War. Less than five years later, I watched them gyrating over London, and joined Londoners cheering in the streets as the enemy tumbled out of the sky in bits and pieces. I watched the Dorniers skulking about Channel convoys of merchant shipping. I was surprised at the evil, predatory aspect that the builders had contrived to work into the profile of these bombers, which stooged about the flanks of the convoy until the Hurricanes and Spits appeared to send them scurrying off to the protection of our gallant ally, France, where Maréchal Pétain was piously appeasing and collaborating with his country's unappeasable enemy. In those days I recovered from London's ruined houses burned-out incendiaries of a pattern identical to those I had pulled out of debris in Guernica — made by the West-Deutsche Stahlwerke in Düsseldorf, complete with stylized German eagle stamped on the case and blackened vents at the base.

The writing on the bomb-case appeared to Gerda Grep, as it did to me, to be as monitory as that on the palace wall was to Nebuchadnezzar in Babylon. It was a timely warning, and British authorities heeded it to the extent of training Londoners in the techniques of dowsing these thermite weapons. One or two would have been easy to handle, but when they fell like rain, incendiaries soon defied control, as the conflagration of London demonstrated; but early familiarity with them induced a certain contempt in Londoners which stiffened their resolve not to be daunted by a cheap incendiary like the Düsseldorf product.

On one of my timid excursions into the countryside in search of the wreckage of a plane brought down by the Basques, my car drew up abruptly beside a roadside dugout, the driver having spotted a plane headed our way. I hopped out of the car and into the dugout, pausing at the brink to admire a magnificent Aquilegia flowering among the roadside grasses. It was a splendid large blue flower, from which I wanted to obtain seeds, but it was too early in the season. While I was scuffing about looking for ripe pods, the planes came over again and I dived into the shelter, thinking to return later in the season when seedpods might be mature; but I never came back to that lovely spot.

A beguiling feature of Basque air-raid precautions was that their sirens, installed throughout Bilbao, were musical. Instead of the hideous cacophony which warned Londoners of hostile aircraft, the Basques had installed sirens which produced melodic chords as they rose and fell; the innovation was startling and drained air-raid warnings of much of the sheer terror which standard cacophony evoked. It was only a detail, but it endeared the Basques to me. I realized, nevertheless, that they had stretched credulity when they boasted of the protection afforded by their "Iron Line", a ring of imaginary field-works which existed only on paper, some twenty miles or so to the southeast. There was no organized protection for Bilbao, so its fall could only be a matter of time. Most correspondents were aware of this, but they forbore to report it lest they give aid and comfort to the enemy; most of us had reached the point where the Basques' enemies were our enemies. The Basques' diet was sardines and rancid olive oil; our diet was sardines and rancid olive-oil. We were not fellow-travellers, we were fellow-sufferers. I thought to improve my diet by purchasing supplies from one of the vessels in harbour; but they turned out to be fishing boats, and all they had was—sardines! A woman on the quay was selling oranges. I tried to buy some; she said something incomprehensible in the Basque tongue — Euskadi — and stepped to one side, to reveal a bushel basket full of—sardines! Grilled, roasted, fried, or boiled, a sardine is a sardine, is a sardine . . . a sardine, a sardine, a sardine, 'dine, 'dine, 'dine! The *Morning Post*, imaginative as ever, sent a magnificent relief hamper to me with ham, beef, sausages, and wine, which kept me happy for weeks.

The end was predictable, and I did not want to witness the entry of the Fascists; nor did I want to get caught up in the scramble to evacuate; so I suggested to Stowe that I had had my share of fun, and would appreciate returning to the perils of Paris. He recalled me at once, and I spent three weeks in a cautious survey of gourmet-Paris, for which the *Morning Post*'s hamper had honed my appetite.

Morning Post correspondents were not highly paid. The paper existed only as long as the Conservative Party was willing to meet its deficit. When this failed, the *Morning Post* died, regretted by everyone who had ever worked for it. It was a delightful paper to be with, correct in its attitude to news, insistent on good paper, beautiful type-faces, and educated correspondents who wrote good English. It rewarded meritorious stories with a cable of congratulations, for which its one-word code was HARROW. I received my first HARROW for covering a Christmas train-disaster at Lagny; HARROWs flocked in — along with hampers — when I was holed up and hungry in Basque territory. The choice of HARROW for congratulations was typical of the *Morning Post*'s wry sense of humour.

The *Morning Post* kept its editorial opinions to its editorial columns. It did not slant or shade the news. The *Herald Tribune* had a close working arrangement with the *Morning Post* and access to all its proofs. We were very happy with this connection;

so, presumably, were they, for when the *Herald Tribune*'s managing editor, Grafton Wilcox, cabled my appointment to Rome, to take over as the *Herald Tribune*'s correspondent there in June 1937, the *Morning Post* farmed me out to the *Sunday Times*, already having a correspondent, Darsie Gillie, and offices of their own in the Stampa Estera Building, both of which they were anxious to retain.

CHAPTER
SEVEN

The Rome appointment came as a great surprise; it had seemed to both Stowe and me that with my background and my recent experiences in Spain, I could mingle usefully with the Spanish emigrés who were clustering about the passes through the Pyrénées. Allowing for the bias which emigrés everywhere nourish, there might still be a rich field for "interpretive accounts" of Spanish developments. It was typical of journalistic reaction, however, that New York decided to reward my services in Spain by sending me to Italy, where every contact with Spain would be hostile, and even the language would be strange.

However, it promised to be an exciting assignment, and Sonia Tomara had already demonstrated that news, such as it was, was accessible, and could be reported, for the most part, without serious constraints, despite Fascist meddling. My predecessor in Rome, Johnny Whitaker, had also tested the fertility of Roman news sources and had revived New York's flagging interest, which until then had given Mexico pride of place in the Latin world, as offering lush markets for American interests, readily controlled by border patrols and a gunboat off the coast. But Mexico's popularity suffered from the discomfiture which "bandit" forces regularly visited on American border patrols.

Italy's popularity climbed as Mexico's fell, so the head office looked sympathetically on the possibility of developing Latin coverage from Rome instead of Mexico City, and syndicating Italian news stories throughout the Latin-American world. It was a shrewd calculation and led to my being hustled off to Rome at short notice, with an allowance of three weeks on the expense account before settling down to survival on my salary and whatever I could dream up as legitimate office expenses.

Having taken a few lessons in Italian before entraining for Rome, happy in the prospect of being my own boss, I had few regrets that there seemed little likelihood of seeing my relatives and friends in Canada for another two or three years. Helen and I had spent most of the summer of 1935 in North America; we had left our son, now a toddler, with his maternal grandparents in Schenectady, New York State, while we travelled first to the Canadian west coast to visit my mother at her home a short distance from Victoria, then to Vanguard, Saskatchewan.

Mother's cottage, built into a hillside which overlooked her flower garden, an orchard, and farmland undulating down to the sea, intrigued me. It seemed the ideal retreat; more than thirty years later, I discovered that my assessment had been correct. Although Mother was far away from the rest of the family, she had carved a niche for herself in the little community. Years later, older residents remembered her as a local "character" who had used a dogcart to which she harnessed not only her dog, but a goat, for hauling wood from the nearby beach. Many also remembered the goats she tethered out to forage alongside the local highway. She didn't lack familiar company either, for Lawrence Fieldhouse and his cheerful, efficient wife, Mary, whom Mother regarded as her adopted daughter, were now living in the neighbourhood with their five children.

As for the homestead and the prairies, I regarded both as dear enemies. While I was in Vanguard, I hated both; the one because even the most concentrated physical labour seemed to bring forth so little in return; the other because the hostility of the prairie and the everlasting wind provided such a contrast to the softer climates of Europe to which I was now accustomed. When it came time to leave, however, I was filled with melancholy, for I realized once again how strong were the emotional ties with my family. Father and my brothers had changed little in temperament, although Eric, a little boy when I'd last seen him, was now a grown man, and I had returned to find a flock of new nieces and nephews, the children of Dick and his wife Hilda. It deeply warmed me, too, that my family wholeheartedly accepted into their midst my wife, Helen, whom they met for the first time on this brief visit.

In Rome, a few regrets I harboured over my absence from Canada were tempered by reports from the prairie during the last two years of the dust bowl which reached its peak after my return to Europe, late in 1935. Some daytime dust storms darkened the skies to such an extent that lamps had to be lighted indoors; farmers, attempting their chores under such conditions, were unable to see the ground from their tractors. Other storms lasted for days; when they were over, most of the soil would be blown off the hardpan, the loose dirt in drifts on the sheltered side of hills, in trees and fences, or just gone. Realizing that farming was not my metier anyway, I was selfishly relieved not to be enduring the added difficulties; whatever storms I was missing out west, it seemed obvious to me that the Spanish martial storm would soon extend to other parts of Europe.

Establishing myself in Rome proved to be a test of initiative, as the *Herald Tribune* frowned upon either a regular office or a bureau as being too expensive. I was supposed to compete with the *New York Times* and make what impact I could on officialdom as a visiting correspondent on a temporary mission. However, moving me and my household to Rome committed the *Herald Tribune* so heavily that it was not too difficult to convince the accounting office that full value from the expenditure could be obtained only by filling in all gaps.

The office accommodations I found were close to those occupied by the *Morning Post* in the Stampa Estera Building, among the most desirable in Rome, besides enabling the congenial relationship with the *Post*'s civilized, knowledgeable, and literate correspondent, Darsie Gillie, to be maintained. One peculiar feature of the Rome offices was that they looked out into a sort of external stairwell which was heavily populated by chimney swifts. Their interminable screaming as they jockeyed for favourable positions established a sort of *leitmotif* for my office, so that I never hear swifts screaming today without nostalgia for my first independent bureau assignment.

The river was among my chief delights at Oxford, and I was proud to be invited to be a part of the Oriel II eight, which in this photograph trails University 2.

Standing next to me is Charles Wayland Lightbody (back row, second from left), the distinguished Canadian historian, who shared with me many of my European exploits and remained a friend until his death.

A photograph of me taken at the Haywards Heath School by one of my pupils there.

(Left to right) My father Philip Richard Minifie, my wife Helen, and my brother Dick, taken on the homestead at Vanguard.

Helen Minifie, my mother Frances Marion
Minifie, and Mary Fieldhouse, with Mary's
children, taken during a visit to Victoria before
the Second World War.

My wife Helen, myself, and Maureen Church,
with my son, James M. Minifie, Jr., in Paris.

James MacDonald Minifie, Jr., a photograph taken during my
years with the Rome bureau of the *New York Herald Tribune*.

Lava and scoriae from the eruption of Vesuvius that took place while I was with the Office of Strategic Services in Naples, Italy, during the Second World War.

I was fortunate enough to get a front-row position for the famous joint interview between the press, President Franklin D. Roosevelt, and Prime Minister Winston S. Churchill, which took place in December 1941.

In September 1946 I received the Medal of Freedom from
Brigadier General Ferenbaugh at the War Department in
Washington, D.C.

Getting aboard the aircraft carrier was half the fun, but I comforted myself that at least I would now know most of what there was to know about carrier operations.

News-gathering in the Italian capital proved to be vastly different from the established methods I had known in France, although there was a provision of long standing for a tipster, comparable to my Parisian friend Léon Bassée, who would clue me in on both Church and State. A minor Vatican official filled the role as far as the Church was concerned, but on the Quirinale or secular side, I was unprotected. Neither was there an equivalent in Rome to the presidential press conferences which I later found to be such a fertile news source in Washington. Mussolini would have scorned such procedure as beneath him, or "demagogy" (of all things!). When he had anything to say, he delivered it from the balcony of the Palazzo di Venezia to the ecstatic applause of the Fascist faithful, massed in the Piazza Venezia for the occasion. There were minimal arrangements for Italian reporters, and practically none for foreigners. They thrust and scuffed their way into what vacant spaces they could find, and accepted them for as many hours as necessary.

I once achieved a place — or at least a foothold — on the gleaming white marble steps of the Vittorio Emanuele monument to Italian unification. But when I sat down to ease my aching back, I was brought sharply to my feet by an officious *carabiniero*, who considered that a sitting position lacked respect for *Il Duce*, even if he were not at the moment visible.

It was not really necessary to be physically present in the Piazza, for loudspeakers relayed every syllable and rustle of proceedings to every café and *trattoria* in town. Even taxis were not immune, for naturally the Italian Broadcasting System carried every whisper, and no chauffeur would risk being caught listening to anything else; it was saturation coverage, setting a pattern which the Teutonic copycats up north methodically followed.

When I was assigned to Rome, I determined to follow John Whitaker's example, and cover everything deadpan, although I proposed to exercise my privilege of accentuating the ridiculous and immortalizing shams by publicity, as far as I could do that under the eagle eye of Fascist authority. My resolve was easier to come by, since I feared that the present Fascist course would lead inevitably to war, and I would just as soon be honourably expelled from Italy before the conflagration broke out. The first three weeks of my Roman holiday I spent enjoying my expense account at a luxury hotel while I found my feet, secured my working papers, including of course the invaluable *tessera* which was roughly the equivalent of the New York police pass or the Paris *coupe-fil*, and hunted for less sumptuous living quarters.

As a precaution I made my number with the Ministry of Popular Culture, where I found Commendatore Rocco, to whom I had been recommended by my predecessors. I found ensconced in a high-backed chair in a magnificently tapestried salon with an exuberantly painted ceiling, a grey-faced man with the tired eyes of a superannuated bureaucrat who dreads any move which might blow up a fuss to the detriment of his approaching retirement and pension.

Rocco assured me that there was no such thing as censorship in Fascist Italy: I could go anywhere, almost, see almost everything, and report discreetly as much of what I had seen as security regulations permitted. There was no censorship, Rocco added, because there was no news either, apart from official announcements, and they certainly could not be censored. Rocco recommended that I stay closely by the official text and enjoy the amenities of Rome. With this sage advice, Rocco looked at me with the face of a Renaissance humanist, and I gazed back at him with what I hoped was a look of credulous but reverent innocence.

Rocco lavished praise on one of my predecessors, Sonia Tomara, while wondering aloud that a woman could be so competent, and a Russian so trustworthy. She had even secured a brief chat with *Il Duce*, at the insistence of his daughter, Edda. There had not been much news in it but it made a good feature piece. This was my cue to make a formal request for equal treatment, and a similar interview with Mussolini. Rocco smiled bleakly at this tactical success, but made no insuperable difficulties to putting the request through channels. Eventually, Commendatore Rocco gave me the word that, while my requested interview with Mussolini was unlikely to be approved for the time being, there would be no difficulty in arranging a private luncheon with his son-in-law, Count Galeazzo Ciano, the Italian Foreign Minister.

My luncheon was to be in the Palazzo Chigi; after overrunning a pair of paper-pushers, I was shown through tall double doors into a modest room hung with embossed leather. I had recognized the signal honour which was being conferred on a newcomer, and had prepared in advance a checklist of luncheon topics, which might not be as innocuous as they seemed. I was prepared to turn the occasion to what profit it could afford, but the boot turned out to be on the other foot, for the Italian Foreign Minister opened up by asking me to tell him frankly what had actually happened at Guadalajara, the Spanish Civil War battle in which a contingent of Fascist militia had been blooded in a Loyalist ambush. I had not been at Guadalajara and despite the many accounts I had received of the battle, I did not know what had happened, so I mentally jumped back and fished out a morsel of history, mentioning Spain as the graveyard of higher hopes than Fascism's, as witness the French disaster at Baylen in 1808. General Dupont had surrendered with 20,000 men there, thus shattering the legend of Napoleonic invincibility. If Old Spain could do that to Bonaparte, I asked if New Spain could be expected to deal more easily with *Il Duce*?

It was a good question, to which I knew the answer before asking, as one always should. Ciano grinned, and I felt that my answer might jog around in much higher circles before its usefulness ended. Having established a certain rapport with my host, I asked him what versions of the affair had come back to Rome. "Mostly Red propaganda," he said, "with which a few misguided people here are trying to stir up trouble. But they are not significant."

Then he launched into a brief dissertation on the art of government which might have come out of Machiavelli's *Prince*. I resolved to read and reread my copy, and then put in a bid to visit the colonization efforts in Libya. He received this well, and promised to turn me over to Marshal Italo Balbo, who was in charge.

He was interested in the reputation in the United States of my immediate predecessor in Rome, Johnny Whitaker, of whom he thought highly. I did not say that some quarters considered copy out of Rome suspect as being too favourable to Mussolini in the Abyssinian crisis of 1935, which had in fact been admirably covered from the first by Whitaker. He had correctly forecast Mussolini's victory after personally covering the training and early field operations of Mussolini's forces. The *Tribune* was tagging along with the general League of Nations estimate that a boycott of Italian goods would bring Mussolini to terms, and that oil sanctions would unseat him. Whitaker had no illusions about this, or about the oil companies. The *Herald Tribune* decided that he had been taken in by Mussolini's propaganda, so the best thing to do was leave him in Rome to sweat it out. Johnny, however, moved too fast, and soon turned up on another war-front: Spain. He compounded his sin by reporting the Franco side, whereas the *Tribune*'s city room was frantically Loyalist. Whitaker had, as it turned out, picked another winner, but since it was not the one the front office favoured, he received little credit for his foresight, or for his ingenuity in accompanying the Italian forces into Abyssinia, from whence he sent brilliant, colourful dispatches of which the *Tribune* was proud, although it winced at the cost of cables from Eritrea. Unfortunately, Johnny succumbed to the temptation of a drink from a pool of water one hot, dusty afternoon. With that drink he acquired some miserable African parasite which ravaged him for the rest of his days and ultimatley carried him off, an unpublicized victim of his professional zeal for first-hand information and personal observation.

I decided I might get a free ride on his coat-tails, so I pointed out that his good reports resulted from the freedom of access he had been given. Without promising anything I then put in my bid for similar treatment. Colonization, the draining of the Pontine Marshes, the creation of the new cities, archeological finds, and Etruscan excavations were all good copy. Ciano suggested I might attend naval exercises at which the exploits of Italy's new light craft might be discreetly mentioned.

Ciano and I parted with, I think, mutual esteem. I followed his career as closely as I could after I left Italy, and could have wished Fate had been kinder to him. He was shot on his father-in-law's orders.

During our luncheon, Ciano also recommended I maintain an association with Commendatore Rocco at the Ministry of Popular Culture, who was understanding and responsible. I liked Rocco, whose task was to avoid being ground between the upper millstone of the press and the lower stone of Fascist susceptibilities. The Italian press was easy to handle. The threat of revoking their Party membership sufficed to bring them to heel. The foreign, and particularly the Anglo-American, press was a very different breed of cat, equally resentful of "guidance" or censorship. One of the Rocco's delicate duties was to work through the files of the telephone-tapping service and to discuss errors of fact or discretion discovered in them without revealing to correspondents that their telephones had been tapped and their conversation recorded.

On one occasion I was called urgently to the Ministry of Popular Culture, where I found Rocco in a terrible tantrum. He ordered me to be at the frontier within twenty-four hours. This startled me, for I was not aware of having committed any peccadillo, and Rocco was uncommunicative, merely calling on me to search my conscience. I did; it was clean. My amazement was so genuine that Rocco suspended sentence, and eventually passed on to me a typewritten report, taken from a wiretap, of a conversation carried over my telephone, in which the *verboten* topic of Mussolini's health did come up. The report exonerated me, however, for it kept referring to the speaker in the feminine gender. It then occurred to me that the culprit was a female who had come in from New York on a scrounging mission and had taken me literally when I told her my office was at her disposal.

Rocco noted all this down on the back of a "charge-sheet", and, with great daring, cancelled the expulsion order, although it had come from Head Office itself. He added a strong recommendation that I ensure that the young woman find herself at and over the frontier as soon as possible. It was many years before I discovered why mention of Mussolini's health, even a favourable assessment, was taboo: the exponent of youth and health, delighting to trot ahead of his Bersaglieri, the pride of the Italian Army, in fact had colitis, a painful inflammation of the lower bowel.

The trotting about and the other physical activities which Mussolini indulged in publicly must have been exquisitely painful in his condition; but had his affliction become generally known, the jibes and jokes of *Senatus populusque Romanus*, who had not had such a target for centuries, would have been spiritually and psychologically unbearable both for Mussolini and for his Fascist Party. How the Germans would have roared! How the Russians would have sniggered! How the Spanish would have derided! In retrospect, these considerations emphasize the restraint with which Rocco, more in sorrow than in anger, complained of the offending medical discussion over my telephone. As I was able to convince him that it was not my voice on the phone, he suggested, as a penitential offering, that I might accompany *Il Duce* on some colourful upcoming visits to his Pontine Drainage Works and the new towns being founded there, an Army review, a Navy review, colonization in Libya with Marshal Balbo, and a close-up view of Mussolini and Adolf Hitler when and if (this was a massive secret, not to be revealed or hinted at under the direst penalty) *Der Führer* visited Rome— which, God forbid, had apparently through some oversight been sanctioned. Signor Rocco explained that he was taking a generous view of my shortcomings in recognition of the enthusiastic tributes to the civilizing and organizing genius of fascism displayed by my early dispatches from Rome. This puzzled me, but I said nothing; least said, least to be mended, it seemed to me. For years I benefited by my reputation for "trustworthiness". It was not until I glanced through the Ministry's files after the Allied occupation of Rome in the Second World War that I discovered that complimentary dispatches written by my predecessors had found their way into my file by mistake, thus endowing me with a useful, if unmerited, odour of sanctity.

For my first three weeks in Rome, I stayed at the Ambasciatori, one of the best hotels. Three weeks was the standard period allowed on the *Herald Tribune*'s expense account while correspondents looked for housing appropriate to their circumstances and the paper's reputation. I favoured the Aventine Hill, as picturesque, uncrowded, high, within walking distance of the office, and still boasting of a tradition of defiant independence which it had long since abandoned. Wandering around the Aventine one day, I spotted a notice reading "Apartment for Rent". It was a bright little place with three rooms and a terrace of its own, looking onto a courtyard, quiet, cool, and clean. Number 8, Via Raimondo da Capua, had a romantic ring, so I rented it at once, confident that my wife would approve—and if she didn't, she could go find a better. At $90 a month that would not be easy.

To this day, I have not found out who Raimondo da Capua was; no history lists him. Perhaps the name was dreamed up by a land speculator who had bought up a vacant hillside and was giving subdivisions romantic associations and fresh-minted antique names. It doesn't matter. The site looked south to the Alban Hills, eastwards to the Sabines, where Horace's farm, with its little brook, *Splendidior vitro*, was holding its own as the authentic *fons Bandusiae* against the pretensions of another claimant far to the south; down below lay the Tiber, and all Rome was at the foot of the cliff. The distant hills shimmered in the sunlight; near by, Judas-trees clothed the plains with imperial purple. Opposite my house, cabbages competed for space with marble pediments of long-forgotten columns, vestiges of a Temple of Liberty.

My wife, Helen, and Don, now aged three, soon joined me. Together we explored neighbouring churches which cherished immemorial traditions, such as the shearing of sheep in Santa Maria Agnese, the fleece of which was used for some of the Pope's raiment. Young Don delighted us by learning Italian very quickly, his pronunciation being considered a model by admiring old ladies whom he made friends with in the nearby park. Naturally, we supported our friendly neighbourhood Sabine farm, well within range for a Sunday picnic lunch, and urged our friends at the American Academy to furnish us with classical allusions; but they lived across the Tiber on Janiculum and did not care much about anything else.

We lived on, by, and for the Aventine. It was not one of the original Seven Hills of Rome, but had always been a place of exile to which inconvenient minorities could be despatched out of sight and mind of rich and conservative aristocrats who occasionally salved their consciences by going slumming to the plebian refuge. One of the flanks of the Aventine had been set aside by Mussolini as a Villaggio dei Giornalisti, where houses and lots could be bought on very reasonable terms by Roman newspapermen. They took the bait but not the hook, and Mussolini had good reason to complain of the ingratitude of the Scribes and Pharisees.

There was a little ragged garden at the back of our apartment that was tended by some nuns. Our maid, who was religious, went there for spiritual consolation and fresh onions, peas, and beans. I gathered mint that grew on the hillside slope opposite the ruins of the Frangipani Castle; the castle courtyard had been turned into a little park, with a terrace from which a noble prospect of Rome opened up. Let into the wall was a marble lion's mouth, probably looted from the Baths of Caracalla. From the lion's mouth a jet of clear, cold water gushed into a granite bathtub. Beyond the park a gloomy spinney of ancient stone-pines gave substance to a legend that Augustus' daughter, Julia, often returned to the solitude which had been her favourite retreat 2,000 years ago. She was not a ghost; there are no ghosts in Italy; she was simply a personage attached to the familiar site. She could be sensed rather than seen; she did not inspire fear, but only a sort of affectionate recognition, such as one experienced at the Pool of Castor and Pollux, at the base of the Temple in the Forum where the myrtle grows.

The emotional attraction of the Aventine would have kept me there forever if it had not been countered by the memory of prairie flowers: *Phlox Hoodii, anemone patens, thermopsis rhombifolia*. I developed such a nostalgia for these insignificant sub-Arctic blooms that I persuaded my Mother to pack some seed-pods in a letter; I solemnly planted these in pots of tufa, regularly watered them, and waited, with all the patience I could muster, for them to germinate. After weeks of suspense I grew a few wretched seedlings which lingered on in unfamiliar soil and climate for a brief summer and then packed up. My nostalgia expired with them. I substituted daily visits to the Forum on the way to my office, and a schedule of studies of surviving antiquities within the city and along the Via Appia Antica and Via Nomentana, pushing as far as I could conveniently reach into Etruscan territory. The material filled out a weekly mailer I did for the *Sunday Times* and occasionally moonlighted in the *Herald Tribune* too. These gave me the freedom of the closely knit Anglo-Italian press corps, where amateur archeologists and bibliophiles flourished and vacant seats in automobiles were not too difficult to come by. Publication in both American and British papers offered the additional security of two embassies to make representations to Count Ciano in the Palazzo Chigi when something in my columns gave sufficient umbrage for poor Commendatore Rocco reluctantly to order me to the frontier. Thus I was able to beat the rap every time, and ultimately left Rome under my own steam in June 1940, only a few days before Mussolini overplayed his hand and became involved in hostilities with France.

Nearly forty years ago, in Rome, telephones were difficult to come by. Thus, my schedule was elastic until the *Herald Tribune* complicated it by renting a voice line, Rome to New York, by the month, over which I could feed from my house or from the office directly to the city room in New York, where the feed was recorded and typed off as soon as it was complete. This arrangement saved much money on cable tolls, provided that I supplied ample wordage daily. The telephone operator in New York occasionally slipped up and put in an unanticipated call— usually in the middle of the night. To avoid a useless charge I would mentally scrape together what I could muster of news and comment over the preceding few days. Being fully awakened I would then throw on a few clothes, wander up the hill to the Frangipani Park, and listen to the nightingales tuning up for the day. It was emotional and beautiful, but it ruined my digestion until my body adjusted to the strange hours. The memory of dawn over Rome still possesses nostalgic power.

EIGHT

Once established, complete with office, tipsters, and telephone, I took advantage of Rocco's suggestion that I cover Mussolini's activities systematically. The first safari was to the Pontine Marshes where the harvest was just being gathered in. Drainage and bonification of these malarial marshes was one of Mussolini's proudest achievements. Over the centuries pope after pope had tried and failed to overcome the marshes, which at one point, in Renaissance times, had crept to the very walls of Rome, giving the Eternal City an unhealthy reputation, which the wealthy avoided by moving to the Alban Hills for the summer, leaving the fever-stricken heart of Rome to those too poor to escape. The popes themselves, having failed to conquer the ailment, escaped it to spend the summer high up at Castel Gandolfo or Rocca del Pap, although the flies there were almost as noisome as the mosquitoes lower down. Primitive surveys failed to route drainage canals through or over the inconspicuous tufa ridge which hemmed in the waters escaping from the aqueducts of antiquity. Mussolini took particular pride in victory where popes and princes—Farnese, Colonna, and Orsini—had failed. He made seasonal pilgrimages to celebrate planting, reaping, and harvesting in the reclaimed marshes.

On a brilliant day in early autumn, I whirled off to Pontinia in a charabanc provided by the Ministry of Popular Culture, which was also demonstrating to a party of supercilious Germans the glories of fascism, at which they glanced with Teutonic disdain. The building of these new towns in the marshes was no mean feat. Modern, accurate surveys had found a course to the sea for the drainage canals and the residual mud bore spectacular crops. Mussolini had given architects full scope to produce convenient complexes of assembly, amusement, trade, and commerce, in a traditional style of red-brick utility construction which adapted itself to the needs of modern distribution in an antique setting. Unfortunately, Mussolini could never resist the urge to be grandiloquent, and the inauguration of Pontinia was to serve also to introduce the new ceremonial dagger which had just been issued to complete the Blackshirt regalia, a sort of Latin dirk.

Appropriate throngs of spectators were marched into Pontinia's piazza. The German contingent was stationed in a balcony on the edge of the square; the Anglo-American press was given comparable places near by. Somewhere near the centre of the crowd a table stood on a raised dais. On the table was a bottle of wine and the new dagger-dirk. Mussolini marched up to the table, picked up the bottle of wine, and raised the dagger on high with an operatic flourish. Thus with symbolical blood and steel would fascism bring into production the fertile lands which had been abandoned by earlier, weaker regimes. But fascism would brook no impediment; let the strong wine refresh the strong soil! With that he brought the dagger crashing down on the neck of the bottle, which held firm; the dagger was shattered.

A gasp went up from the crowd at the enormity of the lèse-majesté. The Germans looked down their noses as if this confirmed their worst suspicions of the incompetence of their allies; they whispered together in their supercilious manner. But Mussolini was equal to the occasion. Grabbing the bottle by the butt, he brought the neck against the edge of the table with a crash; the wine gushed all over it; the crowd cheered, even the supercilious Teutons melted into smiles, and everybody went home happily. The inauguration of Pontinia was not an occasion lightly to be forgotten.

The next founding was less spectacular, but was not without its special charm. The theme for Pomezia would be fruit, but since this is an awkward commodity to parade in bulk, most of the pageantry had to be symbolic. What more symbolic of the productivity of the region than a troupe of maidens in the colourful costumes of the area, or what the nearest farmwife thought would be appropriate? The young women pirouetted, sang, and moved on to the next farm. Mussolini, stripped to the waist and displaying a mat of black body-hair, lugged baskets of fruit, occasionally interchanged with a sheaf of wheat or barley. The sunshine flinted on sweat trickling down his arms and chest. I observed him carefully at close range and there seemed no justification for stories about poor health; he was exuberant in a probably well-calculated demonstration. It impressed the Italian reporters, and it made me resolve to put the health stories on the spike; since they could not be used anyway, I might as well forget them.

Another problem area was his relationship with Clara Petacci, a young blonde, whom Mussolini had set up with a villa on the other side of the Tiber. There was not much to be said about her, even had discretion allowed. She was no Lucrezia Borgia, no Laura, no Beatrice d'Esté. She stayed quietly on her side of the river, and Mussolini lived on his side like a retired Birmingham alderman in a good bourgeois house, the Villa Torlonia, using the sumptuous Palazzo di Venezia only for office accommodations and public appearances on the balcony overlooking the square.

My brief glimpse of *Il Duce* in the Pontine Marshes increased my eagerness to obtain a private interview with him, although I was aware it was unlikely to produce much usable copy, certainly not any roaring exclusive. There are few true "news-beats" fed into high-speed rotary presses. Commendatore Rocco patiently went over these points, but as I persisted, he referred back to the fictitious feature stories which had turned up in my file, finding in them justification for pressing my claims to special consideration. As usually happened, when the time came, I got cold feet, and heartily wished myself out of an assignment from which I expected only embarrassment. I was breathless, as much from fright as anything, but Rocco courteously laid the blame on the long flight of steps leading up to the *piano nobile* which housed *Il Duce*'s reception room. This room gave out on to the famous balcony at one end, while a desk the size of a billiard table squatted in a diagonal corner about fifty feet away.

I had vaguely formulated suitable questions about the Pontine Marshes, which might give Mussolini a chance, if he chose to take it, to generalize on politics; but my attention was riveted on the figure behind the huge desk in the corner and distracted by the marble mosaic patterns of the floor. I stumbled up to the desk, stood at attention, and mumbled something about why the Pontine Marshes had been neglected for so long.

Mussolini leaned forward over his desk, which was as scrupulously clear of litter as a big businessman's, and corrected me. Much had been done over the centuries, but mostly to make matters worse through poor planning and inept performance. The problem had been mastered through science and system, applied by fascism after dukes and popes had squandered their treasure to no purpose; I could see their abandoned works wherever I chose to look, Mussolini concluded, with a sweeping gesture. I nodded and Rocco moved in from the wings, to indicate the interview was over. I determined to squeeze another drop or two out of it, so I suggested that the world had received little or nothing reliable about the development of the Italian colonial domain in North Africa, and that my personal report might carry weight — provided, of course, that I had unrestricted access and freedom to set forth my observations without censorship. *Il Duce*'s face clouded over at this unfortunate word "censorship", but he nodded to Rocco to work something out with Balbo, who was in charge of a big undertaking to settle 10,000 colonists in Libya, which was regarded suspiciously by the French and the Arabs alike. I bobbed a perfunctory bow, withdrew three paces, and sidled to the door, shepherded by Rocco, on whose forehead the sweat of relief made a thankful beading.

There would obviously be no hindrance to a North African expedition, so I quickly queried New York and received an okay on my assurance that it wouldn't cost anyone anything, and should be good for reams of feature copy, besides furthering the education of the correspondent, a by-product which I liked to emphasize whenever I could.

So, in 1938, I found myself among some twenty-five or thirty correspondents of British and American papers who had been rounded up to cover the African expedition along with an equal number of Italian reporters, party members of orthodox views, whose conclusions could be forecast before the "caravan" left Naples.

The colonists, most of whom had been sent on ahead, had been preceded in turn by pioneers who were entrusted with preparing accommodations for the main party. At the head of the operation was Marshal Italo Balbo, a handsome, bearded figure with a taste in colourful capes which enhanced his carefully cultivated resemblance to a Renaissance *condottiere*. He was in high favour after leading a spectacular mass flight of Italian seaplanes from Orbetello, on the west coast, to Chicago's Century of Progress Exposition. This had been a risky, marginal enterprise which had been saved from disaster, so I was assured, by the fortunate and timely recognition, by Marshal Balbo, of an unhappy possessor of the Evil Eye, which caused countless mishaps and delays, until the offender was identified in Orbetello itself and expelled from the aviation camp, whereafter the mischances which had plagued the venture disappeared as if by magic. The planes took off, and in due course put down on Lake Michigan, in full view of Chicago's Michigan Avenue, to the luminous might, majesty, dominion, and power of Mussolini, Balbo, and the Italian aircraft industry, and the confusion of the Evil Eye, which never again exercised or threatened sway over any enterprises directed by Balbo, until his unfortunate last flight over Tobruk during the Second World War, when he was shot down by his own guns. He must have grown careless with success, forgetting to exorcise the Evil Eye, which men ignore at their peril.

The precautions against the Evil Eye are not onerous. A good beginning is to wear, on watch-fob or chain, a small talisman or coral in the shape of a miniature bull's pizzle. This protection may be augmented by other precautions: "making the horns" with the index and little fingers of the right hand while turning over silver in the pocket or fondling the genitals with the left hand; this method was recommended by King Alfonso XIII of

Spain, well known for the Evil Eye. When he visited Rome as an exile, his visits to the movies went to the accompaniment of a continuum of jingling silver as customers recognized and sought to avert their danger. The malevolent influence of *malocchio* is not restricted to Italians.

The King and Queen of Spain were entertained at the U.S. Embassy and lodged at the Ambassador's residence; that night the chimney caught fire! Ambassador William B. and Mrs. Phillips were models of diplomatic discretion and caution, but all Rome gossiped about the strange phenomena at the residence, while newsmen speculated on the terms in which they could be reported to the State Department without causing undue concern. Merchants in the Piazza di Spagna did a brisk trade in amulets and the Embassy resigned itself to abnormal breakages and a high turnover in domestic help, a condition which endured until the King and Queen retired to a country residence.

I was a little nervous lest my long face render me suspect to Marshal Balbo, but a test meeting in an Air Force mess passed off without embarrassment and I, along with the other correspondents, confidently caught the colonist boat for Benghazi.

The occasion was favourable for testing the motivation of the colonists; it was chiefly economic, especially for those coming from the south of the Pontine Marshes, where emigration, particularly to the United States, had been a way of life for generations. A variation in the pattern appeared in this group. By talking to some of them I discovered that their first emigration had not been to the United States, but to Australia. One colonist told me that he had found a job in Queensland where a number of compatriots were settled; he added that they had returned to Italy because of discrimination and hostility against them. But they had no mind to resume their old situation in Italy, so they were giving emigration another trial, chosing the North African colonies as promising a compatible society with a reasonable economic prospect. They looked forward to growing wheat, barley, and olives in the area between the Sahara and the Mediterranean; they had been told that the development of artesian wells would enable large areas to be reclaimed from the desert. University graduates who had felt the itch to wander pointed out that the area had been the breadbasket of the world in the days of Roman occupation, when "Africa", which was the modern Tunisia, was the rich prize for which the Scipios contended with Hannibal and with each other. They produced photographs, taken on an earlier visit, of ancient olive presses and of an olive tree said to have been planted by the Romans in the Jebel behind Tripoli.

The get-rich-quick dreams which the African colonists may have indulged in had been tempered already by their Australian experience, and it was a down-to-earth group which disembarked at Benghazi, prepared to work long hours and live lean, but to give short shrift to such native population as might have survived earlier "civilizing" missions. Most of them had been destroyed or reduced to servile status, living on crumbs from the rich man's table.

Benghazi, on the north coast of Libya, looked like any other small Mediterranean seaport as Balbo's colonists disembarked from their troopships, most of them veterans of the Abyssian Expedition pressed into service as colonial "volunteers".

As an honorary member of Balbo's personal suite, I was rushed out to the first camp, high up on the asphodel steppe behind Benghazi. The spiky asphodel, bearing little relation to Tennyson's romantic herbage on which the Lotus-eaters rested their weary limbs at last, is an infallible indication of poor soil, which should have warned Balbo's scientists against settling their colonists on such terrain. They gave the warning no heed, although even the camels rejected the scrub, which competed with stunted oak and wild olive trees in the gullies for what scanty moisture was available. It was hard to believe that in ancient times this territory had supported five great cities founded by the Greeks and nourished by the wheat and wine and oil produced so abundantly in the area; but the evidence could not be denied. Vast ruined aqueducts at ground level, and underground rock-hewn cisterns collecting seepage from still-active springs, told of advanced irrigation techniques, wealthy occupation, and centuries of luxurious living with secure supplies of food.

At Barce, another Greek foundation farther east along the coast, I tripped over a shard as my guide and I crossed a ruined population centre. I felt that my companion, who was Curator of Antiquities, was keeping a sharp eye on me, so I carefully replaced the piece, although it looked to be an interesting terracotta figurine. My companion picked it up for a brief inspection and slipped it quietly into his pocket. The evidence was overwhelming that the area had been overpopulated and its resources of soil and water overtaxed for centuries before the Greco-Roman establishment collapsed. There were no reserves either of fibrous material or of water to resist the assault on the vegetation carried out by the sheep and goats brought in by Beni Allal in the seventh century when their tribesmen swept in from the western desert and once more overloaded the precarious ecological balance of Cirenaica. Their livestock consumed what ground cover there was, their agricultural methods exhausted the subsoil water, their political ineptitude introduced armies which competed with each other in destroying whatever was left of antiquity to supply the rebuilders of medieval Italy with *giallo antico*, *pavonazetto*, and *verde antico*, with which they embellished their palaces. Meanwhile, the sand pushed on implacably until the Barbary Coast drove its inhabitants to the sea as pirates, thus inviting another, and yet more disastrous, foreign intervention which would complete the subjection of the Moghreb. Americans, French, Spaniards, and finally the Italians, brought "civilization" and change to a land and peoples to whom change was anathema, if not heresy.

In Balbo's scheme of colonization, change was avoided as far as possible. There was no avoiding it for the Arabs, who had the option of moving up or moving out. But preparation for the reception of the Italians, who were to occupy their lands, emphasized continuity of tradition. Each family was provided with a cabin of brick or stone with stucco-and-whitewash-finished stabling for their cattle. Open-hearth cooking was the rule, while baking could be done in the primitive but efficient traditional ovens in which the fire is kindled internally, embers withdrawn by a port, and food inserted to be baked by the heat given off by the ceramic material of which the oven was built. The system called for nice adjustment, but colonists from southern Italy were accustomed to it, as their forebears had been since the days of Homer. They welcomed familiar problems and solutions amid the overwhelming strangeness of this land and people. Use of oxen as draft animals had to be given up, as they could not endure the heat; so the colonist hitched a camel to his primitive plough, and scuffed the surface of his sandy holding before scattering barley in the timeless rhythm of the sower, to be reaped in due course with that most primitive and difficult of agricultural implements, the sickle, and ultimately beaten with a flail or trodden out on the threshing floor by a team of oxen who snatched a surreptitious mouthful as they circled around on their dreary task.

The first time I saw this age-old ritual, I still had in my ears the roar of E. P. Walker's threshing rig as it flung the straw on a golden mountain of debris and clocked the bushels of grain into waiting wagons or the field bin. It was efficient within its limitations, but it did not offer the ballet rhythm of winnowing, in which a shovelful of grain and chaff from the threshing floor is flung up into a breeze just weak enough to allow the grain to plummet to the ground while the chaff drifts away in a golden shower, like Zeus descending on Danae. Given normal moisture and no devastating sirocco from the Sahara, the colonists could practise subsistence farming in Tripolitania, but they could not produce the lush farms and wealthy cities that the French had created in Algeria, or which the Romans, in classical times, had organized to support luxurious centres like Leptis Magna and Sabratha, where marble ruins and deeply rutted street-paving testified to their bygone prosperity.

Mussolini allowed Balbo to rummage for prestige in the shards of past glories, but he was under no illusion about the agricultural limitations of his collection of deserts. Following his policy of national self-sufficiency, and perhaps looking ahead to a possible war, he sought more promising resources, such as the oil or gas that the French had found, although in limited quantities, in contiguous North African territories. Mussolini had poured all his available geological talent into prospecting Albania, with disappointing results, and had even tried out surface indications in Italy with even less gratification. He then committed all his technical resources to the Italian territories in North Africa where his geologists had given him hope of discovering extensive petroleum deposits in the area adjacent to the French territories in Algeria and farther east of them in Libya.

Knowing the determination with which Mussolini had followed every previous lead, I accepted this hope of discovering oil in commercial quantities on Italian-controlled territory as the basic reason for his pouring so much money into the risky colonization venture. He saw the competition for petroleum in the simplistic terms of Jack the Giant-Killer, in which *Il Duce* and the fascist virtues were ranged against the wicked, selfish, monopolist brigands, represented by the Rockefellers, Morgans, and Rothschilds, who were attempting to strangle the infant Hercules in his cradle.

Had Mussolini found oil in North Africa, he would have been able to furnish his Libyan forces with fuel on the spot in the event of war without having to run the gauntlet of the Royal Navy's control over the Mediterranean, which had been tight ever since the days of Nelson. As it was, when the Second World War commenced, his vulnerability proclaimed itself. British warships destroyed or captured four barrels out of every ten shipped to Africa. The drums were loaded on the decks of destroyers which raced across the Mediterranean by night on a dangerous and costly mission that the Italian Navy scorned as humiliating and decried as a demonstration of how little Mussolini and his advisers understood naval affairs. The Royal Navy, secure in its Malta fortress, used the Italian fuel ferry as a training ground for night operations in which they tested out a variety of search and identification devices, while their heavy but agile Tribal-class destroyers out-gunned and outran the light Italian vessels burdened with their volatile deck cargo.

The petroleum deposits which might have made this naval shambles unnecessary eluded Mussolini's best experts. They concentrated on indications along the first coastal ridge in Tripolitania; while they drilled through promising strata, they

105

found no oil. The irony was that there was oil in abundance farther east in Libya, but the experts did not look there until Mussolini was dead and gone, and then they found high-gravity petroleum in quantity at low level and high pressure, which needed only a pipeline to bring it to the sea. Mussolini's career might have developed along much happier lines had the Libyan discoveries been made under his auspices. The thing was so close, and the stakes so tremendous, that I often wondered whether some hostile, anti-fascist, fanatic driller had found traces in Libya which he thought best to suppress lest Mussolini fly too high. I put these doubts to an American oilman with experience in the area, who assured me that they were not well-founded. Still . . . I wonder! History often ignores essentials to concentrate on secondary phenomena. The files of Standard Oil or British Petroleum and the logs of early drilling in Libya might be as important a contribution to Mediterranean history as the Rosetta Stone.

As I drove past the ruins of massive olive presses built in Tripolitania by the Romans, and plucked a twig from an olive tree said to have been planted by Belisarius, I tried to imagine the ceremony as the young tree was dedicated by the triumphant general in honour of the Emperor Justinian: "And don't you stupid scribes forget to put the Emperor's name up near the top of the marker; remember the Senate—we still have one, and the Senators like to be reminded of their importance—and throw in a couple of archaic Punic symbols to remind the Carthaginians that the West is best, always was, always will be, despite these crummy Syrian magicians — don't quote me, but you get the picture. The Empress is quite fond of them, so perhaps we shall have to make sure of our rear if we ever get back to Rome." I should like another slip of that olive tree, as a link between Belisarius and me.

From the tableland above Barce we could look out over Homer's "wine-dark sea", and wonder what malign influences reduced this terrestrial paradise to such a solitude. One of these must have been malaria, which was rampant in Algeria before the French cleaned up the stagnant pools and puddles where mosquito larvae developed in the few days between flooding after a shower and desiccation under the sun; the disease made Rome notoriously unhealthy in the summer months too, and spread lassitude and weakness all along the coast of Italy south of the Pontine Marshes.

Parasitic diseases were recognized and controllable, so the Balbo colonists were free of those hazards, but it remained a question whether they could survive on their thin production of barley, olive oil, and wine. Under much more favourable conditions, the French in Algeria had to be heavily subsidized with special treatment for the harsh wine they shipped in tankers to spike the *vin ordinaire* produced in the south of France for the *petit bourgeois* of the north, or, farther north, for the snobs of Britain. All the pomp and circumstance with which Balbo glamourized his attempt to restore the littoral of "Our Sea" — Mare Nostro — to its ancient splendour could not hide the fact that the land was exhausted, the Arabs were a burden, and the colonists would have to be subsidized in perpetuity by the Motherland. How long would Italy be prepared to bear this fardel? As long as Mussolini was in command, there would be no change, and no good and true Fascist would permit himself to think in terms of any alternative to *Il Duce*, so Balbo swept into Libya in imperial style, set up a marquee on the fringe of the desert, and presided at a banquet to which most of the local potentates, Fascist and native, were invited. He delivered the expected oration about the permanence of Fascist influence and glory which I was happy to have witnessed, such as it was, before it became one with Nineveh and Tyre. He swung his cloak over one shoulder with a spacious gesture which displayed its scarlet lining to advantage as he stalked about inspecting his caravan. Balbo was flashy, but he did things with the spirit one expected from a native of Renaissance Ferrara, where traditionally the wealth of the Po Valley had been used to produce beauty in form and colour of rare intensity.

Balbo enjoyed himself in Ferrara, and took with him on his formation flight to the United States his enthusiasm for the pleasures of the flesh, which, he said on returning, were to be

107

enjoyed there abundantly with a minimum of effort. It was not even necessary to have full command of English, Balbo confided, so long as one mastered two key phrases: "double room" and "beeg bed". I grew quite fond of him on this trip and followed his subsequent career with interest until his death during the war.

Returning to Rome, I busied myself with recording the development of the Rome-Berlin axis. It appeared to me to hold sinister portents for Mussolini's Italy, which found itself in the same position as that held by Italy prior to the First World War, the weakest member of an alliance whose aims were repugnant both to its real interests and to national sentiment.

CHAPTER
NINE

There was feverish excitement over the visit, in 1937, of *Der Führer,* the Apprentice Sorcerer who was giving some apprehension to the Italian Master Magician who had indoctrinated him. The visit was to propagandize the "Rome-Berlin axis". A vast empty warehouse near my Rome apartment was devoted to the manufacture of swastika banners, swastika armbands, and swastika pins, under the supervision of a company of S.A. heavies who seized the opportunity to steal from the warehouse a pretty little torso of beautifully weathered antique marble, which for months I had been planning to abstract through the solid window-grill, but had been reluctant to risk damaging. So I had saved it for those damn Nazis after all! It made me mad, but I covered the visit conscientiously, and had my moments. One of these came when Mussolini decided to impress his visitor with his military might, and mounted a review of what was billed as an armoured division. To me, sitting watching, the tanks seemed by their identification marks to have been drawn for the occasion from scattered depots all over the country. I checked this impression with the U.S. Embassy, and found full agreement from the military attaché, who had also been watching and counting carefully. The attaché, a genial sceptic with whom I often exchanged views and news, was concerned lest this display heighten the contempt, which the Nazis made little effort to conceal, for the military effectiveness of the Fascists, and thus downgrade any potentially moderating influence they might have on the Berlin element of the Axis.

Actually, the attaché told me, the Italians had just developed a new machine-gun which the U.S. Army might be very interested in if the Germans did not get it first. We agreed that it might be a good idea to go up the coast to the range when the weapon was to be demonstrated to the Führer's military advisers. I persuaded the military attaché to drive me in a staff car up to Santa Margherita, a little summer resort on the west coast, north of Rome. An embassy staff car was a useful instrument for cutting through a maze of roadblocks and inspection points which sprang up like mushrooms whenever Hitler moved about. Safely installed on the roof of a shed in which the machine-gun tests were being carried out, the military attaché drew his own conclusions from the frequency and duration of the bursts of fire. When the firing ceased there was a stir below, and I said to the attaché, "By the pricking of my thumbs, something royal this way comes."

Trumpets sounded, the guards presented arms, and out of the right wing, as it were, marched Mussolini, King Victor Emmanuel II, and a third — I forget who, possibly Mussolini's son-in-law, Count Galeazzo Ciano. A moment later, out of the left wing, marched Hitler, with an S.S. general and an Italian army officer. They halted facing each other. Mussolini saluted in style. The King of Italy watched like a boy at a circus. Hitler, looking acutely uneasy, began a half-baked salute, thought better of it, and tried to find a comfortable place to rest his hands. His face was puffy and full of wrinkles, with an unhealthy, yellowish colour around his eyes.

The King broke up this uncomfortable little gathering by taking his party back into the shed; the Germans followed; the leaders drove off with the King, their suite accommodated in long black Mercedes limousines. I never again saw Hitler close by, but I retained a chilling memory of his swollen, flaccid face, his uneasiness, his shuffling feet and flapping hands, which contributed to the impression of instability and nervous excitability that I was horrified to observe in an autocratic ruler of such immense power.

On the way back to Rome I found that the Italian officers who had watched the scene with me were even more apprehensive, for they were chained to the chariot of this monster whose conduct as a guest promised little comfort if and when he returned as master. The Apprentice Sorcerer was displaying a tendency to practise his own thaumaturgy regardless of the consequences to the other members of the coven. My friend Lovatelli said confidentially that he would not compare Hitler with the Emperor Nero for he doubted whether Hitler had the musical and artistic talent that the murderer of Agrippina displayed. Perhaps Tiberius would be a better prototype, since the successor of Augustus perfected the imperial machine which transmuted his will into action on a universal scale, in the heart of Rome or on the far-off shore of the Euxine. The parlour game of identifying the master of Germany with one of the rulers of ancient Rome was a dispiriting exercise; it emphasized the tenacious grip on power which the emperors, with their limited means, had established; the fate of would-be liberators in classical times discouraged modern imitators from attempting much riskier coups against equally ruthless despots, with more sophisticated defences.

The savage torments with which the Nazis executed would-be assassins of Hitler might have sprung from the unstable mind of a Caligula who felt no responsibility to gods or men for his deeds, any more than did Goering or Goebbels whom I saw riding in state along the Via dell' Impero while their leader was fulminating against the modern Sarmatians on the fringes of the Empire.

Elaborate checkpoints closed all access to the Aventine to its normal residents, without, however, offering an impenetrable barrier to newcomers determined, for whatever reasons, to obtain advantageous posts from which *Der Führer* might be seen, if only through gun-sights, as his car sped along the Via dell' Impero. I was in a nervous sweat until he was out of sight and range, for any disturbance which might have been interpreted as an *attentat* would surely have been answered by a burst of rapid fire in the direction of the bleachers, whose occupants would incur a double jeopardy from bullets and panic. We were all glad to see the last of him and to settle back into an easier routine.

In addition to covering the political scene, which centred on

Mussolini's office in the Palazzo di Venezia, I was expected to handle the Vatican, with the caution demanded by the existence in the United States of some 48,000,000 Roman Catholics, each one alert to catch mistakes in my copy. To minimize this risk I was instructed to employ a competent cleric to advise and supervise me. My predecessor had solved this problem by employing a Monsignor Pucci, a minor official in Vatican City, to assess the significance of articles in the *Osservatore Romano*, an official daily which vied in authority and obscurity with *Le Temps* in Paris. I inherited Pucci, a tall cleric supporting on slender means a host of nephews, who produced, as often as needed, a sort of *Pauline, Epistula ad Paganos*, neatly typed on coloured paper, red for the *Herald Tribune*, yellow for the *New York Times*. He also made timely application for places for his clients at important events— the election, coronation, or funeral of the Pope, even an occasional presentation to His Holiness. In addition to Pucci, I relied on the *Catholic Encyclopedic Dictionary*, an authoritative work which I drew on freely for every theological term I had to use and define. It was a fascinating volume, and I wish I had it with me now. With these crutches, beatification and canonization held no terror for me, although Pucci's enthusiasm once brought me into embarrassingly close contact with the bier containing the body of the recently deceased Pope Pius XI. Stationed on the staircase leading from the Sistine Chapel, I was swept away by a descending torrent of choirboys with candles. Riding the crest of the wave precariously was a bier bearing the body of the Pope. At the head of the torrent foaming down the Sistine stairs into the Basilica, I staggered forward, unable to retreat or turn aside. At this point the *Times* man joined me, and never was I more thankful to have the competition with me. The stream debouched into the nave of the Basilica. As we appeared, the two lines of papal guards flanking the fairway brought their rifles to the floor with a crash, and stood rigidly at attention, and then presented arms as the bier drew abreast. At the end of this military corridor, I spotted the imposing bulk of a mitred abbot, wonderfully arrayed, standing before a catafalque, his mitre and cassock glittering with gold braid, his crucifix glistening in the soft glow of our candles. Behind him were steps leading to the crypt where centuries of popes were buried. The mitred abbot guarded access to the steps.

He stood there like the rock which divides the stream of the Tiber crossed by the Ponte Rotto, and the stream of choirboys flowed on either side of him, depositing the Pope's body on the catafalque. I stood beside it, noting mentally the detail of the Pope's robes, and particularly his red leather slippers embroidered with gold thread and his ankles tied together with silver cord.

At the end of the service, I staggered out of the Basilica emotionally exhausted, and found a cable in my office informing me that an assistant would be sent to help carry the load during the election and coronation of the next Pope, and angling for hints about whom it might be. I resolved to keep well away from that flypaper. One might list "i papabili", palpable candidates for the Triple Crown, but even this would be a tricky forecast, like picking a Derby winner from a field of seventy entries. So I decided to concentrate on the externals — the conclave, the Cardinals' thrones, their baldaquins, and the little iron stove in which the voting papers would be burnt and from which the smoke issuing from the chimney-pipe outside would tell the waiting crowds that a new Bishop of Rome, Vicar of Jesus Christ, successor of St. Peter, Prince of the Apostles, Supreme Pontiff of the Universal Church, Patriarch of the West, Primate of Italy, Archbishop and Metropolitan of the Roman Province, Pontifex Maximus, had been chosen.

I delighted in the sonorous roll of titles, reading them off from the Annuario Pontificio, a magnificent compendium of authoritative information to which my new assistant, Barrett (Bill) McGurn, had introduced me.

McGurn was a treasure so perfectly adapted to my needs in Rome that I marvelled at the *Herald Tribune*'s sagacity in selecting him. It appeared, however, that McGurn had done the selecting, and, to clinch it, had paid his own fare to the Holy City, which I deprecated as a very bad precedent, while admiring the enthusiasm which he radiated. I grew very fond of Bill McGurn;

he was both credulous and critical, accepted the financial clout of the American faithful, and was above all an accurate observer. He vastly enjoyed the last stage of his trip to Rome, on the same train as Cardinals Mundelein of Chicago and Dougherty of Boston.

"They didn't like each other," he said with characteristic understatement. "So they travelled in the same train, to make sure neither got here ahead of the other; but they used separate coaches, so as not to be embarrassed by crowds welcoming the wrong man.

"But that's what you'd expect from Jezzies," McGurn concluded. "I know, because I'm one myself!" He recommended getting as close as possible to Mundelein, as a well-informed and powerful figure in the American church, rather than bothering too much with Dougherty, even though his New England see gave him potent support.

"The thing is, the Americans are not popular over at the Power House, but they have the money, so they have to be babied a bit."

He was all for dropping Pucci as an ignoble tipster, until he learned of Pucci's ill-health — he was a diabetic — and his nephews, after which he accepted Pucci as a useful supplement to the *Encyclopedic Dictionary*, and an indispensable intermediary for obtaining observation posts or other favours from the Vatican bureaucracy. I was happy at this realistic approach. I told him of my experience at the Pope's funeral, and we agreed not to press for too-advanced posts at future ceremonies such as the coronation of the next pope. "Just take a sandwich and a flask of brandy, and find a dark nook behind a pillar where you can enjoy them, because it's a long service, and you have to be at the gates by six in the morning if you are to have any chance of seeing anything." Then Bill let slip one of his unsanctified aphorisms which soothed ruffled spirits. "I hope the gates of Heaven are better organized than the gates of St. Peter's," he said.

"Nice!" I applauded. "With a little polishing that could be quite a creditable epigram!"

"I'll work on it at the next High Mass," he returned. "Apropos of which, if you take some brandy and a bun, you're less likely to salivate over the wine and wafers."

This irreverence disturbed me, as my face probably showed, for Bill explained: "I used to be a pretty little crucifer back in Tenafly," he said. "New Jersey was a great gangster hangout in those days, and you had to make it pretty clear right away where you stood. Once you were with the right mob you were okay, and I was soon swinging a censer with the best of them."

I was fascinated but a little alarmed at this glimpse of Bill's career, particularly as reports were circulating from Naples that American gangsters were revisiting their old cabbage patches, but I always enjoyed reminiscing with him about the Early Fathers, New Jersey gangsters, and Washington politicians. Another source of amusement was the collection and circulation of unflattering anecdotes about the Fascist regime.

One of these which had wide currency concerned Mussolini's new motorbike; impatient to try it out, he went roaring around the gravel paths of his Villa Torlonia, scattering pebbles and dirt everywhere. When he came to a halt, a window opened and Donna Rachele's lace-capped head inquired, in the meter of *I Pagliacci*: "La commedia è finita?" These were harmless little squibs which kept Romans at peace with their conscience and caused the regime no great concern, since they were in the long Roman tradition of pasquinades, which were safety-valves for earlier discontents.

I had scope to report freely on these facets of Roman life, which were read eagerly by the Romans themselves when they appeared in the Paris *Herald*, or occasionally, for a change, in the London *Sunday Times*, for which I did a weekly column of Italian news.

These were useful outlets for feature pieces and enabled me to take advantage of the benefits offered by the regime to journalists. Among these were special seats to the opera. I used to attend the open-air performances staged in the ruins of the Baths of Caracalla just below the Aventine. Seats for two lire brought these performances within reach of everyone, and tickets were in great demand. I saw a spectacular performance of *Aida,* with real elephants and a real full moon rising behind the

115

broken arches of antiquity. Just before the show began, Mussolini came in without fanfare, and took a two-lire seat in the row immediately ahead of me. Another favour available to the press was accommodation on limited groups visiting newly opened Etruscan tombs. I joined a group on the theory that one could never tell when an out-of-the-way scrap of information would come in useful either as a colourful, authoritative detail, or as a precaution against error. We visited excavations around Tarquinia which amazed me with their anticipations of stylized forms which would not become current for another thousand years.

After a few months in Rome, I acquired the feeling that I had rubbed elbows with earlier visitors in contacts perpetually renewed, despite chronological interruptions, whenever my feet returned to paths they had trodden earlier. This is the fatal spell that Rome casts over her friends. I used to walk every day from my house on the Aventine to my office in the Stampa Estera Building. My path took me along Via del Mare, the road leading to Ostia. Mussolini ordered its surface to be lowered six feet, an operation which brought to light a legion of marble columns, drums, capitols, and similar debris of earlier buildings.

Striding along one morning near the Theatre of Marcellus, I stumbled over a shard. I took it home, washed it off, and showed it to an archeologist at the American Academy. He reported that the shard was Roman pottery, with a painted decoration in the Etruscan manner, showing it to be a cheap Roman copy of a good Etruscan original, done about 165 B.C., the period of the Jewish rebellion under Judas Maccabeus and the destruction of Carthage by Scipio. By this time, Rome had destroyed its Etruscan rivals, while adopting arts and crafts, utensils, decorative motifs and designs from its defeated foe, no doubt despite the warnings of its old-fashioned worthies, sitting in the little Senate-house (which still stands in the Forum), and inveighing against fraternizing with the enemy, or adopting their manners, morals, or ceramics, to the detriment of the local product. But Etruscan pottery was fashionable, and the price was right. I carried this evocative pottery fragment with me for many years

116

until I lost it during one of my many moves. I regret its loss to this day.

Etruscan relics, and Roman copies of them, intensified my sense of the unreality and impermanence of the present, which living on the Aventine fostered. I waited for a bus beside a wall of tufa brick, built by the Frangipani Pope who had excommunicated King John and laid England under an interdict. The wall surrounded a park on the crest of a declivity overlooking the Tiber. A patrician house had been built in Roman times on this superb site. Here St. Jerome and his amanuensis, the lady Rosella, translated the Greek of the Septuagint into the unpretentious Latin of the Vulgate.

These were trying times for the capital of the world. Barbarians from the heart of Asia, who had never been touched by the Greek civilizing genius, were pressing against the walls raised so recently by the Emperor, who excavated the Vatican hillside to provide the brick for his gigantic defences. The barbarians proved what was to be demonstrated repeatedly after their day —that the most massive defences could always be penetrated or circumvented by a bold, imaginative assault. Aurelian's Wall was no more immune to this law than was the Ligne Maginot 1,500 years later.

St. Jerome correctly read the limitations of the wall. As the barbarians approached, he felt that his divine mission to translate the sacred writings accurately demanded that he obtain a more reliable version of some obscure passages in Isaiah, even if it meant a dangerous and costly journey to Jerusalem to obtain authentic scrolls. Every advance of the barbarians underlined the urgency of this duty. It was imperative to be out of the city before it was cut off by the enemy storm troops; so, by the time the Goths swarmed over the defences and swept up to the summit of the Aventine to command the river approaches, Jerome was safe in Jerusalem, examining scrolls for his revision of Isaiah, leaving his secretary to fair-copy the work in progress.

Rosella might have come to no harm had she remained behind the massive walls of her house on the crest of the hill; but rashly venturing out to the market at the Porta Ostiensis, she was

117

surprised by a Goth soldier before she had gone fifty yards and was cut down as she tried to escape. I located the site of this tragedy opposite the door of my house on Via Raimonda da Capua, and visualized it so often that I half expected the Nazi storm troopers lounging around the Ostian Gate to come charging up the hillside to inspect my documents as I mooned around in a suspiciously detached manner which might have masked Heaven-knew-what sinister designs.

I had no designs whatsoever, which was suspicious in itself; I merely wandered about in a dreamy way, picking up a shard here and a tile there, peopling the Aventine with the rebellious individualists who had lived there long ago and losing my sense of the present in my identification with the past. Rejection of the Establishment was the motif of the Aventine's long history. It began with the earliest social struggles during the youth of Rome, when the triumphant patricians expelled the plebians from the security of the seven hills to the Aventine, which lay exposed outside their traditional circuit, too far from the Forum to benefit from its facilities for assembly and cut off from its wholesale food markets. However, as was to happen so often later, the dissident minority proved more stable and indigestible when isolated than it had been when within the body politic. A troop of slingsmen from Crete, sent to incorporate the dissidents forcibly, had no more success than had subsequent attempts to impose unity by arms; missiles poured into the plebian encampment until their leader, Tiberius Gracchus, led a breakthrough attempt; but the river escarpment proved too formidable. In scrambling down it he twisted his ankle; limping across the bridge almost in sight of safety, he was cut down, and the revolt collapsed. The scene unfolded before me as I stood on the edge of the escarpment, looking down at the muddy Tiber, its bridges and the Isola Tiberina dividing its swift current. I felt myself caught up in the eternal drama of the survival of dissent in defiance of the most implacable attempts at eradication. Beyond the valley of the Circus Maximus, on the other side, the massive masonry of the Palatine survived the combined enmity of time, the popes and the Romans. Bright anemones flourished

118

on the fallen arches of Caligula's mansion; caper bushes clustered on the buttresses of the palace where Augustus received the ephemeral homage of the barbarian chieftains, to be disavowed at the first sign of weakness or need.

It was easy to become so enthralled in this pageant that the familiar landscape of migration, challenge, and survival at home in Saskatchewan appeared trite and unrewarding in the light of the millennial stage of history presented in Rome.

I came across an example of this in the Forum when I climbed a scaffolding which had been set up around the Arch of Septimius Severus. This is the familiar Arch, so near the road that the inscription can be read without difficulty. At the top of the scaffolding a young man was laboriously dusting cornices, cleaning dirt off sculptured marble flowers, and filling his notebook with jottings and sketches. He pointed out to me an area where a word in the inscription had been chiselled off. "That was Caracalla's brother Geta," he said. "He disagreed with the Emperor, and became a non-person, never referred to, his name chiselled off all monuments, obliterated. It was worse than exile; the victim just ceased to exist. Let's go down and look at that block of peach marble on the ground."

Here was another florid inscription to another most distinguished soldier and citizen (name chiselled out).

"That was probably Stilicho," my guide surmised. "It fits the chiselled gap. He won a number of remarkable victories over barbarian invaders, in the later days of the Empire, but with a barbarian name like that, he naturally fell under suspicion, and the Senate disenfranchised him, so off came his name. Even today, Gibbon has only the briefest reference to him — but he would be worth a long memoir, if I could just find the materials in all this dump heap."

I asked him how long he expected to remain in Rome.

"Until I've finished Stilicho," he said. "There's so much to be done, and it fascinates me. There are a dozen of us here, with nothing to do and nothing to go back to. We start in at the American school over on the Janiculum, and we end up here in the Forum, or in some of the Etruscan digs." He explained,

119

"That's the newest Rosetta Stone challenge, deciphering Etruscan inscriptions, such as they are. That'll keep us here forever."

"Expatriates," I murmured.

"Dirty word," he said. "That's exactly what we're not. We live in this culture as we never could back there. We relate. We have our wheat, and wine, and oil, and the time to enjoy them."

I asked him if he didn't have some particular scenes or sights or even smells of his home town that he longed for. He said there were none. "And particularly, there's no dame I can't live without," he added, emphatically.

The intensity of my impressions of Rome was magnified by the recognition that my assignment was not permanent, and that my Roman holiday might be cut short by a single indiscreet word uttered or written which might give anguish to the Ministry of Popular Culture or umbrage to the Palazzo di Venezia. Aware of this threat, I made the best of my opportunity, visiting churches, shrines and monuments, *trattorie* and *bars Americaines*, with the fidelity of a Cook's tourist packing a lifetime's memories into a transitory visit. My enthusiasm spurred Pucci and McGurn to imaginative projects like walking the perimeter of the Aurelian Wall, noting variations in the brickwork and deducing appropriate theories about the changes. This was a large order; since the circuit of the walls exceeded twenty miles, there was great variation in the type of brick and the construction pattern. Consequently I was neither surprised nor perturbed to learn that an earnest German group was undertaking the same mission — to be carried out with Teutonic thoroughness, I felt sure. I hoped indeed that the German group would expedite their study, for signs were increasing that the fragile peace would not long endure, and that "the Empire", to which Mussolini was raising a captured Ethiopian monument, would not outlast another war, in which case studies of Roman defences might be somewhat academic. That last summer in Rome, A.D. 1939, stands out in memory with the inevitability of a Greek tragedy, as Mussolini dared the Fates with theatrical poses and bellicose gestures, stumbling ever closer to the disaster for which neither he nor the country was prepared.

I kept myself in a state of readiness to leave Rome at a few days' or hours' notice if I felt that remaining there would be inviting internment. Then, on May 15, 1940, I received this cable from the *Herald Tribune*'s New York office:

DECISION MADE TODAY SEND LOCAL REPORTER HOMEWARDS SOONEST FOR OBVIOUS REASONS STOP WANT YOU LEAVE PERMANENTLY AND QUICKEST POSSIBLE FOR WHATEVER REST NEEDED THEN TEMPORARY CHARGE LONDON BUREAU STOP CAN YOU ARRANGE INTERIM COVERAGE ROME

Early in June I confided my wife and son, who were American citizens, to the good offices of the American Embassy, which arranged for their safe transportation to the United States, and then myself took a train for Paris.

I had lived in Rome for three years, the happiest and most rewarding of my life. On the reverse side of the coin is the acute nostalgia which now sweeps over me every time I think of Rome. I see myself panting up the steep side of the Aventine, past the little nunnery and the wood of crowded stone-pines where an Emperor's daughter found peace; past the garden where our maid Maria gathered herbs. While I long to return, I fear lest high-rise hotels will have blocked off the view of the Alban Hills and the Sabines too, bringing noise and bustle to destroy the immemorial tranquillity of Santa Sabina. I yearn for the keyhole of Sant-Anselmo through which you can peep at the dome of St. Peter's, and the Square of the Knights of Malta under the catalpa trees, heavy with white and purple flowers. Vain regrets! the most futile of spiritual pastimes, afflicting every traveller mentally revisiting scenes more beautiful than reality in the afterglow of memory.

A few days after my departure from Rome, on June 10, Italy declared war on France and Great Britain, as the Germans broke through the Maginot Line, so heavily oversold and so weakening to French morale. It was clear from my sleeping-car window on the northbound train that things were not going well. Interminable trains of matériel, guns, tanks, and trucks moved slowly westwards — away from the front. At Paris there were no porters, no taxis, no trucks. Fortunately I was travelling light, and managed to board a bus whose driver said he thought he would leave for the Arc de Triomphe before long, provided his gasoline did not run out. I encouraged him with fifty francs to start before he had idled away his fuel.

The bus was still half empty when the driver made it leap forward, roar down Boulevard Raspail, cross the Seine, and swing into the Champs-Elysées as if the Germans were after him, as indeed he may have thought they were. I made him stop at the rue de Berri long enough for me to get myself and my bags to the sidewalk, while he prodded me to be "Vite! Vite! Allez! Allez!"

It terrified me to be driven like a maniac through what was normally the busiest section of Paris, with hardly any pedestrians to be seen, no streetlights functioning, and hardly any other traffic moving. It was a paralysed, invalid city. I was glad to reach the solid-functioning Paris *Herald* building at 21 rue de Berri, where the office factotum, Mlle Brasier, was knitting up what strands of order were left against the time when the Germans came, which, she thought, could not be far off. Meanwhile, the railway line to Le Havre was still intact; she urged me to seize the occasion while it lasted, and I, nothing loath, did so. It was obvious from the general apathy and confusion, the failure of morale, that there would be no spectacular resistance from Paris this time.

The windows of the boat train from Gare St. Lazare to Le Havre had been hastily and amateurishly frosted, presumably to deter spies. As we rolled through the countryside I felt no regret at leaving France, only a vast relief that I should be spared the sight of her rape, which seemed inevitable. Crossing the Channel by what must have been one of the last steamers to ply its way between the French and British coasts, I was secure in the knowledge, too, that my wife and young son would by now be on their way to the United States, where arrangements had been made for them to stay with Helen's parents in Schenectady, far away from the European battlefields.

TEN

Only one day after leaving Paris, I was in a comfortable Southern Railways coach, speeding towards London through the impeccably groomed English countryside, where every hawthorn tree had its quota of blossom, and every blade of grass was in place. The contrast between France and Britain in 1940 could not have been more striking, and I found it comforting to realize that British stolidity would not be upset by French flightiness, and that, in short, there'd always be an England. This impression was emphasized on arrival at Waterloo Station. There were porters and there were taxis, and no difficulties were made about taking me to an address in Chelsea where the *Herald Tribune* had arranged hard-to-find accommodation. The room was conveniently placed for public transportation, but soon proved very inconvenient with respect to the bombing pattern, for it lay across the Thames from the Battersea Power Station, a natural magnet for every enemy bomber which penetrated the coastal screen. The misses landed in and around Chelsea. They made night so hideous that I took to reading Fauré's *Social Life of the Insect World*, to take my mind off the violently antisocial life in the non-insect world; but when a "sleeper"—a delayed action bomb —landed in the backyard, I decided it was time to move, even though it meant leaving the telephone with which I'd managed to establish contact with the Canadian group which centred around Matthew Halton, then correspondent for the Toronto *Star*, and Andrew Cairns, a Canadian wheat specialist who was director of research at the Ministry of Food. With the optimism and initiative of his Scottish forebears, he had just furnished a house in Hampstead with magnificent glass, then to be had for a song, but virtually uninsurable, and mahogany furniture, Chippendale style, made to order with a wheat-ear motif. It was as solid as Andy himself, and as wonderful for morale. I stayed with the Cairnses for a few days, but it was obvious that, despite my ration cards, I was a nuisance. Once again, the bureau managed to wheedle a room for me, in the Waldorf Astoria, near the offices at Bush House. Since this could properly go on the expense account, I did not demur, but I soon tired of it, and moved yet again, this time to the Savoy, where I took a suite on the fifth floor, with a magnificent view of the river just below Hungerford Bridge.

This, however, was a major rail artery, and was subjected to the same intensive enemy attention that the Chelsea site had attracted; the Savoy management, however, had thoughtfully provided a vast refuge underground, The River Room. A brochure in my suite informed me, "This room is provided with special protection from blast and splinters. The inner wall is fourteen inches thick; the outer wall, five feet distant, is nine inches thick. The brick joints of each wall are strengthened with steel mesh, and the two walls support each other by sixteen connecting steel rods. There are nine floors of steel and concrete above The River Room. The air-raid shelter is immediately below." In this stronghold, guests could sleep in reasonable comfort and complete safety, on a paillasse and treads, army style. More than a hundred were accommodated, without overcrowding. I used it several times for an undisturbed night's sleep during July 1940 when German bombers were intensifying the raids on British airfields and vital industries which culminated in the start of the Battle of Britain the following month. Subsequent events proved that I would have been well-advised to have continued using The River Room, but I liked to wake up in my fifth-floor suite, then to breakfast off grapefruit (I did not inquire where they came from), eggs, toast, and ersatz coffee, while I watched the Spits weaving designs in that incredibly blue sky while the customary river traffic quietly held its course during that long, lovely summer of 1940.

The grandstand view I obtained of the South Bank and the Thames bridges warned me that the bulletins of the Ministry of Information were as unreliable as those of the Spanish government during the Civil War. Was there any reason to suppose that communiqués about the success of the convoy system bringing food supplies and raw materials into Britain from the United States and Canada were any more reliable? I thought not, and decided to use such merit as I had acquired in official circles to obtain a personal unconducted tour of the convoy system.

I used the oblique approach; after a dull week in which there had been few raids and no spectacular fires, I asked one of the Ministry of Information officials whether there wasn't something exciting to write about. He replied that he was going to dig some badgers at his place in Worcestershire over the weekend, and if I wanted to see some real excitement, why didn't I come and stay with him? I accepted at once and took with me a canned ham I had requisitioned from American friends. Badgering, I found, was cold, damp work; the badger dug faster than we could, and the dog who was supposed to hamper him soon lost interest. So did I, but by that time I had made my number with my host, and it was only a question of which convoy I would prefer to join. I ordered my preferences like this: Atlantic route, from the Western Approaches out to 20° West and back; East Coast swept channel; English Channel Convoy. We referred to these trips as "boating", as if we were planning to go up the Thames to Maidenhead to find relief from bombing. It was a simple subterfuge, but it eliminated a risk that my absences from the press room might be collated with the approach of important convoys. All these routes had been sporadically under enemy attack, and in August 1940 the Germans had made extravagant claims of cutting Britain's lifeline by totally blockading the waters around the island. I would see for myself, and write as much of what I saw as I could get through censorship, enough at any rate to convince New York that they could take my word for a state of fact or mind, regardless of what the wire-service specials said.

London was becoming increasingly uncomfortable both by night and by day. From September 7, 1940, intensified German bombing had raised casualties to 300-600 killed daily, with between 1,000 and 3,000 injured. In addition, the Germans alleged that their long-range guns emplaced on the heights above Calais had closed the Channel to shipping bound for London. I went around to the Ministry of Information to ask about these claims; MOI rose to the fly and I struck hard. Only a day or so later, I received my first "boating party" invitation in the form of an Admiralty authorization requesting that arrangements be made for my accommodation on board a convoy escort vessel leaving Portsmouth on September 17.

I was given a berth on the newest Hunt-class destroyer for the next convoy-escort duty through the Straits of Dover. The "Hunts" were the Navy's joy and pride, designed with convoy protection in mind, and well-endowed with four-inch, high-velocity guns in twin turrets, and ample radar, the newest and most highly secret development — so closely guarded that even the word could not be used, lest it give some inkling of its purpose and components. Another most sensitive item was IFF — Information, Friend or Foe — beam-reflecting apparatus for the discovery and identification of approaching aircraft. These items reassured me that "our side" had made vastly important technical advances in the understanding and use of electronic devices. These facts reconciled me to working under censorship, for I realized how important it was to keep the enemy in ignorance of them until he met them in battle. I could see clearly where some careless phrases, if picked up by enemy ears, might give away the entire order of battle. This was not what I was there for and I played it safe from then on, deliberately turning away when sensitive material was handled. Along with much novel equipment of a more-or-less-experimental nature, the "Hunts" relied heavily on the well-tried ASDIC, the first of the great anti-submarine detection devices. Its low hum, like a contented cat, calmed my nerves when "Hunt" was in dangerous waters. By comparison with other vessels on which I sailed later, "Hunt" was a dream ship. She had an open bridge, which gave her watch a clear view of the air approaches, and a much better gunnery control station. In addition to this, the open bridge was warmer than the glassed-in bridges of the American "four-pipers" that the British were then buying from the United States, as the outward flare of the bulwark deflected the wind, and it had the sporting attraction of a good covert when the pheasants are rocketing. The open bridge was also more advantageous for conning the vessel alongside a pier or wharf, and took much of the hazard out of tying up to the oiler.

The convoy assembled at Portsmouth was a covey of small freighters, the unglamorous errand-boy vessels which took most of the load of provisioning London and the cities along the Thames Estuary. They were slow, and their skippers scorned the idea of "keeping station" Royal Navy style; so the convoy had a rather ragged appearance, but they kept up a steady pace. By the time darkness had fallen, they were ready for the really tricky sector, the narrows between Dover and Calais, where I felt as if we were right in the muzzles of the German batteries, as we were unquestionably well within their range. I stood on the bridge, wishing to God the skipper would douse his cigarette, which glowed like a light-house beside me. I do not know how many miles the glow of a cigarette will carry on a clear night; if I had reasoned it out, I should have concluded that it did not carry very far. Undoubtedly the merchant skippers were doing exactly as we did, and I could never detect the faintest gleam or glow from any of them, but my imagination saw them as so many beacons for an alert enemy to train his guns on. On that night run, I generated a hatred of cigarettes which was helpful to me later when doctor's orders compelled me to renounce tobacco. My fury made it easy to kick the habit as a sort of revenge for the scare it had given me that night.

Enemy guns were not the only hazard in the narrow straits. The skipper's cigarette had barely come to full glow when I heard the characteristic pulsing vibrations of a two-motor plane cruising overhead. The skipper ordered the challenge letters to be flashed up to him. There was no answer. The aft turret swung around. "Try him again," the skipper ordered. This time an

127

answering signal came from the aircraft. The First Officer checked it with his code book. "Wrong letters, sir," he reported. "What do we do now, sir?"

"Sweet F.A. is what we do now, First!" the skipper replied (spelling out the letters in full). "That's Jerry, for sure, by that motor pulsation, and we're not going to get into a dogfight here in the Straits, so tell those silly sods on No. 3 turret to lower their guns and secure." Turning to me he said, "You might as well go below and get some sleep while you can, before some silly bastard in Dover notices the lights and opens up."

I was ready enough to take his hint and staggered down to my bunk and slept until we tied up at Tilbury. As soon as the sun was over the yardarm, whatever that may mean, I looked in at the wardroom, and found everyone sampling a pink gin. "How shall I write up the log, sir?" the First Officer inquired.

The skipper set down his glass. "Nothing to report," he said. "Routine passage."

Ashore, back in London, the bombing continued in force. Raids were more serious and effective, and were accompanied by the insidious comments of the traitor, "Lord Haw-Haw", who developed a particularly effective tactic of warning where the next night's strike would hit, and then venomously "commiserating" with the victims who had stood their ground despite the "friendly" advice of Lord Haw-Haw to move. Even with Lord Haw-Haw's dire predictions, or perhaps because of them, and despite some talk of an invasion, the British, as a nation, seemed not to waver in their courage and determination to overcome the enemy. German targets varied; London was not the only British city to suffer Luftwaffe attacks. On November 10, 1940, the industrialized medieval cathedral city of Coventry was blasted, in a supreme effort to crush British industrial resources and demoralize the population. For similar psychological reasons, the slums of southeastern London, whose inhabitants had the worst of both worlds by day and by night, were subjected to massive bombardment. The Cockneys had no commodious underground refuges such as the Savoy provided, but noisy, crowded, uncomfortable berths in the underground "Tube" or brick "dog-kennels" in their backyards. My office boy informed me that both forms of shelter were unpopular. "We 'adn't counted on this," he admitted after a particularly destructive all-night raid. It was the first sign of faltering morale I had detected and I considered it so ominous that I reported it at once to my friends at the Ministry of Information. They, too, recognized the danger and added more barrage balloons with wire slung between them to the defence of London's slumland. I felt that I had contributed my two-penn'orth to the defence of whatever we might be defending, and that, in a back-handed way, I was justifying my expense account, which living at the Savoy had inflated to a startling figure.

It was possibly a desire to reduce my expenses for a while which prompted *Herald Tribune* New York officials to suggest, late in November, that I take the "rest" which had been recommended in the cable advising me to quit Rome earlier in the year. Having endured several months of nerve-shattering noise and confusion in London under heavy bombardment, I felt a request to return to the United States for a brief vacation before continuing my duties as London bureau chief might be looked on kindly. My application was duly approved, and I spent Christmas 1940 with my wife's family in Schenectady; to my great regret, time did not allow a visit with my own family in Saskatchewan.

Once the festivities were over, and I had reassured myself as to the welfare of my small family, I felt it time to return to London, for that city in wartime was a newsman's heaven, as long as he could take it. Fortified by my leave, I saw no reason why I could not take it "for the duration".

By January 1941, transatlantic travel was a questionable luxury, denied most civilians such as I, so I leapt at the chance to return to Britain by Pan-American "Clipper" flying boat, an opportunity afforded by the decision of Wendell Willkie, the Republican presidential nominee defeated by Roosevelt in 1940, to assess in person British prospects of winning the war. Willkie was at least the titular head of the Republican Party and had his eye on the 1944 nomination.

Despite his defeat, Willkie was still the darling of the *Herald Tribune* and the despair of the Republican wheel-horse politicians, who never knew, any more than Willkie did, what he was likely to do or say next. This made covering him a lively assignment, and I was ecstatic when I was given the nod, with a warning that I was not to deify him. But neither was I to reveal to the faithful that he had feet of clay, which even the *Herald Tribune* was beginning to suspect, while Colonel McCormick's *Chicago Tribune* gave them front-page treatment and all the pictures the page would carry. Bertie McCormick did not want "another demagogue" in the White House; F.D.R. was bad enough, but this guy was worse, and the British, as usual, had already taken him into camp. It was clear that my assignment was a ticklish one, which would require a good deal of innocent legerdemain, but which promised a wealth of front-page bylines, and quite possibly some nasty notices from the *Chicago Tribune*. However, I could afford to ignore these tributes, and would have been disappointed had they not appeared, as I feared would be the case, when months and years went by and no word was said. Ultimately I got a good blast, levelled, however, at Rhodes Scholars generally, who, it appeared, were termites eating into the solid, wood framework of the United States. However, this did not get into print until long after I had been assigned to cover Willkie's bold venture into cookie-pushing with royalty in Buckingham Palace, a project which was bound to have serious, possibly fatal, consequences for the independence and future of the rebellious colonies.

It was obvious that there would be no call for full society-page coverage of Willkie hob-nobbing with the nobs, so my way would be clear for a straightforward, factual account of his words, deeds, and itinerary, which would enable me to size up the man and to estimate his chances of winning the Presidency and his likely policy if and when he got to the White House.

As a wet-thumb report, I warned the editorial bull pen that, while Willkie cultivated a robust appearance with his shaggy-dog fur coat, he was not in fact sturdy, and habitually overtaxed his strength in the performance of what he considered to be his

duty. Like many men of his build, Willkie was extremely susceptible to colds, which took a heavy toll on his heart. In this
situation the path of wisdom would have been to take life easily;
but no aspiring politician could afford to do that, and Willkie was
too committed to hedge his bets now, or to betray the followers
who had staked their political futures on his success. He was the
victim of his charisma.

My estimate of his character was confirmed on his whirlwind
trip to England. The airline had offered Willkie accommodation
on the new "Clipper" flying boat for the flight via the Azores and
Lisbon, which it was pioneering, and for which it needed big-
name publicity. Willkie was the name; I was included, with two
other newsmen, to ensure publicity.

Willkie was luxuriously accommodated in a cosy cabin when
we set off from an airfield in Maine; I had space next to it, where
I dossed down to spend an uncomfortable night listening to ice
breaking off the wing and scraping against the side as it was
borne away. I thought the airline was taking a terrible risk by
flying its "Clipper" in icing conditions; it had more faith than I
had in its de-icing equipment. However, we survived, and by
mid-morning we were peering over cliffs at the tiny harbour of
the Azores, into which we splashed like an elephant. Willkie
insisted on going ashore, where he was received as enthusiastically as if he were already President. He made a speech which
was interpreted as an offer of statehood, shook hands with
everybody, and was borne shoulder-high in triumph. It was
superb, but it was not politics, for there wasn't a vote in the
crowd.

Back to the "Clipper" and a scary take-off that just cleared the
cliffs around the harbour, a short flight, then Lisbon, and down
into the Tagus, choppy with a cross-wind which caused the
"Clipper" to heel over until the wing tip caught the waves and I
thought we were in for a ducking in those filthy waters. However, the pilot righted his ship, revved up the engines, and
brought her in. As we taxied up to the landing pier I saw with
relief a swarm of colleagues well to the fore in the welcoming
crowd. This eased my mind of worry about how I could get the

story off to New York from a country where I did not know enough of the language to call a messenger. However, my colleagues were lavishly equipped with cable-company pads, headed "presse collect"; all I needed was to fill in the script. My friends had also seen to it that rooms were ready for Willkie and his party at their favourite hotel, where there were no back exits or secret stairways; all visitors could be checked coming and going, and the management was not too strict about filling out identification forms. This made it an ideal haven for intelligence operatives, more commonly described as "spies"; and the pillars and palms in the lobby all had furtive figures lurking behind them, stout figures with bristly moustaches and goat's-beards on their fedoras. It looked like an ensemble from *Der Freischütz*; they turned out briskly next morning to wave good-bye. I am sure they knew as well as we did that Willkie was flying on to England by land plane, and it was no trick to figure his estimated time of arrival. Equipped with the ETA, Messerschmidts or Dorniers could stooge around the approaches waiting for the big prize. However, the pilot fooled them. He took a long sweep up the coast of Portugal, checked in over La Coruna, where he was sure to be reported, and then swung back to sea in a wide loop to south and west.

"We'll pick up heavy cloud cover west of England," he assured his passengers, "and move in to Bristol through it. Couldn't wish for a better screen."

This both reassured me and gave me a certain malicious glee at the thought of all the cumbrous, expensive apparatus of espionage in the Azores and Belem and of patrols on the approaches to the Bristol Channel frustrated and brought to nothing. It was the first of many examples which came under my notice of the futility of espionage when an up-to-date Baedeker would be much less expensive both in money and in lives.

Normally, prolonged flying through cloud makes me nervous, but on this occasion I welcomed the concealment it gave. However, it was a relief to drop through the swirls of vapour and see the neat, verdant fields of England comfortably below us, with hedges and lanes, cows and barns, as unchanged and unchangeable as if there had been no invasion threat since Bonaparte broke up the camp at Boulogne.

At the Bristol airport Willkie was welcomed by a brisk young man from the Foreign Office whose rucksack suggested that he had combined an official mission with a walking tour in the Cotswolds. His easy informal approach delighted Willkie, whose bluff friendliness assured the British official that his advance notices had not misrepresented either the character or the sentiments of his illustrious guest. Willkie, in turn, was relieved to find that he could fill the role of supporter and not just pallbearer; he was not wasting his enthusiasm and committing his prestige to a worn-out champion with no more fight left in him. On the contrary, he soon found out that there was plenty of fight left in the British and that their confidence in victory was undiminished. It was important that Willkie should have reached these conclusions from his own observations, for he was aware that there was well-financed defeatist propaganda back home, in strata where anglophobia was practically an article of faith, a life style. It was to counter this attitude that Willkie had staked his reputation, and if he had been at fault, there would be plenty of opponents back home to remind him of it.

The British government, admirably briefed by their representatives in New York and Washington, and, for once, assimilating the intelligence, made it clear that Willkie could go wherever he wished and see whatever he wanted. They shrewdly kept officialdom out of the spotlight, and let Willkie take it all, since he enjoyed it. They were careful not to favour Willkie in the matter of rations; if the formula was a little slender for a man of Willkie's bulk, they let it be known that something could be arranged. But Willkie would have none of special privilege; in making do as everyone else did, he found hope in the fact that, by and large, rich and poor fared alike.

So he wandered about bomb-shattered streets in London, talking to survivors and marvelling at their determination not to give way before "a pack of foreigners". He made copious notes, to be used on his return to the United States to assure Doubting Thomases that they were not being asked to bolster up an already lost cause. Eventually, Willkie flew back to Washington where he wanted to mend his political fences. Fate was not kind to him; the man who had been nominated as Republican candidate for the Presidency in 1940, by 1944 became the man no party wanted.

Willkie's departure from London removed a valuable news source from the scene, but at that time there was no dearth of stories in the city. Part of my regular beat in London was the United States Embassy, where I not only obtained weekly briefings on American news from either the First Secretary or the Counsellor, but also reported my comings and goings on assignments for the *Herald Tribune*; the purpose of the latter exercise was to keep the Embassy informed as to the movements of the employee of an American newspaper, and, if necessary, to report to my American wife what my fate had been. The United States Ambassador until October 1940, when he requested to be relieved of the post because of his trying experiences in a German target zone, was Joseph P. Kennedy, Sr., for whom the British had acquired great dislike on the grounds of some off-the-record remarks he had made to three Boston newsmen, one of whom had published and was consequently damned. Kennedy had commented that the British had no clear idea what they were fighting for, and added his opinion that they could not possibly win the war.

I met Kennedy a few times between my arrival in London and his departure; on those occasions, there was an instinctive lack of empathy between us. His manner was abrupt, and the famous Kennedy charm, so apparent in his sons, was absent. Only one meeting with him do I remember well. I questioned him concerning an unsubstantiated rumour that secret information en route from the Embassy in London to the State Department in Washington was being leaked by the United States Embassy in Dublin to German agents in Eire. Ambassador Kennedy replied that it was a mistake to assume that there were links between the two embassies, but in any case, he was not responsible for the actions of the United States Embassy in Dublin. His attitude, one shared by most of his staff, was that the war was of no concern to

Americans or the United States; further, he displayed an inherited distrust of the British which he may have learned at his mother's knee.

After his return to the United States, however, a statement of Kennedy's, which had been passed on to me in London, alerted me to a story which was not only of special American interest, but which also took me on another "boating party". Commenting on a defence agreement between Britain and the United States, which arranged for the transfer of fifty aged American destroyers to be used in convoy duty, Kennedy said that the deal was "the worst ever" and that "when all the facts are known", they will "shock the American people".

The vessels, "four-pipers" which had been sold by Washington to the British government, made their first Atlantic crossing in the late autumn of 1940. I went down to Plymouth to watch them come into port after their hazardous crossing—hazardous because they were designed for service in sheltered Caribbean waters, and had been mothballed for twenty years in the Potomac, with minimum maintenance, before F.D.R. struck a hard bargain with Churchill in Britain's hour of need, and traded them off for a string of bases in Newfoundland, Bermuda, the Bahamas, Jamaica, Trinidad, and British Guiana. For closer inspection, I picked the newly renamed H.M.S. *Caldwell*, for no better reason than that my cousin Harry Ashmall farmed at Caldwell; the name stood for something solid and reliable. I found little of that nature aboard and my previous "boating trip" on the sleek "Hunt" had left me unprepared for the *Caldwell*'s defects. No. 4 stack was jacked up by a block of wood, and stayed by guy-wires; the base was too corroded to support the stack independently. The bridge, which was glassed in, unlike that of the "Hunt", sported two compasses, the mechanical box, which was out of action, and the standard magnetic job, which was still awaiting setting—the specialist who was to have rearranged the magnetic plugs in the casing had not turned up. Prominent on the bridge was a roll-indicator. "It jams at thirty degrees," the First Officer informed me in reply to my question about the ship's ability as a firing platform. Mechanics were tinkering about with two fifty-calibre machine guns, and the First Officer told me grimly that they had never been fired in anger, or indeed in any other way, and he hoped they never would be. The deck was cluttered with four-tube torpedo mounts, armament which had long been discarded by every other navy as inefficient and dangerous. It came as a horrid shock when I realized that H.M.S. *Caldwell* and her sister "four-pipers" lacked even the primative shield of ASDIC, anti-submarine detection devices, besides having neither radar nor sonar. The "four-pipers" were in fact nothing but scarecrows, intended to frighten away raiders by their appearance. No wonder *Caldwell*'s crew was sullen at being used as bait for a shark. In addition to her other deficiencies, *Caldwell* was heavy to handle, with an extravagant turning angle which made keeping station a constant struggle, and she was wet; water boiled through her scuppers and drenched clothing and equipment stowed away below. She was in fact a real pig of a ship, and I would not have blamed the crew if they had jumped ship en masse; but they did not; to the best of my knowledge the desertion rate was very low.

It was a problem to know what to do with this information. Obviously I could not give aid and comfort to the enemy, the sons of bitches who had been making my life in London so miserable, but on the other hand, the *Herald Tribune* would expect some return for my time and expenses, exiguous as they were. I solved the problem by compounding it, on the grounds that my visit gave inadequate data for a definitive story; so I asked my contact at the Ministry of Information for a boating jaunt with the "four-pipers", specifically aboard H.M.S. *Caldwell*.

CHAPTER
ELEVEN

This request confirmed MOI's suspicions about my sanity; they insisted that all identification marks on my clothing and all papers should be removed, in case of "accident" and of my body being picked up by hostile hands. I promised, for the same reason, that I would take no notes or memoranda while aboard. Finally, in February 1941, I received a railroad warrant and a letter to the Naval Officer Commanding, Western Approaches, and set out for the Fleet Oiler, Mersey Estuary. When H.M.S. *Caldwell* came in to refuel, I should swarm aboard and make my number with the skipper, if I could. It was a haphazard arrangement, but it worked. On February 26, I found myself taken in hand by the Chief Petty Officer, given the drill and a berth, and introduced to the wardroom as "a gentleman from the press". The CPO strongly advised that I dispense with undressing, since, in the event of Action Stations being sounded (four blasts on the siren), the sooner I was on the bridge in my duffel coat, the better. He also advised a practice run before Lights Out, as strange companionways were tricky to navigate in the dark.

I had good reason to be grateful to the CPO for these friendly suggestions. That very night I was awakened out of a sound sleep by the sinister din—one . . . two . . . three . . . FOUR wails on the hooter. I was up on the bridge faster than I had believed possible. The First Officer gave me brief recognition. Everyone was peering into Stygian blackness. The Navigating Officer said: "That profile—might be the *Scharnhorst*." The famous German

137

pocket-battleship had eluded the Allied blockade and was somewhere at sea. First Officer negatived the suggestion: "We wouldn't be here this minute if that was the *Scharnhorst*," he commented practically. There was some exchange of views about calling for the recognition signal, and putting a shot into her if it did not tally, but this faded out when someone recognized the strange object as an old merchantman converted into a convoy aircraft carrier with a couple of planes and a catapult to ward off enemy scouts or bombers. Characteristically, the convoy commander had received from his superiors no word of her mission, and an imbroglio had only been avoided by the commander's readiness to take an uncalled-for risk by not challenging her. An enemy auxiliary cruiser, raiding commerce, could have destroyed the convoy in the interval in which she was free from interrogation.

All this was very stimulating, but it was not good copy, since it could not conceivably be written until long after the war. So far as I was concerned it was a non-story and not worth the risk to life and limb involved in covering it. However, I was committed to the escort squadron assigned to pick up an incoming convoy at 20° West, and accompany it back to home port, Western Approaches, so I resigned myself to the discomforts of an outmoded destroyer on the open Atlantic, and got what sleep I could. I was awakened one night by a furious rattling and banging, part of which was occasioned by an inkwell which had broken out of my desk and was accompanying the metal wastebasket in a steeplechase around my cabin; but this was only a frill; the heavy clanging and rattling was somewhat more serious, so I stumbled up to the bridge to find out about it. The First Officer greeted me: "I'm just writing up the log," he grinned. "Reversed engines to avoid unidentified floating object." He added in an explanatory aside: "It was the Isle of Man, if you must know!" I grinned back, lying: "That eases my mind. Floating object, eh?" At the same time I was wondering whether he intended noting in his log that the steel containers ranked on *Caldwell's* deck, aft, which I knew were depth charges, fortunately set for a certain delay, had broken loose when the vessel reversed to avoid the "floating object".

Being now established as a reliable auxiliary to the ship's company, I was advanced another grade by the Navigating Officer, who beckoned me around the corner of the radio shack. "You wouldn't happen to know what that bright star is up there to port?" he asked. "I could get a good fix on it if I knew what it was." Only occasional stars showed through broken, scudding clouds, but it was no trick for me to recognize Arcturus; position, colour, and magnitude allowed of no mistake. "You're sure of that?" the Navvy queried. "Positive," I assured him. "There's the tail of the Bear — two stars of it anyway, and there's no other first-magnitude star in that quadrant."

This made my number as a very knowing fellow, and from then on I was referred to as "The Ambassador". I didn't follow their reasoning, but " . . . mine not to reason why . . .", so I happily accepted the tribute and asked if I could be seated at mess handy to a stanchion. This request was occasioned by an incident at lunch, when the cruet had broken away from its mooring and had somersaulted down the table, over the First Officer, and down to the floor where it sideswiped the ship's cat, which had been swaying before the fire like a metronome; she fled to refuge under the companionway, and crouched there glowering for the rest of the voyage. We fought our way doggedly into the southwesterly gale until we reached 20° West, our rendezvous with a small convoy of freighters, as fragile as a little flock of sparrows, scudding before a mighty indigo cloud which nearly reached to the zenith. As we turned — a terrifying manoeuvre in that weather — I observed in the east another cloud equally sombre and menacing.

"Aye," said the First Officer gloomily, "we fought a sou'wester outwards, and we'll fight a nor'easter back . . . *if* our fuel lasts! She's been drinking it like an elephant, and we'd better have a clear run to home port, or else . . ."

In this quandary, it was impossible to sheep-dog the convoy. We cut our speed to the most fuel-economical and set course for the Mersey Estuary. If the convoy scattered, that would be just too bad; nothing we could do about it. Those gallant little freighters rose to the occasion as if Rudyard Kipling himself had been there to chronicle their triumph. They kept station, with us and with each other. I felt duty-bound to keep them under observation, as if, in some occult way, they might drop astern if my eyes were taken off them. I watched until my eyes ached. They bit into the seas while spume swept over their bridges and foamed out of the scuppers in torrents, as we fought our way around the north of Ireland, the meanest ocean bowl in U.K. waters; but through all this *sturm und drang* the convoy held together and on course, while the weather relieved us of the strain of watching the skies, a merciful respite. We made the Mersey Estuary with a few gallons to spare, but some unfathomable signal from CNO Western Approaches, instructed us to lie at the entrance of the channel. "Silly old fart!" said the First Officer. "We'll have to keep some way on her because of the current. That means we're bound to run out of fuel. Wonder where the Admiralty finds these relics?"

"Agnes Weston's Home," I suggested, mentioning a recently controversial seamen's charitable institution. This cheered up the First Officer, who ordered "Half-speed ahead, and damn the CNO." We forged on for a minute until the Navigating Officer shouted "Oiler ahead! Tie up alongside!" At that moment, the fuel ran out and everything stopped—engines, winches, rudder servo, compass. Through good luck and seamanship, she hove to just windward of the oiler, and the breeze pushed her gently alongside. A line was thrown out and grabbed aboard the oiler; we were pulled in and berthed by manpower, almost derelict. The First Officer wiped the sweat from his head and face. "The hand who flung that line is going places," he said. "So's the fellow who secured it. I'll tell the CPO to get their names. That's as close a thing as you're likely to see, Ambassador, but I'd be just as glad if you didn't write it till this bloody war's over."

"Armistice plus twenty," I agreed. "There'd be a tot of rum breaking out now?"

"Let's go below," the First Officer suggested, "though I'm afraid it's only gin. The Navy ain't what it used to be, but even so, a drop of Mother's Ruin will do us no harm."

We went below.

Ashore, I found everyone in a great stew over German motorboats, which were making hit-and-run raids on shipping, trusting to their speed and low silhouette to protect them. They carried one torpedo for armament. It rarely struck target, so very little damage was done, but the possibility of attack disrupted traffic, diverted escort vessels from more important tasks, and kept up pressure on the supply lines. The Germans beefed up their attack by dropping mines from aircraft into the shipping channel; these airborne mines incorporated new bedevilments. One type rested on the bottom and was activated by the vibrations of a ship's propeller; it was not very successful, being, characteristically, too sensitive and delicate to stand the rough treatment of the aerial mine-layer. So the Germans rushed development and production of a new device on which they gambled heavily — the *magnetic* mine, which was exploded by the magnetic impact of a ship's hull passing over it. British scientists defused this monster with the "degaussing girdle", a metal cable which was laid around the hull, and in effect demagnetized the ship. It was a superb triumph, simple, imaginative, and effective; it conquered the threat of the magnetic mine. I found this hard to believe when the news was passed to me with bated breath by the Information Officer, so I used my understandable scepticism to get authorization for a "boating trip" in April 1941 up the East Coast swept Channel from Harwich to Cromer, where the German mine-laying planes had been intensely active.

Harwich was dreary and discouraging. The station platform was dominated by a large poster giving detailed instructions on procedure to be followed in the event of invasion. The gist was "get out fast, but don't clog the roads with refugees" — a neat trick if you can do it. By the time I had worked through this "Refugee's Handbook" I was tempted to go back to London, but pride forbade. I was committed; there was no retreat. I wandered down to the inner harbour and had no difficulty identifying my minesweeper, a battered but business-like former Iceland trawler.

I found the skipper eating steak-and-kidney pie at the bottom of what looked like a prairie well-shaft, a vertical companion-

141

ladder which dived into the hold, where a bridge-table, set with white napery and silver, displayed the remains of the pie and some bread and cheese. I showed the skipper my orders, and sat down at the table while he read them. He suggested that we both go ashore to the Mariners' Arms and have a chat with such worthies as we could find in the Saloon Bar. There we would get intelligence on the war, the weather, and the "Oropesa float", the most recent and supposedly still most secret device for dealing with moored mines. Like most wartime secrets, it was common knowledge among the habitués of the Saloon Bar. This was not such a vital security leak as it appeared. True, the Germans could have picked up all sorts of information, but with so much misinformation as to cloud the credibility of the truth. Furthermore, no German operative could hope to survive the diagnosis of accent which went on in the Saloon Bar. I have always regarded my speech as the King's English, untarnished by any regional or class accent—a well of English undefiled, you might say. But I had not been in the Saloon Bar more than the time it took to order a pint of old-and-mild before bets were being laid as to whether I came from North Staffordshire or South Yorkshire. My voice production must have been Central Staffordshire, but I could well have picked up from Jim Pearson on the prairies a tendency to turn vowels into diphthongs, and occasionally to use a "Yarkshire pudd'n" turn of phrase that habitués of the Saloon Bar would identify and appreciate at once. No foreigner could have met that test.

To the skipper of the minesweeper, this exercise in phonetics was a better guarantee of my reliability than all my official papers. He took me aboard without more ado, and turned me over to the Chief Petty Officer with his blessing. The Chief Petty Officer of any well-found naval vessel combines the military functions of Quartermaster Sergeant and Regimental Sergeant-Major. He knows where everything should go or is hidden, he supervises the rum ration and knows where the extra tots are kept, he knows when the issue of dress shoes comes in, and where to go for them. The CPO, H.M. Minesweeper No. 325, explained that the ship, having started her career as an Iceland trawler, had amenities not generally found on His Majesty's ships. These included sleeping quarters aft, sumptuously panelled in mahogany that discreetly concealed tiers of bunks equipped with individual reading lights so that the off-duty watch could entertain themselves with reading or games like chess, draughts, or halma without disturbing everyone else in the wardroom. Mostly, however, they just wanted to sleep!

Having shown me my quarters, the CPO suggested that I might like to watch the Oropesa float being launched, since there were still several hours of daylight. I went on deck and found the float, a battered metal "potato" about six feet long, with lugs placed on a bias, which drew the float away from the vessel and held it about 200 feet distant, almost on the surface. A cutter with jaws like a gigantic steel shark was held at an appropriate depth below the surface by a paravane or kite. When the cable attaching the mine to its anchor was severed by the cutter, the mine floated to the surface, where it was exploded or sunk by a rifle shot. The first swath of a sweep was the tricky one, for the confines of the field were only approximate. After that there was no great problem; the sweeper merely followed the lane cleared by the first swath, with its float reaching into the field like a mower with a scythe. Shipping was warned to keep well away from us by a huge red flag hoisted between the masts.

One afternoon as we were droning quietly along with the float well extended on the starboard beam, the skipper exploded into a torrent of oaths. A small vessel, decked out like ourselves, was approaching us head-on down the channel, as yet unswept. The intruder was operating a noisemaker designed to explode acoustic mines well ahead of her — which was just about our position. We all lay prone on the bridge on the theory that the body could absorb shock in a prone position better than upright. The only man on his feet was the helmsman, who sidled us past the intruder keeping clearance to a careful minimum. The skipper gave the intruder's skipper a piece of his mind and received as good as he gave, in broad Yorkshire.

At dusk the float was hauled in and equipped with a small light, which looked very picturesque as it bobbed along on our starboard beam. But with darkness, the North Sea chill set in. I went below, climbed into my snug berth and fell asleep. I was awakened about two in the morning by the CPO telling me that if I wanted to see the float brought in, I should go on deck with him immediately. I declined. I had seen all of minesweeping that I could digest. What I wanted at that moment was sleep. I did not get much, for hauling in a float, possibly entangled with a mine, was a noisy operation. It all had to be done in darkness, for there were aircraft above, and intermittent flashes from the neighbourhood of Harwich suggested that a full-fledged raid was in progress.

At daybreak we turned and headed back to port. As we entered the inner harbour, ominous gaps in seafront buildings testified to the night's activities. The skipper turned to me and slipped his false teeth into place. He pointed with his thumb shorewards. "Better come back with us for another sweep with that new gear," he said. "It just ain't safe ashore."

I felt however that my paper would prefer some message from me dealing with the previous night's raid, so I regretfully said no. I did not relish the idea of returning to the bombing routine after this pleasant boating jaunt, but thought it possible I might organize an expedition into the Bight of Heligoland with a motor torpedo-boat. Flotillas of these gadflies darted in and out to keep the German garrison on the *qui vive* and to map any new minefields by tracking the course enemy vessels took through them. I put in my bid as soon as I got back to town, but for some unexplained reason it hung fire. Possibly I was getting more sensitive information out, despite the censor, than the services cared for. They were so uncooperative that the only other party I was able to set up was a brief run with a flight of light U.S. planes modified to serve as medium-range patrol planes. I also found that New York was turning against these expeditions as involving more risk than the story was worth.

It was apparent that I had failed to convince the *Herald Tribune* that London was in fact the front line, and much more dangerous than positions manned by the fighting services. This was discouraging, but I complied, and resumed my old beat—Ministry of Information, Whitehall, the Chop-House, my office in Bush House, and my bedroom at the Savoy. New York was front-paging everything I sent, but reported difficulty in finding volunteers to share or relieve my workload. Wives added their objections to their husbands' distaste for an unknown but evidently uncomfortable and dangerous assignment. Ultimately Joe Barnes, a tough bachelor, got the message, and was flown across before he could change his mind. Barnes, I thought, was too eager to grab the best stories for himself, but he agreed to confine himself to "actuality", and leave political comment to me. It worked as well as such arrangements between two ambitious, conscientious reporters ever do, and turned out unexpectedly well for Joe when I was taken off the scene as an air-raid casualty on April 15, 1941.

I was sitting in the Savoy's underground bar one evening enjoying a quiet drink while listening to the bumps and crumps drawing steadily nearer as the enemy attacked the Hungerford Bridge. Missing the bridge they concentrated on its approaches, among which the Savoy was a conspicuous target. A very near miss sent a shudder through the building, followed by the sound of showers of broken glass. I began to worry lest the blast and the glass might have destroyed the blackout curtains in my suite. In that case my bedroom lights would be a beacon for every raider in the area. I decided, although reluctantly, to go up and turn them off. My misgivings were justified. The curtains were in tatters and all lights were blazing. I turned them off and went into the adjoining bathroom. The bath was half-full of splintered glass; I felt thankful I had not been enjoying my evening tub when that happened. With a feeling almost of relief I returned to my bedroom, and peered cautiously out at the fires burning in half a dozen centres on the South Bank. I thought of our office boy and hoped his home had not been hit. As I stood there I was horrified to see a dark shape float down past my window. I recognized it as a landmine attached to a parachute; I had seen one hanging from the Hungerford Bridge the other day. The parachute prevented the mine from destroying itself by the impact of its ton of metal and explosive dropped from two or three thousand feet. Fright froze me. I was unable to move from the window until I heard the monster clank on the pavement and fall onto its side without exploding.

"Another dud!" I thought, as I thankfully wiped the sweat from my brow and strode to the door. I stepped into the corridor, closing the door after me quickly, only then discovering that I was unable to lock it because I had left my keys on the dressing table. I turned back to get them. As I opened the door, there was a great flash of light, and something struck my right eye. The only thought that came into my mind was: "I'm glad it wasn't my best eye." I had noticed some time before that my right eye did not focus as precisely as the left one. I put a folded handkerchief to my eye, and made for the elevator doors. The operator received me with a single word: "Hit?"

"Yes. Take me to the dressing room in the basement." There, a volunteer nurse bent over my eye as I sat on a chair. I anticipated bad news when she drew in her breath sharply in an unprofessional display of revulsion at what she saw. "If you're not too shaky on your feet," she said, "I think we'll take you to the Royal Westminster Ophthalmic Hospital. It's the best place in London."

I got up. She took my arm and led me outside. On the other side, a fire warden helped me stand up. He complained about "people mixing drinks in times like these". This seemed to me to be grossly unfair, for I had stayed steadfastly to one potion — Scotch and soda — all evening; but the warden seemed to feel that it was riotous living by the wealthy which had brought this vengeance on him personally. The street outside was ankle-deep in glass. As we shuffled carefully through it in the direction of the volunteer ambulance waiting for me, I heard the unmistakable throb of a German bomber overhead. My heart failed me: "There they are again," I muttered. "I can't stand any more of this."

The nurse's morale was beginning to waver, too, for she replied crossly: "Don't be silly. Here's the ambulance. Get in." A few minutes later I was snug in bed on the top floor of the Royal Westminster, with another row of those damned glass windows facing me when I turned on my left side, and the sky alive with bright sparks of tracer bullets, climbing slowly, slowly towards an enemy who showed neither fear nor regard for them.

I remembered to ask that Joe Barnes be alerted at the office and a cable sent to my wife in the United States, giving my whereabouts and concluding, "Nothing serious." The orderly protested, "No eye injury can be anything but serious."

With that I was given a sedative, but the drug was not powerful enough to put me to sleep; it barely dulled the pain in my eye. Some time about midnight I was aware of Joe Barnes bending over my bed; I complained about the glass windows facing me— glass was anathema. Joe agreed; he hauled a mattress into a dark, unglazed corridor, I joined him with a blanket for each of us, and there we spent the night comfortably enough, although my absence from my bed gave the night nurse a fit until she discovered our retreat, when she gave us a well-earned lecture on hospital routine and its observance.

It struck me then, and more forcibly since, that Joe Barnes' visit to me in hospital that night was one of the most outstanding acts of charity I ever heard of. I asked Joe what it was like outside.

"Bad," he said. "They are still coming down and I counted sixteen fires all around us; if they ever unite it will be another Fire of London." They did not unite; the indomitable fire-fighters struggled throughout that fearful night, and subdued them one by one.

By next morning our world had returned to what we had learned to call "normal". The milkman made his appointed rounds, noting in his pocketbook the gaps in his roll of customers. Charwomen came by with mops and scrubbing brushes complaining of the sand, mud, and plaster tracked over their clean floors. The night fire-fighters caught what sleep they could before daylight dwindled and bombardments began again.

I was visited by a great eye specialist — so outstanding he was addressed as "Mister", not "Doctor" or "Professor". He murmured noncommittally at first, but came back later to ask if I would agree to an operation which might save my eye, though not its vision. I agreed; after the operation, the specialist informed me that he had put two stitches in the "white of the eye", but he feared that the retina had been displaced or ruptured, in which case, I would never see again with that eye.

Gradually, I made the acquaintance of most of the ward, all eye-patients. It was not very helpful, since, having had experience with ophthalmasthenia, they with one accord forecast that the wounded eye would have to be removed. This was borne in on me too, as the left eye grew gradually less powerful. I remembered the case of a young man on the *Lake Manitoba* on our way to Canada, who was totally blind because an injured eye had been allowed to impair its mate until vision had been lost by both. Therefore, I was neither surprised nor shocked when my specialist confirmed lay opinions. The news spread as if by telepathy, for soon after he left, an attractive young woman was shown in. She sat down, pointed to her eyes and asked, "Now which of these is glass?" She moved them left and right, and I was unable to detect any difference. "Nobody does, and they feel just the same," she exclaimed as if proving a debating point. "So you see it won't make any difference to your looks, and it will prevent the other eye deteriorating." Without more ado, I okayed the removal of the right eye, on condition that the surgeon described the operation step by step, in which case I agreed to a local anaesthetic, which the specialist said was preferable as giving the operating surgeon a better chance of dealing with the muscles of the eye that was being removed. The ten days to two weeks following the operation were tense times for me; the vision in my remaining eye seemed to continue deteriorating and in my anxiety over this phenomenon I began having nightmares about tapping around with a white cane for the rest of my life. Joe Barnes and other patients in the ward tried to keep up my morale, an effort which culminated in the words of an old lady next door, who said, "I'm so sorry to hear that you're going to lose your other eye after all."

At that point, Maureen Church, a pretty girl who had been my son's governess in Paris, decided that my morale and health would be improved by a change of scene — such as a cottage in the New Forest. Maureen, who had rallied around while I was in hospital with frequent calls, chatter, and readings, plus a synopsis of the bomb damage overnight and an estimate of morale in southeast London, as measured on my office boy's gauge, managed to organize such a retreat, plus a room for herself which would enable her to avoid the nightly London shambles. The cottage was a treasure, to find which must have taxed all the wiles and ingenuity of a pretty young woman; however, I profited by the treasure without searching too closely into its acquisition. I took gentle walks among the ferns and young growth, noting with relief that my remaining eye seemed to be recovering and focussed well on blue. Wild hyacinths were easy to bring into sharp focus; red or yellow flowers presented more difficulty. This woodland idyll ended with my transfer to Wilton, a country house in the Cotswolds owned by Lady Reid, a relative of the Ogden Reids, owners of the *Herald Tribune*.

In the blue-and-silver morning of the Avon Valley, I tasted all the delights of gracious living in an English country house. The library was well equipped with leather-bound volumes which paid tribute to the taste of an eighteenth-century country gentleman. It reminded me of Oriel College's library, replete with volumes of sermons, natural history, Boswell, and Gibbon. When the country gentleman and his lady modernized their interests, W. H. Smith & Co. attended to their re-education.

The cellar was stocked with port, laid down in '88 by Lady Reid's predecessor and sipped cautiously at infrequent intervals. The cut-glass decanters which sparkled on the mahogany sideboard dispensed this nectar until the fad changed and it became *de rigueur* to bring the bottle, cobwebs and all, to uncork it with exquisite delicacy, and to circulate it "way of the sun". The decanters remained, a sparkling souvenir of fickle fashion.

My bedroom windows were high under the roof of the pillared portico; I looked out at the marble acanthus leaves of the capitals, floridly undercut, where generations of swallows had made their nests. I awoke to the continuum of hirundine twittering as the feeding routine commenced for the day. It would have been sacrilege in that ambience not to have taken a cold bath, so I came down, shivering and shaking, to the breakfast-room for a ritual English breakfast of oatmeal (Scottish), bacon (Canadian), and eggs (Irish), followed by finnan haddie (Scottish), or a bloater (Yarmouth), leading up to toast and marmalade (Dundee). By this time some of the hoarfrost had evaporated. Feeling returned to my fingers. I was ready for a brisk stroll down to the canal at the foot of the paddock, as the grassy hillside leading up to the house was called. I delighted in the Grand Union Canal—its locks were so sturdy, its bridges so confident in the potential of well-laid brick, and the stillness of its shallows so hospitable to small fry, that "the cut", as it was vulgarly nicknamed, became one of my favourite haunts. The Grand Union Canal and its ancillary works—locks, bridges, lock-keepers' cottages—advertised the durability of good design. Its charms were enhanced by a certain melancholy which clung to it as to an aging beauty, long the toast of the town, whose architecture and construction were so sound as to be enhanced and embellished rather than ravaged by time. As I stumbled through the grass, savouring an occasional sprig of sorrel, my melancholy tendency was intensified by the brown hue with which A. E. Housman's verses shadowed the landscape. This was very beautiful, but it had no future, indeed it possessed only the most tenuous relationship to the present. It lived in the past, and so did the gracious lady and her memories which filled the house. While enjoying this foray into the eighteenth century, I realized that it was fortunate for me that I had to earn my living, otherwise the temptation would have been irresistible to hang on, in some innocuous role, with no more future than the house, living in a world of make-believe and surreptitiously buying tickets on the Irish Sweepstakes, like the rest of the household. I was flicked out of this dream-world, like a fish on a line, by an abrupt message from New York asking me to return as soon as I felt able to do a day's work. Head office hinted that a post in the Washington bureau might round out my experience while giving me a private peep, as a *voyeur*, at the intimate dance of Empire. The Managing Editor further suggested, as a conclusive argument, that it might be advisable to return before I became an expatriate.

150

There were no options open to me other than to obey the summons, although I was reluctant to return to the United States. I had expected that my injuries, suffered as they were in the line of duty, would have assured me a cushy billet in the overseas service, but the desirable posts had been pre-empted while I was *hors de combat*, and on principle, overseas appointments were made by the head office, not by subordinates on the spot, however informed they might be of the local needs, opportunities, and pitfalls. It was all part of the journalistic mystique which insisted that tradition in appointments and similar matters have precedence over innovation. I knew enough about "front office" working to be aware that trying to buck the system would be a grave mistake, as injurious, even if successful, as a calamitous failure would have been. It would turn an armoury of sharp office knives against the would-be subverter of established newspaper habit and tradition.

So I made no more than a token demur, for the record, and prepared to start all over again on whatever rewrite desk I might be assigned to. Visas were obtained in surprisingly short order, largely because of my status both as a foreign correspondent and as a *blessé de guerre*, which I made the most of, wearing a large black eye-patch with a wide black band. Transportation to the United States I solicited from my friends in the Ministry of Information; the speed with which I obtained it made me doubt whether it was granted in reward or relief.

Leaving Britain was a wrench, for I was beginning to feel at home there, and I wanted to be on hand for the invasion of the Continent, the "Second Front", which I knew was coming. I did not know when, but changes in the concentrations of LSTs (Landing Ship, Tank) were a pointer and a calendar. Of course many ruses, including feint movements, were adopted to confuse both the enemy and neutral observers; I think, oddly enough, that the enemy was taken by surprise by both the number and the location of the landings. However, I missed Operation Torch, although by that time I was back in Europe after a brief stint in the United States.

TWELVE

The pleasant New Forest landscape slid by as I was driven down to Bournemouth from which, on June 14, 1941, I left, bound for New York aboard one of the stolid "Short" flying boats. Soon I was bouncing around on the choppy waters of the Tagus off Lisbon, then we pushed on to the Azores—unchangingly beautiful and venal—and so to Bermuda and Norfolk, Virginia, where I had a plate of Chincoteagues to celebrate my return to North America. There had been nothing worth reporting about the rest of the voyage except for the startled exclamation of a customs officer in Bermuda who wanted to know what, if anything, I was hiding behind my eye-patch. When I showed him he exclaimed, "Good God! Maimed for life!"

The reaction did not cheer me up, although I recognized the sympathetic intent. However, a warm greeting from Whitelaw Reid, the eldest son of the owner and publisher of the *Herald Tribune* re-established my confidence in my ability to survive professionally. Unfortunately, I had overrated my physical capacity to recover. I had no reserves of strength, and my patience, never my most outstanding characteristic, had been worn very thin. The Reids were models of understanding and goodwill. Helen and I were invited to the family home at Purchase, a sumptuous estate developed in the Hudson Valley in the days when conspicuous display was essential to the success-rating of the acquisitive robber barons. Gradually, as summer wore on, my health improved sufficiently for me to return to work in the *Herald Tribune*'s New York newsroom.

My reception there was cordial but embarrassed, for nobody

knew what to do with me. I ended up sweating it out again on the day or night rewrite desk, decoding cable-ese copy from the *Trib*'s overseas correspondents and fleshing out the bare bones of their stories from my own recollections and clips from the morgue. However, I comforted myself with the reflection that, despite the waste involved in using an experienced foreign correspondent in the position I now occupied, the copy I had edited would be reasonably accurate because of the specialized knowledge I had accrued abroad.

Avoiding errors rather than assembling data is always a reporter's major problem. Errors have an extraordinary life expectancy. They pass from originator through plagiarist to rewrite man and on through the chain until they reach the wire services, by which time they have become an article of faith which no newspaperman dare contradict.

A prime fount of erroneous material was the up-state correspondent who was paid by the column-inch, and needed a great deal of unnatural history if he was to fill in the gaps left at the end of the legislative session at Albany. In the vacation he moved across the state line into Connecticut, a rustic state where all sorts of odd happenings could be reported without fear of denial. Every evening the night rewrite desk expected him to call in with some prodigy worthy of a place beside "Lady into Fox" in the annals of unnatural science. We printed the items opposite the obit page, which featured other snippets of local, national, and international folklore. All too soon obits came to be recognized as my particular charge, until I committed a heinous offence, which earlier in my career might have cost me my job.

One busy night just before the deadline, I was called into the reception room to deal with an agitated lady who had a carton of cigarettes in one hand, and in the other a tender obituary notice of her husband. He was not a man who deserved more than a couple of "sticks", but she had provided a full half-column and was determined to get it printed. I disliked the idea that my services had to be bought, so I sweet-talked the lady, took the cigarettes and the obit, and went back to the night desk, where I laid them down and promptly forgot both.

The poor lady was understandably upset that her loving tribute to the dear departed should have been overlooked, and she raised so much hell about it that I urged that obits be transferred to somebody less fallible, leaving me to concentrate on the cable desk, where I would be less dangerous since all my attention would be focussed on transcribing cable-ese from our overseas correspondents.

New York had changed little since my first days on the *Herald Tribune* staff, and I loathed the city's grime and noise with a cordiality unassuaged by time. Increasingly, boredom made my job almost intolerable and I longed to be where the action was, which was certainly not in the newsroom or on the rewrite desk. At a particularly low ebb, my cup was sweetened by the discovery that I had been insured against death or injury while I was in Britain; consequently, the insurance company came across handsomely. The examiner for the state of New York generously found that I had sustained embarrassing facial deformity which called for compensation too; so I was relatively well-off as a result of my trials. I put my money into a down payment on a house in Washington and applied for a transfer to the capital. This relieved the *Tribune*'s dilemma about my future, particularly as I made no difficulties about my position on the bureau staff which was already crammed to bursting with stay-at-home worthies who had picked themselves the best jobs — White House, Senate, House, State Department, Pentagon—and were not disposed to move over for a newcomer, no matter how deserving. I had neither status nor beat, but functioned as a swing man, or dog-of-all-work, which gave me access to the White House, State, and any other department worth cultivating, although I was always on sufferance. It was limiting and irritating to be always supernumerary — the invisible and unwanted guest. Bert Andrews, the *Herald Tribune*'s Washington bureau chief, was jealous of, and I think a bit unsure of, his own position, although he enjoyed the firm support of Mrs. Helen Reid. Despite this he was careful not to encourage competition; any heads which sprouted up too high were soon lopped off on one excuse or another. Sometimes the only way to get rid of uncomfortable examples, shining or dull, was to get them dispatched to an overseas bureau, where they would have to survive the jealousies of the cable desk, the telegraph desk, the city room, and their colleagues overseas. The successful took a long look at their prospects and waited for an opening on the *New York Times*, which paid three times the salary and was generous with expense accounts, or, *faute de mieux*, the wire services — Associated Press, United Press, or even International News Service, if the worst came to the Hearst, as we used to say.

Washington in the Forties was a reporter's dream world. In contrast to London or Paris, it cherished a subversive heresy about the right of the people to know what their masters were up to. The architecture of its public buildings followed patterns established in Imperial Rome; the President, enthroned in the White House, enjoyed authority and wielded power in A.D. 1941 which T. Claudius Nero Augustus might have envied in A.D. 69, with the additional bonus that, unlike Nero, the President had no need to fear rebellion in the provinces or revolt among the generals, MacArthur excepted, although there were more than 150 of them commanding some 2,000,000 well-armed troops. When the President travelled, his small but select praetorian guard preceded him, vetted the route for enemies, and discreetly frisked visitors for concealed weapons. Taking their cue from the Palace, as irreverent reporters occasionally dubbed the White House, government departments maintained heavy mimeograph machines — and sometimes portable ones too — which operated heedless of the eight-hour day, vomiting out reams of what might grossly be called propaganda, but, more accurately, "information". It was presented not only in plebian mimeographed pages, but aristocratically, as printed folders with handsome type — Roman, Italic, or bold-face — on thin, strong paper with attractive rubric and colophons. Above all, these documents were authoritative, and libel-proof. Another well of information, not necessarily undefiled, but authoritative also, was the printed record of hearings held by the appropriate committee on every bill, amendment, or resolution introduced into either House. They were voluminous and exhaustive; a copy bound in a green paper cover lay on the desk of every legislator, along with the text of the item under consideration.

By the time a conscientious or inquisitive reporter had ploughed through 1,500 pages on hearings before a good committee like the Senate Standing Committee on Foreign Relations or the Select Committee on Standards and Conduct, he was well-informed, not only on the subject matter of the bill, but on who wanted it and why; or, as we used to discuss in *ad hoc* sessions on the white marble steps leading up to the Senate Caucus Room, on the second floor of the Senate office building: "Who got screwed and who got the three dollars."

Valuable as they were, the printed records were no substitute for personal attendance at hearings. For one thing, they were often savagely edited versions of the original official stenographers' script. In so-called "sensitive" areas, the cuts often made the record meaningless. Furthermore the dour, censored, printed record cannot convey the sensation of imperial magnificence afforded by the baroque marble frieze, the solid marble columns, and the bronze fittings of the Senate Caucus Room with which Nero, Domitian, or Caligula need not have been ashamed to adorn their palaces on the Palatine Hill; a modern Tacitus might have drawn a moral from them on the parallel decline of simplicity and public virtue in the mighty republic which dominated its known world as surely as Imperial Rome ruled its dominions in the days of the Flavian emperors.

I used to amuse myself, when the hearings dragged, by adapting the inscription on the base of the column of Marcus Aurelius in the Piazza Colonna in Rome to fit the pillars adorning the Caucus Room of the United States Senate. It went like this:

> divus ROOSEVELT IMPERATOR AUGUSTUS,
> Sarmatiis, Parthis, Germanisque
> Bello maximo devictis,
> Triumphalem hanc columnam,
> Rebus gestis insignem
> > Dedicavit.

The White House regulars enjoyed this bit of historical transposition, along with any other crack levelled at F.D.R.

156

Although my position was so lowly that any perquisites I acquired came rather as an act of grace than a right, by waiting interminably in the White House lobby and pushing shamelessly at the right moment, I thrust myself into the front row of F.D.R.'s press conferences in the Oval Room, at the famous desk covered with knick-knacks — Democratic donkeys, ash trays, lighters, and cigarette holders.

As the months passed and opportunities presented themselves for me to observe the behind-the-scenes power politics in the capital, Washington's appeal became more apparent. The traumatic events of April 1941 faded; it had been a momentous year for me, providing as it did the chance to purchase the architectural gem in Georgetown, a suburb of Washington, where my wife, my son, and I made a delightful home. Apart from the loss of my eye, to which I was gradually adjusting, the only other cloud on my horizon was my mother's illness, diagnosed, during a vacation she spent with us, as cancer. An operation halted the spread of the disease and she was eventually able to return to her home in British Columbia, but her former vitality never returned, and ultimately she died in 1946 while I was overseas.

The second year of the Second World War was memorable also for its fast-breaking news stories, among them Japan's surprise attack, December 7, 1941, on the Philippines and Pearl Harbor which caught the American forces there unprepared, resulted in enormous losses both of men and matériel, and ensured the United States' entrance into the war.

First report of the attack was phoned to me by Bert Andrews, my bureau chief. After a brief discussion we decided that I should go to the White House where press would be briefed as information became available. A great crowd milled outside the White House; inside, a throng of newsmen had gathered, including representatives of all the major dailies and periodicals, as well as some reporters none of us had seen before. Both groups appeared shocked and disbelieving that the Japanese offensive could have taken place while peace negotiations were still in progress. Presidential Press Secretary Steve Early made his first announcement early in the afternoon; there were few details at that stage, but his announcement that President Roosevelt would speak to the nation next day created ripples of excitement among the press, for it indicated that the United States would be actively engaged in war before too many hours had passed.

Press conferences with Early continued at regular half-hourly intervals, with reports of destruction becoming worse as the day wore on. It appeared that at least one battleship and a destroyer had been sunk at Pearl Harbor, while others were seriously damaged, and a large number of planes had been destroyed or crippled. Severe criticism was levelled at the Navy, which was accused of being "asleep", but I pointed out the virtual impossibility of warding off a surprise air attack in time of peace.

By next day, Monday, December 8, it was clear that losses, already known to be serious, were worse than was originally thought. At Hawaii, five battleships and three cruisers were lost, three were less seriously damaged, many smaller vessels were sunk or disabled, and 177 aircraft were destroyed; many hundreds, military and civilian, were killed or wounded. On Capitol Hill, where Congress was to meet, thousands, mostly women, huddled behind barriers in the cold, clear sunlight. The building itself was packed and the press gallery was so full as to be almost impossible to get into. Each paper was issued only one admission ticket to the gallery, so Bert took the *Tribune*'s. When proceedings commenced, I found a chair in the reporters' room outside the gallery, and stood on it peering through the glass doors, although it was impossible to see much; F.D.R.'s speech was indistinct from where I stood as the loudspeakers were not functioning, so it was not until night that I heard the complete text when it was rebroadcast.

After the President's speech, I went in and watched the House vote for war, 388 to Jeannette Rankin's 1. It was a strange experience for me to see the old-time isolationists confessing their sins.

The United States' declaration of war on Japan, closely followed by the British declaration, set rumours abroad, swiftly denied by Steve Early, that Churchill would visit Washington. Just before Christmas, I sat waiting for Wendell Willkie, the Republican party leader, still the *Herald Tribune*'s white hope despite defeat in the 1940 election, to return from the White House. Roosevelt had sent for him secretly, and the Reids feared that "the spider", whom they abominated, as only socialites can abominate a socialite socialist, as a black sheep, a traitor, a Judas, and a success, had spun a web to entrap the innocent fly, Willkie.

Early in my Washington career I had been assigned to cover this potential David who might knock off the Goliath F.D.R. My duty was to record every word and deed of Willkie's that was fit to print; such a mission was supposed to keep us both out of mischief, for the Reids hoped that a reporter eternally on his heels might check Willkie's habit of sounding off on all occasions, timely or untimely. And if, despite these precautions, Willkie floundered into heresy, the *Tribune* counted on me to cover it up or explain it away.

I galloped off on this assignment joyfully, for it released me from the cullion's role in the bureau; everything I wrote about the Great Man would be "must" copy which nosy little mice on the telegraph desk would nibble at their peril. However, before I had been with Willkie for a week, I realized that I had fallen into the Scylla-Charybdis trap awaiting the special correspondent, who should neither love nor hate his assignment but regard it with a cold, impartial gaze, assessing good and evil with equal gusto, and confiding all editorial matter and his own sentiments to the "turn-page". It was the antithesis of the *Chicago Tribune*'s policy, which habitually printed thinly-disguised editorials as front-page news. I fell for Willkie, and soon found myself ignoring his mistakes, correcting his syntax, glossing over his exuberant brashness, and presenting my readers with the idealized caricature of a cool opportunist of statesmanlike reserve, who could be counted on to tread circumspectly among the broken glass bottles of American politics at the federal level. Treading circumspectly was the last thing that would have occurred to Wendell Willkie; no bull in a china shop more enjoyed the clatter of Dresden, Meissen, or Chelsea *objets d'art* stamped underfoot.

While he went in to see Roosevelt, I holed up in Blair House nearly opposite the White House; there was only one postern gate by which he could escape unseen, and I was positive Willkie did not know about it. Sure enough, he came bustling out of the West Entrance, and posed for the cameramen outside the door, where the portico pillars made identifying background. I was happy to see there were no microphones about, so he had not said anything about his interview.

He came back to my room at Blair House, bustling with importance and secrecy. Vowing that he would not reveal the great news, he let himself be drawn out until he muttered something about "Great man ... coming soon." He seemed to feel that by keeping his voice to a whisper, he was not violating a confidence.

I guessed, "Churchill ... Don't tell me ... I know it."

"How did you find out?" Willkie asked innocently. "It's top secret."

"We have a London bureau," I hedged, "and I'll have to cover him."

It was a grim time for the democracies. The United States Pacific Fleet was sitting on the bottom of Pearl Harbor, H.M.S. *Repulse* and *Prince of Wales* had been sunk. The Japanese were on the march. Great pressure was building up in the sticks to concentrate on the Pacific and let Europe ride. It would have been a popular but fatal decision for the President to make. To be sure, many disasters were ahead: Singapore, Hong Kong, and Manila would fall, but Alamein was only five months ahead. At this Christmas the grand alliance was founded, the European Theatre was given priority, the Congress and the American people would, however reluctantly, accept the decision. F.D.R. and Churchill had a rendezvous with destiny, and I was there when the appointment was made, to hear Willkie report it. Further, he told me that Churchill and F.D.R. would give a joint press conference at which some of these matters would be unveiled.

There I was with another potato so hot I could neither hold it nor drop it; so I hurried back to the office, phoned the news to the desk, securing a pledge that they would check it with the

London bureau, and run it as if it leaked from Whitehall — an innocent deception. This shot my exclusive all to hell, but it was worth it, since we beat the *Times* anyway, protected my source, and secured great credit for me among the knowledgeable.

I was determined to be on hand for the Roosevelt-Churchill press conference and got my credentials lined up early so that I was sure of admission to the Oval Room where the President worked. I had learned some of the back ways and private corridors by which newsworthy visitors could slip in and out unseen, if they wished, which was exceptional and newsworthy in itself. By using these skills ruthlessly, I turned up in the front row at that most famous press conference of them all.

Franklin Roosevelt and Winston Churchill were a pair of prima donnas, neither prepared to cede front-and-centre to the other. F.D.R. sat at his cluttered desk with a cigarette in a long holder. He had placed Churchill well to his right. The British statesman, pink and bland, with his inevitable cigar, was almost out of camera range and well out of earshot. It was deliberate, I don't doubt, but it boomeranged.

As we burst into the Oval Room, after an agonizing wait, Roosevelt, fitting another cigarette into his long holder, half-turned to his guest muttering, "They're an awful bunch of wolves, you know. And I'm going to throw you to them. Go ahead."

Churchill, clutching his cigar, stood up, and delivered some platitudes about his pleasure in meeting his distinguished friend. But his voice was so thick and his speech so slurred that even I, in the front row, could hardly make out what he said, and of course there was no mike or amplifier, though there was a recording device concealed under the bouffant skirt of a doll — on the side farthest from Churchill, but well within reach of Roosevelt's voice, and for that matter, of mine also, for I later heard a recording of that episode. F.D.R. sat back in his swivel chair, looking smug. He knew quite well that the British Prime Minister could not be heard by reporters at the back of the room where they were crowded ten deep.

But they were not of a mind to take this lying down; someone far back sang out "We can't hear you" — and someone else amplified "We can't see you either." Spurred by this challenge, Churchill stood up, turned and clambered onto his chair, fortunately solid. From this vantage point, he waved his cigar, gave his personal V-for-Victory salute, and said simply: "Here I am." That brought the press into camp. The *Chicago Tribune* girl forgot the tough questions she had come to ask. Churchill could have run for the Presidency against F.D.R. himself and Franklin D. knew it, without necessarily relishing the fact.

The following day Churchill repeated his triumph by bringing Congress into camp too. I went up to the Hill for that. The galleries were packed, and so was the floor, for a joint special session fills every available seat, and this was extra special. However, by peering over the heads of my colleagues, I managed to keep Churchill in sight as he brought the house down with his opening comment: "If my father had been American and my mother British, instead of the other way around, I might have got here on my own." Congress appreciated the practised politician, and after that his speech was frequently interrupted by applause. He had Congress in his hand, and soon afterwards he rounded up the rest of the nation when, with full radio coverage, he turned the switch which illuminated the giant Christmas tree on the south lawn of the White House.

Churchill had the genius which made even his random remarks poetically and politically effective.

"I have the honour to add a pendant," he said then, "to the necklace of Christmas goodwill and kindness with which my illustrious friend, the President, has encircled the homes and families of the United States."

Franklin Roosevelt met Churchill measure for measure in his skill as a politician; he was also a consummate actor with a dramatic sense that enabled him to conceal from the American public the full extent of his crippling paralysis. Few people outside Washington realized his complete reliance on his heavy steel leg braces and canes for support; any movement was painful and difficult, yet sensitivity for his political image helped him overcome his handicap. F.D.R. played to his audiences with unabashed enthusiasm, knowing that a wave of his hand or hat could bring thousands into the Roosevelt camp.

In the days before assassination became a fact of American political life, it was relatively easy to gain access to the President's Oval Room at the White House, or to the souvenir-filled library where he worked at Hyde Park. F.D.R. was friendly, affable, approachable, and a good source of news when he chose to be, or when Steve Early chose to let him be. He made a point of knowing all the regular reporters by name, exchanging quips which frequently had the press corps in roars of laughter, in which he joined.

But press conferences could sometimes be a nightmare for reporters unwise enough to phrase their questions carelessly, for F.D.R. was not a man to suffer fools gladly. "That was a stupid question," he would comment, his famous charm disappearing, to be replaced by a black scowl. Those who crossed swords with him under these circumstances rued the encounter, for it was not pleasant to be taken to task publicly by Roosevelt. Fortunately such instances were rare, for F.D.R. was far too great a man and too generous a character to engage in continued warfare against a member of the press, though he found it difficult to resist needling offenders occasionally.

Hob-nobbing with the President, observing the events of 1942 when Churchill once again visited Washington, and developing news sources on the Hill, nonetheless failed to disguise the fact that I was fifth wheel in the *Herald Tribune*'s Washington bureau. Feeling that I was filling in time to no purpose, for there was nowhere for me to go with the *Tribune* at that time, as the most interesting beats had been taken over by reporters so magnificently healthy neither disease nor death seemed likely to carry them off, leaving a space for me, I bid my colleagues farewell, and joined the Office of Strategic Services, Psychological Warfare Branch, at higher pay.

CHAPTER
THIRTEEN

The O.S.S. was a bowl of the oddest fish I have ever seen assembled in one container. It was sired by Colonel W. H. (Wild Bill) Donovan out of F.D.R.; one of a bevy of boards, commissions, divisions, offices, and services spawned by the New Deal, which fought each other more fiercely than the enemy and proved their directives orthodox by bureaucratic blows and knocks.

O.S.S., like its confrères, was staffed by newsmen whose papers had folded or bureaucrats whose jobs had evaporated following some high-level consolidation of their offices, departments, missions, or posts. Its immediate parent was the Office of Facts and Figures, a strange assembly of rumours and ciphers, which had somehow managed to attract to its orbit Elmer Davis, a Rhodes Scholar who had helped me find a job when I landed in the United States in 1929. Davis, a popular newsman and magazine writer, one of the pioneers of news broadcasting, delivered, valiantly and nightly, a carefully balanced, impartial commentary on the news. He would leave his office immediately afterwards, before the abusive telephone calls began.

Once it had been established, O.S.S., like any other bureaucratic creation, had to elaborate a role for itself, together with a Table of Organization packed with plums for astute office politicians and bran for the working stiffs. Some bureaucratic magician found premises for the new hush-hush department in an abandoned brewery, the chief virtues of which were that it had ample ground space where independent buildings could be erected, and nobody had to be ousted to accommodate us, which would have occasioned an interdepartmental feud to end all feuds. Having invented a name and found quarters, it now had to develop a mission, which is bureaucratese for justification of existence, or in a simple term, a job. After other expedients had been exhausted, Colonel Donovan went in person to the White House, sold a bill of goods to F.D.R. in a fifteen-minute interview, and came out with a "mission", which soon became known as "the golden directive". Moses with the Tables of the Law could not have been more welcome than Donovan and his "golden directive" which was submitted to critical exegesis, analysis, and interpretation, until every drop of authority had been squeezed into the bureaucratic flagon, and distributed into a hundred waiting cups. It authorized practically everything anyone could think of, including printing false money. An operation of this scope could not be conducted without arousing the liveliest curiosity in the press, which had to be fobbed off without being so browned off that the story would be on every front page in the country. There were some juicy items which would have rejoiced every rival group in the establishment and made the press happy to boot. One of these items was the occasion when a harassed secretary left a highly confidential document in the safe together with a batch of freshly printed false money. She closed the self-locking door and went home. A few hours later President Roosevelt called urgently for the document. Terrified at the prospect of being unable to produce it or to recall the dialling code, the young woman remembered that one of her boyfriends had just taken a special course—of which Colonel Donovan was very proud — in safe-breaking and lock-picking. She sent him around to show his mettle, but when he got there, he found that a neat hole had been drilled in the wall of the safe and most of its contents had been removed — all except the critical document. He removed it thankfully, and in good time it floated across the President's desk.

This, however, in no way discouraged the bureaucratic mandarins, who had their eyes firmly fixed on the happy prospect of obtaining access to practically unlimited jobs, funds, fees, and expenses which need never be accounted for, and which could be cleared with Congress in silence on the grounds of security.

The essential was to find or invent a stunning title that would reveal nothing and justify everything. The Office of Strategic Services was ultimately selected. It had everything, including a parody on the initials O.S.S., in which they were interpreted as Oh So Social — which had more than a spice of truth in it.

The Operation was modelled on British Intelligence, which at that time was extravagantly admired, in so far as it was understood through the uncertain medium of best-seller fiction, or on the reports of our own operatives who were allowed to polish up their techniques by riffling through the files of the very people from whom they learned "dirty tricks". It was more through luck than good planning that they were neither shot nor electrocuted, for they were apprentice sorcerers who asked for trouble and had no loyalists.

The first few weeks of my stint with O.S.S. I spent harnessed to a desk in Washington, although I had been assured by Colonel Donovan that my experience as a European correspondent would ensure my eventual transfer overseas. Waiting for that golden moment, I spent much of my time interpreting some of the gems of misinformation that floated across my desk in contributions from amateur agents whose imperfect command of English was offset by an exuberant imagination and nourished on arcane fiction. So much of this "intelligence" was rubbish that I was reluctant to pass it on under the lurid red SECRET tab at the top of the page. But much money and many jobs were involved —my own among them—so I compromised by drawing my pay and maintaining my "security".

Among the jigsaw-puzzle pieces of intelligence I saw was material which indicated that a highly secret operation, having as its ultimate aim the invasion of Sicily, was about to be mounted in North Africa. I was determined to be on the Sicilian team, and working from the inside through my former *Herald Tribune* colleague, Johnny Whitaker, I obtained my objective.

High on the list of O.S.S. priorities was a series of broadcasts beamed from North Africa to mainland Italy, designed to allay Axis suspicions of the Allies' planned Sicilian landing. We innocently went to the trouble of engaging a pair of Sicilians to broadcast the messages. Unfortunately, their native accent convulsed Italians who, on picking up the send in Rome, Florence, or Milan, thought they had stumbled into a prose version of *Cavalleria Rusticana*, and wondered what kind of country boobs we must be to think that anyone who cherished "la lingua Toscana in bocca Romana" could be influenced by this comic-opera dialect, which our high-powered transmitters poured into their ears.

However, the German invaders were also listening, and their intelligence correctly deduced from our use of Sicilian personnel that we planned a descent from North Africa on Sicily rather than against Sardinia or Calabria as we had tried to persuade them. Reasoning that our next move would be at the heart of Sicily, German Intelligence recommended to their generals reversal of an earlier plan for withdrawing from the western mountains and concentrating around Aetna in favour of a solid defence of the heart of the island around the strong-point of Caltanissetta-Enna, the geographical centre of the island, with poor roads, few communications, and little local produce to sustain an invader. As so often happened in that war, Allied stupidity paid off. The German commanders, strong in logic though they were, could not believe that we would show our hand so indiscreetly unless we had some double play in mind.

Even though General Patton pranced around Algiers in light, summer-suntan uniforms (though he dressed his GI troops in full-weight uniforms), the Germans still discredited their own intelligence estimates, dismantled their western defences, and concentrated on the romantic Aetna salient where the amenities were there for the asking. As they had shipped Italian currency plates to Catania there was no problem about printing all the money their armies in the island needed, leaving the paper to be redeemed or discarded by the next occupants. It was an agile method of modern looting, and it left us with a problem that we in turn met with equal dishonesty by issuing dollar currency identical with standard Treasury notes except for the seal, which was done in gold rather than blue or green. Gold-seal dollars were legal tender throughout occupied areas, but not for shipping back to the United States. It discouraged hoarding, which might otherwise have been a problem. This venture into coun-

167

terfeiting was highly successful, making nonsense of Gresham's Law that bad money drives out good; the two currencies coexisted happily. Oddly enough, no objection was raised to gold-seal dollars, even in the United States. They were evidently not returned in sufficient numbers to create a problem.

A less successful O.S.S. operation, just before the Sicilian invasion, involved Italians we collected from the New Jersey Palisades, gave a pressure-cooker indoctrination, and shipped to Rome, where they were immediately rounded up and shot or shipped to the Pontine Islands, then a convict settlement. Years later I met in Rome a friend of long standing, who asked me in amazement where we found these characters, for their Sicilian-American accent declared infallibly their birthplace, breeding, mission, and future (which would be as "nasty, brutish and short" as the philosopher Hobbes could wish). There was no need of torture to bring them to confession; their clothing, speech, even their voices, shouted aloud to Italians that they were enemy agents, but such poor ones as to justify maintaining them under supervision, or even providing them with phoney information, rather than having them replaced by competent newcomers. It was the classical double-whammy in espionage, and the intelligence they sent out was so untrustworthy that we never did discover the whereabouts of Mussolini until the Germans, whose intelligence was much superior, found out where he had hidden himself and captured him in a spectacular coup which made us look very silly indeed.

We had envisioned *Il Duce* in the Pontine Islands, which we even raided once since they were easily accessible by sea. There were guesses (for they were not much more) that he had taken refuge in an ancient castle of one of the Sicilian barons, a remote fastness not too far from Mount Aetna, which was well known as a smuggling centre and now might have some very important contraband, since our regional representatives reported mysterious comings and goings.

When O.S.S. set up a unit in Sicily, I looked into these rumours which kept the province agog with curiosity. I discovered that the Baron Gordoni operated a still in the hills back of Messina. In the keep of his feudal castle he fortified an already potent wine grading fifteen degrees with an *eau de vie* that knocked me out when I sampled it at lunch. I spent the afternoon asleep on top of a pile of feather beds, which the Baron had stored in his castle as a hedge against the inflation which he foresaw following this stupid war, with which he was thoroughly out of sympathy. Not only had it violated his treasured isolation, but it had made it impossible to get adequate medical attention for his eye, injured in a brawl in Messina. Furthermore, what else but the war could be blamed for the spread of sullen resistance to work on the part of his employees? "Not so long ago," he confided to me as we stood on the terrace overlooking his vineyard, "the women whom I hire to harvest the grapes used to pile the baskets high, and carry them up the hillside on their heads, singing as they climbed, out of pleasure in their work." He added gloomily: "They don't sing any more, which is a very bad sign. Pretty soon they won't work either, they'll join the Mafia up in the hills and come to no good."

I clucked sympathetically at this indication of the decay of pride in honest work. But he reassured me that it was not all dead, since the women still raised geese at the back of the castello, and made the down into the feather beds I had so enjoyed earlier in the day. "Just so long as those damned socialists and republicans don't get at them to turn their heads," he continued. Times will improve, particularly if the Allied soldiers forbore to tell tall stories about America and all its household machines and money and good times. "If it was so good there, why did they come back to Sicily?" he inquired.

I seized the opportunity to retort: "They came to uncover the secret radio sender which is located somewhere around here and puts out much enemy propaganda." He hurriedly denied any complicity, and invited me to search his castello. He suggested that Germans who had remained behind in Messina when the High Command evacuated the island might be responsible. "Or even," he hinted with intense roguery, "even your own people in Catania, who have installed an odd crowd, mostly *mafiosi*, and print a paper which preaches nothing but subversion." I bridled a bit at that, for if he thought so poorly of the Catania paper, what did he think of our Palermo paper, *Sicilia Liberata*? He thought poorly of it. So did I, for entirely the opposite reasons. He thought it was subversive, full of communist propaganda. I thought it was stodgy, Tory dogma, a betrayal of all the principles we were supposed to stand for.

The odds were against us. Mussolini had enrolled all working journalists in the Fascist Party. If we brought them into our liberation papers, everyone would feel that nothing had changed, and all the anti-Fascists would vociferate — and with reason — that their steadfastness, which had cost them dearly, in money, liberty, even life, had been for naught.

> Say not the struggle naught availeth,
>   The labour and the wounds are vain,
> The enemy faints not, nor faileth,
>   And as things have been, things remain.

Clough's poignant lines fitted the post-Fascist scene too precisely for comfort. However, we took aboard Sig. Loverde, former editor of *La Tribuna*, a fat man whose halitosis was so pronounced that we felt confident that he would not enter any conspiracy or cabal against the Psychological Warfare Branch, since no closed cabinet could endure his presence for long enough to draw up a new constitution—always the first requisite of revolutionaries. We interviewed him across a huge desk which kept him at a livable distance. We also pulled out of the *maquis* an eager, youngish writer, slender as Casca, but without envy. Spinelli's knowledge of Mafia mentality enabled him to sail very close to the wind, writing deadly editorials with a knife in every line, and borrowing two of our military types to escort his shipments of olive oil, pressed in the hills, from his own wild trees, to his home in Palermo.

As a further precaution we sent Spinelli with a weapons-carrier to collect the earthenware vessels of oil, and a jeep to escort it, with strict orders not to be overtaken by night in Bugheria, a Mafia-dominated suburb of Palermo which set the price for old wine, young women, and assassination, with exemplary integrity. What you paid for you received; what you did not pay for, you also received, without undue delay or satisfaction. However, the Mafia had an Achilles' heel, which we took advantage of. Most of them came from Brooklyn, and a threat to send them back to "Brookolino" was usually enough to keep their extortions to a reasonable wholesale-retail ratio, and their intelligence reasonably accurate.

Here we found great benefit from our connection with British Intelligence. We adopted their security classifications, merely changing terminology. Thus, all our stationery was headed "Confidential equals British Restricted, Secret equals British Confidential, Top Secret equals British Most Secret". We also set up parallel departments. Special Operations (so) played within its limitations the role of British Special Operations Executive (soe); Special Intelligence (si) duplicated British Intelligence Services (is); but Morale Operations (mo) had an individual role without British counterpart.

mo had had a very limited life-expectancy until Colonel Donovan came back from the White House flourishing the "golden directive", which authorized everything we could think of. We thought of plenty. About that time, Vesuvius blew its top, and lava poured in a red-hot stream down its cinder cone. A special committee was convened in O.S.S. which seriously discussed the possibility of channelling the flow into a Plutonic V-for-Victory pattern, emulating Churchill's famous wartime salute.

However, lacking the technology for carrying out this splendid propaganda triumph, we dropped it, fortunately without publicity, for shortly afterwards another vent poured more lava streams down the cone. These united to form a majestic, fiery, spectacular, unquenchable M, visible all over the Bay of Naples, to the consternation of our friends and the delirious excitement of the Fascists, who hailed the phenomenon as a heavenly witness to Mussolini's virtues and a portent of his triumph. We made a feeble counterattack along the line of the hellish origin of the eruption, and the damage it wrought to the owners of farms and vineyards within its radius.

The better to assess this, I whistled up my jeep and set out for Sorrento, across the bay. It was a good excuse for a trip which I longed to make, so I drew up and signed a trip-ticket which would authorize me to poke around anywhere in the area. The justification for this was that it would enable me to advise the

Psychological Warfare Branch and O.S.S. in Washington on how the disaster should be handled propaganda-wise. To my surprise I found that the damage was minimal, and the benefit enormous. The earth was covered with black scoriae—volcanic cinders—which the peasants were frantically digging into the soil. In the fertile coastal plain, the eruption was hailed as a great blessing, since it had not been accompanied by earth tremors which would have damaged or collapsed buildings, and the scoriae were fertilizer of the highest quality, free and bountiful, excellent for the vines and promising a bumper yield of cauliflowers, the major cash crop. I reflected on the need for a constant flow of background information. Lacking this, we could have made ourselves look very foolish indeed if we had beamed propaganda to the area deploring the eruption as an unmitigated disaster, and holding Mussolini responsible for it. I made a note to fire off a warning to this effect to Washington as soon as I got back to Naples, and to add a further caution against sounding off about topics on which they were not fully informed.

A notable offender in this class was Mayor Fiorello H. LaGuardia of New York, who had mike-fever, and never missed an opportunity to address his compatriots. Unlike a volcanic eruption, which he otherwise resembled, the Little Flower was an unmitigated disaster to Psychological Warfare in Italy. In the first place his accent made him sound like a Yorkshireman explaining to Somerset what culture was all about. As if that were not enough, he poured out a bounteous cornucopia of promises —rations increases, bread, meat, and flour—which we had not a hope of fulfilling. Neapolitans in our zone had a pocketful of Japanese persimmons and that was all. They puckered the mouth without satisfying the belly. The sidewalks of Naples were spotted with the remains of the persimmons, trampled on by disillusioned Neapolitans. Furthermore, the army had established a vast food-and-clothing dump on the hillside in plain view of the hungry, ragged inhabitants of Naples, who would have marched out in droves and looted it, but for the heavy guards we placed around it, with orders to shoot if necessary. In addition, the dump was some miles away, and difficult to reach without a "borrowed" car and "borrowed" gas.

It was quicker and safer to exploit the docks, where the confusion attending the discharge of LST's and army freighters offered almost unlimited opportunities to the adventurous. We estimated that we lost 40 per cent of everything landed on the Naples docks. It made me mad to think of the futility of the lives and ships we lost freighting matériel across the Atlantic and through the Mediterranean, to be pilfered by a gang of thieves in Naples.

I had cruised on convoy escorts in the western Atlantic, so I knew what a trial this operation could be. Burning with anger, I determined to pay a surprise visit to Pompeii, where we had an emergency landing-field and a dump. The airfield had just been bombed, and eighty fighters parked around its perimeter had been destroyed. It was the largest single loss of aircraft we suffered in the entire Italian campaign, and I wanted to establish the pertinent facts about the disaster. Was the field properly defended? Were the aircraft dispersed and sheltered by bunkers? Or were they just lined up on the tarmac, a tempting target?

It was not all bad. The station presented the sloppy, unmilitary aspect which most of our installations quickly took on; but there were plenty of good bunkers, although the aircraft had been left outside them. While we were there, Vesuvius started blowing off again, the scoriae crashing onto the roof of our car. Fortunately, the roof was metal, but this was not wholly reassuring as scoriae the size of cowpats thundered out of a rapidly darkening sky, while the air reverberated with thunderous explosions. I looked cautiously out at the sky. A huge, indigo cloud towered to the zenith. It was rent by vivid chains of lightning. On the ground, sizeable branches were being hammered off trees by the impact of the scoriae.

It was time to get out, if we still could. We plunged the car through nearly a foot of black ashes. It was a powerful Plymouth, and it ploughed strongly through the debris, until we came to a stout brick-and-stone barn. We cut and ran for the barn with a folded American Sunday paper protecting our heads. We stood in the high arched doorway, as possibly the safest part of the building; then I began to wonder what would happen in the event of an earthquake, which might well accompany this eruption.

While I was sombrely contemplating this possibility, my companion turned to me saying: "How long did it take to bury Pompeii in 69 A.D.?"

A squall of scoriae knocked down a horse and stripped a nearby tree of branches.

"How long?" I replied. "Oh, one long day and one long night."

At that moment, the intensity of the fall diminished somewhat. "Let's run for it," I said. We stumbled through the scoriae, plunged into the car and started the engine. With a great heave, the car ploughed through the volcanic debris and into a violent rainstorm that was followed by a pounding hailstorm. Holding course, we drove through these strata into brilliant sunshine. Looking back, a blue-black cumulus towered to the zenith. Ahead the road was dry; we did not wait to see any more, but raced back to Naples, shaken but full of gratitude to our Plymouth, a make for which I have retained admiration and affection, together with the memory of that horrifying day at Pompeii. Had the eruption continued for another hour or two archeologists by now might be digging out our skeletons, for exhibition in a new War Museum. I had no mind to be a celebrity to be viewed for a dime. I decided to limit my personal, on-the-spot reports to items which could be covered from the Singer Building, where my office had been established in downtown Naples.

Keeping out of danger, however, was not as easy as it seemed. That very night there was a heavy air raid which made my billets on Posilippo dance. I glanced cautiously through my blackout curtains, which we conscientiously used *pour encourager les autres*. The view appalled me. Not only was Vesuvius pouring out red-hot lava, but the Germans had dropped a string of flares over the harbour. They floated slowly down, pouring a deadly light on the freighters riding at anchor below. In flagrant disregard of regulations, Neapolitans were driving about with their automobile headlights full on. A small machine-gun unit was sending ineffectual, red tracer bullets into the sky, reminding me of the London air raids. The foreground was brilliantly lit by the flashes of the anti-aircraft battery established immediately behind my billets. I had not felt so conspicuous since I lay in a ditch in the Basque campaign, trying to take shelter from a fighter which was manoeuvring with deadly persistence to get me in his sights.

I reached for my tin helmet and went outside to check on our lights. In the courtyard, I found a British soldier on guard, nervously fingering his rifle, while spent anti-aircraft pellets pitter-pattered all around him. He challenged me.

"What are you doing here?" I asked him, ignoring the conventional reply to a challenge.

"I don't know, except going crackers," he said, with British restraint.

"Go inside," I ordered. "There'll be no action around here tonight; and if there was, you couldn't stop it."

He needed no second invitation. I followed him in, and after a drink of boiling water poured over ground tea-leaves, sugar, and milk powder, which the British favoured rather than coffee, I went to bed and slept ten hours.

Next morning I found showers of messages from Washington, demanding samples of the unit's output. It appears that these were needed to ensure funds and continued Congressional support for the operation. I hesitated to comply until the messages became urgent commands. There was not much point in sending individual pamphlets, surrender passes, or forged documents, without a report on how and where they had been put into enemy hands and their observed effects obtained from prisoner interrogation.

Such information, however, would endanger the lives of our operatives behind the lines, and be awkward for ourselves if captured, since it would pin on us all the label of espionage which some of our personnel in Washington were foolishly claiming for themselves. Furthermore I was collecting samples of our documents and reports, hoping to take them home with me for my private records and for ultimate publication after security

175

had been satisfied. Many of these operations, especially those carried out by the British, would make fascinating and instructive reading for decades afterwards. I surrendered them on pledge that they would be given back when I returned. However, they were consigned to the military records buried in Fort Knox, and to this day I have not been able to obtain or even to see them. I wish I had been less conscientious, for they would have been valuable, both as guides and as warnings, for a long time— particularly the schedule of do's and don'ts that we drew up.

For instance: Don't promise more than you can perform. The Germans played a clever trick on us in Naples, by spreading the word that as soon as the Allies came in there would be bread in abundance and a healthy meat-ration too. They knew this could not be met, for they had themselves eaten most of the bread and meat in town and had evacuated the rest. Consequently the first popular reaction to our occupation was bitter disappointment, turning to resentment and hostility when it was discovered that full rations would go first to the military, while civilians got what remained. Our most apparent contribution was the everlasting Japanese persimmons.

I never found out who organized the vast supplies of persimmons which poured into Naples—some worthy bureaucrat, no doubt, who wanted us to have plenty of antiscorbutics, and was influential enough to commandeer the material and the shipping to deliver it on top priority.

I was so disillusioned by persimmons that I was ready to throw in my hand when something occurred which restored my faith in what we were doing. This restoring agent was a case of typhus— only one, but in the overcrowded conditions, the dirt and grime of Naples, the wreckage of buildings, and the lack of medical facilities, the stage was set for a runaway epidemic which would be a disaster for our military effort.

The Psychological Warfare Branch got to work, fast. We cleaned out the house where the outbreak occurred. Then we sent loudspeaker trucks to instruct all the inhabitants of that street to muster at the Singer Building "for an interesting operation".

Typhus is carried by the body-louse which lives and breeds in hair, particularly the pubic hairs. Fortunately it is very susceptible to pyrethrum, a botanical insecticide, of which we had an ample supply in powder form. We explained this to the Neapolitans who came to see us. Then, with a flit-gun full of pyrethrum powder, we called for volunteers from the women. They filed into a small adjoining room. Flit-gun under dress, flak-flak, "Here, take some *caramelle per i bambini*" — exeunt, giggling. It was a roaring success. Next day we sent for a new supply of candies (caramelle) to cope with the crowds. By the end of the week, the danger area had been sanitized; there were no more cases. We had stopped a potential typhus epidemic dead in its tracks, the only time in recorded military annals that this had been done.

You might have expected (if you did not know the military mind) that P.W.B. would receive handsome recognition, perhaps a medal or two, for this spectacular victory. But the generals were too busy pinning medals on each other to notice us, and although ultimately I did receive a decoration, the citation made no mention of the Typhus Triumph, which in its way was as important as Alamein, and cost no lives. That puts me in mind of the sardonic French joke:

Question: How is the greatness of a general assessed?

Answer: By the number of casualties he sustains.

While Typhus Triumph was a tremendously useful operation, it was not covered by any directives. Our job was to pump out propaganda by radio and press to bolster our side's morale, and beat down morale behind the German lines. Allied Forces Headquarters in Algiers (A.F.H.Q.) reminded me of this, and urged that my unit perform its allotted function.

Thus, following the Allied forces as they moved northwards up the Italian boot, I eventually found myself in Rome with the American army four days after the Eternal City was liberated on June 4, 1944.

Rome knew many conquerors in the Second World War; first, there were the Germans, who entered as allies and remained as overlords; next came the strange tribes from Eastern Europe, whom the German tidal wave had washed from their homelands to deposit on this strange strand; there were the Ghoums, Negro

177

troopers from Mauretania whom the French had posted in their mountainous sector of the Italian front; finally there were the Americans—God's gift to young women, rich and gullible, with all the money and cigarettes in the world, as well as access to the military Post Exchanges, where silk stockings were available for young women who were willing to be captured by handsome young soldiers (or even by old soldiers, provided they retained their P.X. cards). Along with the troops came reporters, who were even more of a captive girl's dream, for not only did they have access to Post Exchanges, but they were so guileless, so ready to be conned out of all they temporarily possessed, and they talked endlessly of Washington, New York, and other American power centres. Naturally, their girl friends might, by various sleights of hand, be infiltrated into the United States.

On my arrival in Rome, I drove at once to the Aventine, where I had found shelter and content for three beautiful years before the fragile vase of Western society was shattered by the Second World War. I parked my jeep in the Piazza of the Knights of Malta, an exquisite area designed by the printmaker Piranesi to look like one of his own works. Nothing had changed in the time I had been absent, and I felt a surge of relief coupled with a great desire to see friends made during the period during which I had called Rome my home. I drove the jeep away from the Piazza and parked again near the door of the Church of Santa Sabina. Unlocking the "boot" I took out a one-pound tin of coffee, more precious than gold. I took this to the beautiful house opposite, as a present for the Albertinis, whom my wife and I had known in happier days. That night I slept in their home on a cot near a window overlooking my jeep, in which more coffee was hidden.

The coffee famine the American forces found when they entered Rome was a paradoxical result of Mussolini's dreams of Empire. He overran Ethiopia, but found that this major source of native coffee produced bitter berries, unacceptable to Italian taste. The conquest drained the regime's supply of foreign currency with which to buy the abundant coffee production of Brazil or the more-esteemed Costa Rican berry, and the war, which brought with it trading difficulties, made coffee of any type virtually unavailable in that nation of coffee drinkers.

178

Aware of this situation, I kept supplies of green berries under lock and key. It was a more powerful inducement than money, and it obtained for me undreamed-of privileges. The green berry is preferred by afficionados, for they can vary the roast to their taste, grinding it only immediately before use, so that none of the flavour escapes. The aroma, however, pervades the block, causing the nostrils of passers-by to flare with appreciation.

Even the American GI's who were exploring the Aventine in off-duty hours took to walking around the Church of Santa Sabina, pretending to examine the ancient doors, but sharpening their appreciation of the artistry with which they were carved by an extra whiff of the divine fragrance which filtered out of the Albertini *espresso* censers, and drifted over the curtain walls of the ruined Savelli stronghold on the crest of the Aventine. In its day it had been a fair haven for the Savelli Pope Honorius III, who laid England under an interdict in King John's reign. The enclosed garden is now fragrant with orange trees, scions of the original planting by St. Dominic in the garden of Santa Sabina near by.

I frequented that lovely garden whenever the pressures of the military became too onerous. Normally we trotted along on a loose rein, the military being too busy planning victories or explaining away defeats to bother with the Psychological Warfare Branch as long as we did not agitate for more transport or rations. We were careful to avoid this, for any demand for more jeeps or "K rations" would have called attention to the abundant supply which we had "acquired" by purchase, barter, or discovery, untended. Our jeep, for example, had been "captured" on a field of battle in Sicily by a Mafia type from whom we bought it for gold-seal "Trade Dollars".

We also had a "command car" which had disappeared from a British Army dump near Caltagirone, in their sector of Sicily; it was a great prize for which we traded a truckload of tea — the finest Assam leaf, which had arrived, chest and all, in a shipment of mines which checked in by mistake at Syracuse because the skipper was an old Classics specialist who could not forgo viewing the site, so graphically described by Thucydides, where the Sicilian Expedition perished in the fifth century before Christ.

The "command car" was a cross between a jeep and a station-wagon, ideal for transporting Very Important Military Persons, but not good for much else, and was viewed with envy and hatred by Brigade Headquarters, with desire and fury by Third Division, with malice by xv Corps, and with spite by Seventh Army.

That we were able to hold onto such a treasure against this horde of pirates was a tribute to Psychological Warfare's resourcefulness and the Command's incompetence. We also had a six-by-six (in American, a truck; anglicized, a lorry), a splendid piece of equipment big enough to transport a flat-bed press *and* a portable offset job. With this equipment we could set up shop in any captured town and within minutes print off proclamations to the people, telling them to mind what we told them . . . or else! We could also run off leaflets with good cuts and colour work for mass distribution among crowds as fast as they could be written.

We soon moved from propagandizing our friends to decontaminating our enemies. We invented a technique of doing up our subversive leaflets into a roll about the size of a mortar bomb or twenty-five-pounder shell, which we could place behind the enemy's lines with great accuracy, affording us much diversion and them reluctant admiration and dismay. We varied our own output by printing documents found on prisoners. The Germans were a particularly rich mine; the letters those poor fellows received from home were heartrending tales of disaster: the meat ration had been cut, diphtheria was epidemic, the children were sick, doctors were scarce and surly, electricity failed with dinner in the oven, and Willy was missing on the Russian front. We burst into tears reading these doleful narratives, but we printed them off, suppressing names and other identification marks, and fired them back over the enemy lines, together with a FREE PASSAGE to Canada for the bearer who brought it into our lines. We didn't need to invent propaganda; they gave us the script and we used it.

As time and the war went on we expanded our operations, advancing from shell-delivered leaflets to newspapers dropped from planes. It took some arm-twisting to induce the United States Air Force to substitute bundles of papers for bundles of bombs; the brass was particularly sticky, suspecting that the truth—if that was what we were purveying—would do nobody any good. At first, they insisted on checking every issue themselves before it could be fired off, but they soon tired of that, and tried instead to get publicity for themselves into the sheet. Fortunately, Lord Trenchard took a dim view of this and put his views so cogently before Bedell ("Beetle") Smith, Eisenhower's Chief of Staff, that a special order was issued giving sole authority and responsibility for psychological warfare to the Psychological Warfare Branch. With an A.F.H.Q. order backing us, we felt that we had unlimited authority to do as we thought fitting, and we made the most of it.

German troops were tough material to subvert. They were good soldiers, but as the war ground on, the *Wehrmacht* filled the gaps in their ranks with inferior troops, levies from nationalities overrun on the eastern front—peoples who had no love for the Russians or for the Germans or for dying in a cause that was without interest or emotion for them. We pelted these conscripts with propaganda, going to extreme pains to use their own language, no matter how remote, until we realized that they were illiterate; at that point we concentrated on their NCO's, assuming that they would be able to read and would pass the word on to their rank and file. Sergeants and corporals were our targets, and we registered many hits with gratifying results in surrenders.

Thousands of Kazaks came over to us. We treated them well and gave a special bonus of tobacco to a few hardy souls who were willing to be infiltrated back to spread subversive rumours behind the lines; it was surprising how many volunteered, in full knowledge that capture would mean death under torture. It said something for their courage — or their simplicity — that they would take such risks for a cause not their own, for a mythical democracy which they neither understood nor desired. But they had a sort of Asian resignation and endurance, and as long as they had food and shelter for today, hardships were accepted philosophically as a part of the eternal balance of life. It was a real problem to know what to do with these Kazak deserters. We solved the problem by doing nothing, following the tested principle that if a problem could be ignored long enough, it would go away of its own volition. Ultimately the Kazaks went away; I don't know where they went; they simply evaporated.

Decades afterwards, when the war and its Four Freedoms had long been forgotten, I was driving through the Carpathian Mountains on some arcane mission when I saw a herd of horses in the valley below being driven eastwards through the pass by a wiry, wild-looking fellow on a wiry, wild-looking mount; he carried a lance and wore a pointed Kazak cap with a big red star on the peak. I wondered what camp he had escaped from, but I did not stop to ask. He had found the Fifth Freedom—his home range — and I did not propose to inquire further into how or where he had acquired the cap.

I wondered if his ancestors had ridden similar wiry horses through the Alpine passes, driving their cattle before them, down the roads to Rome some 1,700 years ago. Perhaps he retained some atavistic memory of finding a gap in the crumbling walls and scrambling up the Aventine Hill to make merry with a roast kid and a skin of wine divided among the women— for women always flock to meet a conqueror and take his money or his gifts and angle for a job for their brothers, their cousins, their fathers, and their sons, in return for whatever they have to trade.

As the fall of Rome was followed in swift sequence by the Normandy landings, the capture of Florence on August 12, 1944, and only a few days later, successful amphibious landings on the French Mediterranean coast between Marseilles and Nice, it was apparent that the Germans were on the run. The prospect of European peace was no longer an impossible dream. Knowing there was some likelihood of being shipped back to Washington when the war ended, I drew up a catalogue of my unit's activities over the past few years: X number of leaflets printed and distributed; Y newspapers revived or founded; H hours of broadcasting from S stations; P prisoners interrogated; and A agents introduced behind the enemy's lines. In retrospect, viewed in April 1945, after the German divisions in Italy were forced to capitulate, the most significant achievement of P.W.B. was that, in the final advances, our teams rushed ahead and occupied printing presses and radio stations before the communists got in. Had we not done so, Northern Italy from Milan to Venice and Trieste would have been deluged by hostile communist propaganda; the task of winkling them out of their shells would have been fearsome, and the outlook for the restoration of democracy in Italy would have been poor indeed.

Our next concern had to be Austria, for on April 12, 1945, the Russian Army "liberated" Vienna, leaving the entire country vulnerable to communist indoctrination. I was in Florence at the time; with the end of the Italian campaign in sight, plans were afoot to disband the Psychological Warfare Branch in order to form in its place two information teams which would be used to prevent the proliferation of communist propaganda. One team was to go to Germany when peace terms had been negotiated, the other's mission was in Austria, where the aim was to provide the Austrian public with alternatives to Russian news sources, as well as with some entertainment. To my joy, I was appointed deputy chief of the newly named Information Services Branch destined for Austria; I arrived in Salzburg the first week of June 1945.

Red White Red radio, focal point of the Austrian information network and named for the colours of the country's flag, went into operation in Salzburg soon after my arrival there. Under the able management of Hans Cohrssen, a German-speaking American who had been with P.W.B. in Italy, Red White Red was soon broadcasting from stations in Linz, then Vienna, using a motley array of equipment captured from the Germans or shipped in specially from the United States, and set up by Austrians assisted by American military and civilian technicians. The radio station's immediate success was due largely to Cohrssen's brilliantly conceived idea of the *"Suchmeldungen"*, daily broadcasts of the names and whereabouts of people hunted or misplaced, or queries for those missing in the war. This service, often imitated, but never equalled, was responsible for bringing together thousands of families and friends.

Neither was the printed word neglected; using old Psychological Warfare Branch techniques we took over printing presses, first in Salzburg, where we set up *Salzburger Nachrichten*, then in

Vienna, where *Wiener Kurier* was established in a building next door to the Red White Red station. As resoundingly successful as our radio broadcasts, both newspapers are still in existence today.

Vienna, when I reached it in July 1945, had already been divided into zones administered by the four "liberating" forces, Russia, Britain, the United States, and France, leaving a central area international. Business was conducted by the four powers at the Allied Council, the city's governing body, during frequent and interminable meetings that I had to attend as one of the American delegates. Every word uttered had to be translated into the languages of all four occupying forces, and, additionally, into German for the benefit of Austrian participants. To me these meetings, verbose in so many languages, constituted the height of boredom, and I would sit slouched at the table, shading my sleeping eye, and allowing the glass eye to keep watch. Occasionally unexpected questions would catch me unawares, but I usually managed to field fast-spins by commenting judicially, "Gentlemen, I think this matter needs further consideration."

Tedious as Allied Council meetings may have been, they nonetheless allowed me to observe how amiable were relations between the four powers. Britain and the United States displayed great warmth and cordiality towards one another; the French, being new to the coalition, were more reserved, though not necessarily less friendly. Only Russia refused to permit any fraternization between its delegates and those from the other occupying armies, and the latter used jokingly to refer to "being caught in the nyet of circumstances".

Russian suspicions of anything Western were confined to their hierarchy. I was once halted by Russian soldiers at Sanct Pol, on the road to Vienna. They wanted my wristwatch, which they knew to be good because it had a round face, not an oblong one — it being well known, even to Russian soldiers from the provinces, that square wheels don't work. But a round watch, and with an illuminated dial, that was prime. I was resigned to losing it as the price of ransom, but the soldier dipped into his wallet and came up with a sheaf of thousand-mark notes, the Russian equivalent of the American gold-seal currency, which he thrust at me, peeling them off faster than I could count them. I tried to stop him, as it was only a $15 P.X. watch, but he insisted—so in the end I swept on minus my watch, but plus several million Reichsmarks, which I duly cashed with the U.S. authorities for something like $250. I remember the little peasant with affection, and hope his ruthless masters in the Soviet apparat did not deprive him of his treasure when he was finally returned to his home east of the Urals. Most returning Russian soldiers, it was reported, were shaken down at the Siberian border so that the home folks should not be exposed to the visible evidence of the sybaritic life style of the democracies, where a common soldier could pick up such treasures.

Vienna in the days immediately after the war did not completely live up to its reputation for gaiety. Many of its finest buildings lay in ruins or, like the Opera House, had been partially destroyed; the traumatic entry of Soviet troops had deeply shocked many inhabitants; food was at a premium. Liberated and liberators alike often went hungry, but the native Austrian exuberance gradually began to reassert itself, and as the country's finest musicians and singers gathered to perform once again together, Mozart's beautiful music echoed through the concert halls.

My time was spent mostly in Vienna and Salzburg, but weekends gave me the opportunity to visit and explore new areas. Life seemed very good until one day in November 1945 when I was travelling on the Salzburg-Linz train and was suddenly overcome by a series of mysterious pains. A military doctor diagnosed my problem as hepatitis; I was taken off the train at Linz, hustled across railway lines, hauled over the couplings of a stationary train, and driven off in an ambulance which delivered me to a nearby hospital. It soon became apparent that what I had suffered was not hepatitis but a severe heart attack. Working on the principle that a change is as good as a holiday, the medics shipped me to Salzburg by ambulance, where I once again lay in a hospital bed, this time for several weeks. Friends rallied around, enlivening with their visits the dreary days I spent recuperating.

When I eventually left the hospital it was for further convalescence at Österreichischerhof Hotel, a new officers' billet in Salzburg, overlooking the Salzach River. My friends and the scenery pulled me from melancholy contemplation of my future, or lack of it; little by little I regained strength and optimism, walking ever-increasing distances by the river, always accompanied by some kind soul anxious to provide encouragement during the exercises.

By April 1946, I was fit enough to return to the United States where I then had to face the prospect of finding a congenial job, compatible with my talents, education, and experience, also bearing in mind the state of my health. Fortunately there was no pressure to make hasty decisions which I might later regret, for my doctors recommended a further rest of six months before I attempted any gainful employment. The occupations for which my qualifications might be important would be teaching, for which I had no taste, advertising, which I was afraid of and did not cotton to, or journalism. And all the time the ideal of returning to Canada was present; but I feared lest men, manners, and attitudes would have changed so much as to be as foreign to me as I would appear to them.

I still thought with nostalgia of the sub-Arctic flora of the prairies, or the flowery treasures of the boreal forest, but these faint images now received competition from more recent memories of medieval walled towns with well-stocked bookshops and trattorie, Petrarch and pasta, Dante and dates, Vienna and waltzes. This struggle in my mind had to be resolved before I could make an irrevocable decision about my future employment; as a final, though perhaps desperate, resource, I also had my father's farm back in Saskatchewan, with which I had developed a sort of love-hate relationship that endures to this day.

However, my return to the prairies was a disaster. The shack my father had built had collapsed under the impact of wind and weather. Skunks and badgers had forwarded the process by excavating under the joists. Such precious books as I had collected in my prairie boyhood had fallen into the cellar and become the natural prey of mould and mice. I made no substantial protest when my brothers, managers of the farm since my father's retirement in 1943, bulldozed the wreck into the cellar, on the grounds that if it was left in its decrepit condition the cattle would fall through the flooring and injure themselves.

But with the destruction of the shack my last strong tie with the prairies was broken, and I longed only to get away from the everlasting wind, the stinging dust, and the brutalization of life that they promoted. At last I fully appreciated the immensity of my father's pioneering achievement. Only now I understood the full impact of the decision he had made at the age of thirty-five— to cut loose from the security of the life he knew, among the friends, kindred, and surroundings of his youth, to face the challenge of uncertainty, a stranger in a strange land, where even the horses needed a different accent and strange commands.

I returned to the United States secure in my knowledge that I'd never make a farmer, though at the same time I also resolved that eventually I would make Canada my home. With those decisions behind me, I made another: that I would return to the *Herald Tribune*'s Washington bureau if there was still space for me. My experience and training should have made me an ideal novelist; to give myself a sense of purpose in the remaining weeks of my convalescence, I started to write a book. I was well aware of the comfortable living that some of my former colleagues wrested from their publishers; day after day I laboured on, knowing in my heart that no amount of special training would ever transform me into a Literary Lion. Subsequent rejection slips demonstrated I had been correct in my self-assessment. So it was with some relief that I returned to the *Tribune* in October 1946, where the main requirement made of me as a correspondent, albeit low on the totem pole, was to write fact, not fiction.

CHAPTER
FOURTEEN

Postwar Washington had changed greatly from the city I had known before joining the Office of Strategic Services in 1943, not only in style but also in atmosphere. The flamboyant, ebullient New Dealer, Franklin Delano Roosevelt was gone, dead at the apex of his career, leaving as replacement Harry S. Truman, an undistinguished but doughty senator from Missouri, unexpectedly propelled into one of the most prestigious positions in the world. Homespun and honest himself, Mr. Truman found in his political hierarchy men aptly nicknamed the New Romans. These potent Washington forces sacrificed to the same gods of unlimited power as their ancient counterparts, although they had been alerted against these concessions to all-too-mortal gods by a British historian who warned: Power corrupts; absolute power corrupts absolutely. Washington was worth a study in absolute power. Mr. Truman, to his everlasting credit, fought against the prejudice and intolerance he encountered among these men when the issue of world communism and its inroads into American society preoccupied the minds of some Potomac politicians unscrupulous enough to attempt a grab for personal power at the expense of others, in both government and private life, who were unable to defend themselves against charges of un-American activities. The American inquisition, spawned by the Smith Act of 1940, operated in the name of God, Law, and Democracy, at a time when the United States was redefining its policies towards its former ally, Russia, and towards China. It sought to frighten all citizens into orthodoxy by persecuting some who had lapsed into the heresy, many years earlier, of belonging to the Communist Party or one of its affiliates. Not long after my return to the *Herald Tribune*'s Washington bureau, Cardinal Spellman, speaking to army and navy chaplains on the arrest, by Hungarian communist authorities, of Cardinal Stepinac, warned against "the brutal bludgeons of communism". In November 1946, a full-page advertisement in the *Herald Tribune* trumpeted against "the menace of Red Fascism", a curious contradiction in terms, but one which stirred the imagination of the gullible, led to the commencement of a search for Reds under every bed, and culminated in the so-called McCarthy Era, during which Washington became a hotbed of malicious gossip, friends turned foe, and nobody was safe from the accusatory finger of Senator Joseph McCarthy.

Part of my job with the *Herald Tribune* was to cover the "McCarthy hearings". I listened with silent outrage as the ignoble senator peppered proceedings with: "Point of order, Mr. Chairman, point of order . . ." and questions beginning, "Isn't it a fact . . . ?" I came out of these "hearings" with an acute realization of how serious a defect it was that the American congressional system, in some ways so much more sensitive than parliamentary democracy, was unable to rid itself of an incubus like McCarthy, despite the widespread aversion he aroused in millions of solid citizens. In a parliamentary set-up a hostile vote might have forced his resignation, but there was no such machinery in the Senate. Ultimately, McCarthy solved the dilemma himself. He committed hara-kiri by attacking a fellow senator. He had slandered with impunity private citizens and had grossly abused, persecuted, and reduced to desperation eminent, able, and conscientious public servants by impugning their loyalty with baseless charges of political irregularity; victims of his haphazard malice saw their careers and futures ruined with no more recourse to justice or reparation than had a Roman citizen who came under the unfavourable notice of Nero. I knew men whose careers had been destroyed by this monster and I longed to be able to avenge my friends by denouncing their destroyer. I heard, at second hand, that he had sent his secretary on a lengthy furlough at the expense of the tax-payer, to give her a chance to conceal the fact that he had impregnated her. But while rumours like this — and worse peccadilloes—were current on Capitol Hill, there was no way of letting the public know the facts.

McCarthy's self-destruction, when the Senate to a man took notice of the fact, came in a careless hour when "Tail-Gunner Joe" took on the diminutive Senator Tobey of New Hampshire, referring to him as "a natural phenomenon, since he has neither belly nor head". This was perceived at once to have been a mistake, for as McCarthy's sidekick, Senator Jenner, observed, "You can say what you like about the ordinary Joe and nobody gives a damn, but a Senator is a different breed of cat." It was Jenner's contribution to American political tradition, and it was profound, although perhaps unflattering to that great deliberative assembly, the U.S. Senate. Senator Tobey saw his chance for a double play to vindicate himself, and to restore the Senate's tarnished image when he announced from the floor one day that "the Emperor has no clothes on".

McCarthy's downfall was mourned by few; while the witch hunt he had instigated continued for several years, it was conducted with ever-lessening vehemence, and left Washington reporters, myself included, time to observe more brilliant luminaries of the Senate.

There was a hoary tradition in the Senate that the "common touch" could be preserved and retained by an affected folksiness which featured downgrading the English language through deliberate sloppiness or emphasis on Americanisms. Southerners were particularly addicted to antique usages which stressed their identity as Confederates without any Yankee alloy. Other senators had to resort to striking dress or mannerisms.

The Texans tried to ride both horses, with unhappy results. "Old Tawm" Connally, for example, affected a rancher's bluntness. By virtue of seniority he introduced new members to the Chamber, assigning them seats high up on the rim of the hemicycle with a promise of advancement to the patrician front rows with time and good conduct, and warning them that it was "draughty up there", but if they felt the wind whistling too keenly around their legs, they would be well advised to glance down and make sure nobody had stolen their pants. Aside from

190

this jovial streak, Senator Connally was a heavy, sadistic, old bully who sought to offset his lack of distinction by oddities in clothing, such as his string-tie, cowhand pin, and untidy disarray. He affected contempt for anything foreign and disdained the manners and courtesy of the New England delegation, and particularly the Bostonian Kennedys, as effeminate and weak. Senator Connally was nevertheless a potent force in the Senate, which he ruled by fear. He demanded and received favours from the ruling president, and from the vice-president who presided *ex officio* over the Senate, which he repaid with contempt. Even the powerful Kennedys were awed. Lesser men trembled at his wrath. He ruled his state like a Persian satrap, but with no more loyalty to the ruler in Washington than the rebellious satrap Tissaphernes in Ionia had to Cyrus in Persia.

Senator Connally bullied little Senator Tobey of New Hampshire, but he was careful not to take issue with Jenner or McCarran, still less with Joe McCarthy, who made the Senate their washpot.

Despite a few questionable characters, the United States Senate in my day assembled a group of distinguished citizens who toiled like dogs, during long hours, for little credit and much abuse, uncertain of the tenure, with the bogey of re-election forever haunting their slumbers.

It has become a tradition among cartoonists to portray senators as bumbling old men with stubbly beards and protruding bellies. The caricature is untypical. The senators I watched were for the most part slender men, clean-shaven, with neat haircuts and generally conservative clothes; Senator Connally was an exception. Daily, they drove themselves unmercifully, sitting attentively in committee from nine to noon or later, taking their seats on the Senate floor as soon as it convened, usually about two o'clock. Each senator sits there alert and wary, lest a watchful reporter in the press gallery catch him nodding, or an opponent try to slip over a unanimous-consent fast, one which will bring howls of rage and anguish from his state unless he detects the hook and rises to his feet to make the standard objection concealed in the formula: "Reserving my right to object, I wish to declare in measured terms my unmeasured rejec-

191

tion of this insidious proposal ... ", and so on, as long as the senator can enunciate, standing beside his desk. If he moves more than three steps away to restore circulation to his aching feet, he loses the floor. The president *pro tem* of the Senate recognizes the gentleman from somewhere else, and away go his chances for fame and re-election, all because of a weak bladder and forgetting to attach his urine bag before he came on the floor. In the evening he must attend some dinner for visiting worthies or important voters, and then stagger off to bed to have his sleep interrupted by impertinent telephonists.

The senator arises early and hurries off to breakfast at the Senate cafeteria, where his table must be open to visiting firemen and self-promoting political climbers. He gets rid of them on the valid excuse that his most important committee convenes at 9:15 a.m. to consider the bill which he introduced on the Senate floor yesterday, and which he must now conduct hearings on. No wonder he develops high blood pressure, arteriosclerosis, calculus, and other ailments due to long hours, irregular diet, tension, uncertainty about the future, and regrets for the past.

The rigid rule of seniority, which governs every post a senator can aspire to, demands that he give absolute priority to re-election. If he fails to hold his seat, he slumps to the bottom of the ladder, and all his investment in seniority is wiped out. The wonder is that under such handicaps a group of citizens of such high calibre convene in the south wing of the Capitol, where they have functioned with — on the whole — such signal success, for nearly two hundred years.

As the Senate tended to relieve stodginess by eccentricity, the House also made a deliberate study of the unconventional. Thus one member, a Southerner, always turned up in a black frock coat with a red carnation in the buttonhole, while Tinkham of Massachusetts set a spanking pace by dying his full beard purple. There was no competition, which I thought a pity; the hemicycle could have done with an extra spot or two of colour, like geraniums in a bed of ivy.

I ordered the *Congressional Record* delivered daily to my office, and made a point always to leaf through it before filing it carefully. This was important, because every six months or so, it produced a voluminous index, drawn up with meticulous care. This was a gold mine, and since few of my colleagues were aware of its value, I had the field to myself and was forever panning out little nuggets, such as editors like to frame in "boxes". Since the insertions in the *Record* were libel-proof, being privileged, it was sometimes necessary, when I allowed enthusiasm to outrun discretion, to hurry up to the Hill to get a squib into the *Record* before it began to fester. I always had a few legislators on hand whom I could rely on to rise and say: "Mr. President, I ask unanimous consent that the conclusion of my remarks be inserted at this point in the *Record*," and the presiding officer would drone out: "Without objection it is so ordered."

Capitol Hill is a rabbit-warren of burrows and tunnels, some equipped with the electric monorail line, others merely for walkers. I studied them carefully during my years in Washington, until I was able to take visiting firemen, editors, and similar nuisances on an impressive underground tour, popping up surprisingly in a garden, a park, an office building, or a public gallery. It was practical knowledge, for it cut minutes off my time from the lobby to a free telephone line, which often enabled me to beat the ticker with my story, a feat which was regarded with more admiration than it merited, since any fool reporter could learn his way around the underground in a few days if he put himself to it seriously.

In the course of one of my exploratory rambles, I rolled into the Senate monorail platform on the front seat, usually reserved for senators, but vacant when I climbed aboard that day. As I stepped off, I was approached by a lady who asked for my autograph. I obliged. Then she asked: "What state are you from, Senator?" I suppose that the handsome pigskin portfolio, acquired from the Office of Strategic Services, which I always carried, stamped me as a legislative giant. I replied, "Virginia, Ma'am," knowing my accent would pass for the North Face — Alexandria perhaps — and that there were hordes of Menefees in the Old Dominion if she cared to challenge me. She chose not to, rather to my regret, for I was prepared to gratify her with an ancestral tree going back to George Menefee, whose seven-teenth-century will bestowed hogsheads of tobacco on deserving relatives unto the third and fourth generation.

A lode which I worked intensively with great profit was the Pentagon. I concentrated on the U.S. Marines, who were treated like stepchildren by Army and Navy types, and were only too happy to get some of their own back by suggesting lines of approach which an inquiring reporter could follow with benefit to himself, his paper, the country—and the U.S. Marine Corps. The Marine Corps specialized in amphibious landings and in "close support" of ground troops. The Army and Air Force did lip-service to this role but skimped on pilot training, making its efforts far more dangerous to its own side than to the enemy. The Navy developed its specialized theories about naval support of ground operations, and the Air Force thought its job had been done when it had plastered everything in sight with the most powerful explosives it could lift. Marines, skimping along on one-tenth of what the Air Force annually wasted, were only too happy to reveal the "soft underbelly" of the monster, and I was only too happy to stick my little pin into it. The Marines gave me my chance.

I had got to know the United States Marine Corps through my careful reading of the *Army and Navy Journal*, in which an article by a Marine Corps colonel had stood out like a gem among the standard service dross. I was so impressed that I got in touch with Colonel Robert Heinl, U.S.M.C., and found him informed, articulate, and competent. Also he understood that the only way the public could support what the Marine Corps was doing was if the public was told what the Corps was doing at that time—fighting for its life against the Army, which was trying to snatch one of its four divisions, and the Navy, which was trying to rip off its Air Arm, in alliance with the U.S. Air Force, which wanted its close-support role, and the planes, money, personnel, rank, and Table of Organization which went with it. By judicious publicity I exposed this murderous cabal, and after that I could do no wrong with the Marine Corps. The other services put me on the "enemy list", but since they had never bothered to give me more than the back of their hand, I had no compunction about screwing them every chance I got—and they gave me plenty. I never enjoyed myself more; the Marine Corps tipped me off to likely stones to look under, and it was no trick at all to uncover fantastic military incompetence and waste while innocently commenting on the efficiency and relative economy of the Marine Corps.

This was not just a propaganda gimmick. The Marine Corps had qualities which I recognized and approved. For instance, the Marines cultivated discipline, while the U.S. Army still believed that "permissiveness" paid off in initiative under stress. A U.S. Army company in those days fell in like a disorganized rabble, slovenly in dress and bearing, pushing permissiveness to the point at which a group slouched off rather than marched away. The Marines on the other hand cultivated "spit and polish", and marched as if they meant it. They had the advantage of a long, honourable service tradition which the Army, having less, affected to disdain. One of the Marines' cherished regimental memories was that there had always been Marines in Washington even during the War of 1812-1814, when the occupying forces were Marines: British Marines, to be sure, but still Marines. The Royal Marines appeared in Washington again as Winston Churchill's bodyguard, and they looked impressive standing sentry at the northwest gate of the White House, with a U.S. Marine on the other side, both of them polished up to the nines.

The Marines specialized in one of the most difficult operations: sending landing parties ashore to establish bridge-heads, and then organizing combined operations by land, sea, and air forces to extend and amplify the bridge-head into a permanent base and depot. It demanded exquisite precision to observe the time-table, which was essential to preserve the operation from becoming a shambles; precision obtained only through careful planning and endless exercises. Heinl secured a post for me at one of these practice drills, which assumed an infantry assault after intensive aerial preparation. The Marines would provide the assault troops; the Air Force would do the softening-up job.

"They've been yammering for years about taking over our air and its role in combined ops," Heinl said to me. "Now we'll give them their chance, and you might be interested to see what they do with it." He knew damn well what they'd do with it, but he wanted me to see for myself.

I jumped at the chance. Heinl warned me that in case I wrote anything about the show, it would be carefully vetted for security, but I was more interested in informing myself than in writing up this particular show. I figured that a good grandstand participation would give me a yard-stick against which I could assess bolts of press-relations embroideries, and a pair of shears to cut them down to size. It would be a "constant", like the physicist Planck's, but in this case "Minifie's constant". I cherished the idea. So I sat happily in the bleachers one sultry afternoon, watching medium bombers dive-bombing the target. It was impressive, but I wondered whether the precision would stand up to sophisticated anti-aircraft defence.

"We're bringing in an Air Force heavy to take care of that," Heinl assured me. "And there he is... over there! Hold on to your seat!"

I suggested that perhaps we were unpleasantly close to the target area in case any drops went wild. He answered: "They'd better not! I posted plenty of brass down in the front row to make sure of that. . . . But watch it! Watch it! Here comes the big one now, out of the west!"

I turned, to see a tiny shape wheeling in the western sky. He was making a target run; columns of dirty smoke towered into the sky like thunderheads.

"Hullo!" I commented unkindly. "He cut his load a bit early, didn't he? Fell a bit short."

No answer from Heinl. The tiny plane-profile turned, heading back the way he had come.

"Where d'you suppose he's headed for now?" I asked.

Heinl replied grimly: "He doesn't know it, but he's headed for Indochina."

This startled me, but I recognized it as a first-class nugget of information, which might develop into a bonanza if I started panning. There was not much to be got out of the Marines on the subject, and they were uncomfortable under my questions. They were obviously committed in Southeast Asia, since the Air Force had heavy bombers there—as the unthinking exclamation of my cicerone had revealed; it was obviously considered a hardship-post to which dumbo pilots were being assigned to get them out of Headquarters' hair — a standard operating procedure.

As soon as I got home, I pulled out my file of brochures and maps put out by the oil companies for shareholders. I had invested in an occasional share or two of the big international oil firms, for the sake of such information on their activities, or some of them, as was deemed advisable for shareholders to know. I was not surprised to find that they were pouring money into costly off-shore drilling in Southeast Asian waters with very favourable indications for profitable discoveries.

With this under my belt, I went to see friends in the State Department who had levelled with me in the past with confidences which I had not abused. Sure enough, they said, "Keep an eye on those parts. They're getting real hot." They reeled off names: Cambodia, Laos, Thailand, Annam, Cochin China—the debris of the French colonial empire which was lying around for anyone to pick up.

The Department's Far East desk was resigned, pointing out that it had been too heavy a financial burden for the French to carry any longer, so why on earth did Uncle Sam want to adopt this horse-leech with two bellies that would be an interminable drain on his money, men, resources, morale, and international goodwill, just to ensure security and a clean title for the big oil corporations who have crude running out of their ears already? I left that question to the experts, and they are still trying to puzzle out some answers.

I never joined enthusiastically in the popular parlour game of "Seeing Reds under Beds". I once horrified my State Department contact by suggesting that it would serve the communists right if we poured the whole can of worms into their laps and let them try to cope. "That would never do," said State, "they'd soon have all China's 700,000,000 inhabitants under their control." I was never very impressed with this argument. Trying to "control" that vast people had absorbed all the energies of the Mongols and the Manchus for thousands of years. Control of China had been too much for Britain, France, Germany, Japan, and the United States, jointly and severally, despite a hundred years of capitulations, concessions, customs dues, and lavish expenditures of men and money, on the excuse that tea and silk were not luxuries but basic commodities for which China was holding the West to ransom. I recalled how profitable the West had found it to destroy the Chinese monopolies. Italy acquired new industries by raising silk-worms and planting mulberry trees to feed them on; and tea was soon shown to be as brittle a monopoly as silk, since it grew as exuberantly in the mountains of Assam or the hills of Ceylon as in China. So all the legends about Chinese monopolists holding the West to ransom were blown up by the first application of facts.

A similar fate attended the effort to create a monopoly of coffee, which exercised the world in the interbellum years. The monopoly once enjoyed by the province of Yemen, in southern Arabia, where the true Mocha is still produced, was destroyed by plantations in Java, Ceylon, Surinam, and Jamaica, while the market was overwhelmed by unfettered production in Brazil, which bore down the price so disastrously that coffee was actually burned as fuel to keep the markets under control.

I was surprised to find both Congress and the Marine Corps following the coffee crisis closely. Heinl pointed out that Puerto Rico was a very important Marine Corps base and training area, hence politically sensitive. In the same way, any political disturbance in Costa Rica, Nicaragua, or Honduras created exquisitely sensitive tremors along the Panama Canal. The Marines were particularly allergic to any mention of Nicaragua, where the "bandit" Sandino had led them an embarrassing chase, forever surrounded and forever slipping through their fingers in a serial thriller that reminded me of the adventures of my boyhood hero "Captain Montana", the prototype of all Captain Midnights. Heinl admitted ruefully that Sandino had outfoxed every task force sent to destroy him, but claimed that his very successes had been used to obtain weapons, aircraft, and specialized equipment from Congress.

When the next Central American revolution broke out, I conned the bureau into okaying a trip to the Scene of Diction, as I put it, but only on condition that it did not cost the paper even the fare to Brownsville, Texas, which was just across the Rio

Grande from Mexico, and therefore just the place from which to cover high jinks in Honduras, the bureau thought.

I promoted a ride on a Navy plane proceeding to Houston for manoeuvres, and was soon stowed away comfortably aboard a carrier—I forget just which, but I believe she was the *Saratoga*. When I wrote "comfortably" I mis-spoke myself; nobody is comfortable aboard a carrier. Since they carry enormous quantities of high-test aviation gasoline, smoking is strictly *verboten*; matches have to be parked on embarkation, and shoes must have no steel trim which might create sparks. During night operations, carriers are a bad dream.

I had a berth under the flight deck. A returning plane landed on the deck and crashed into the check-rope with a noise as if the entire ship were coming apart. One of the landings failed to follow Standard Operating Procedure, which resulted in a strange pattern of crashes, punctuated by a loudspeaker voice from the bridge, demanding to know "What has happened?" I would have liked to know myself, but no bullhorn answered the bridge, so I swung out of my berth and dropped to the floor in the dark, nearly crippling myself when I caught the edge of the deck on the way. I limped topside and was promptly shooed down below again, until the wreckage of the plane had been dumped overboard and the loose gasoline cleaned up. I was no great company at breakfast, but still felt I had to rise to a challenge and test the merits of the short-run catapult which had just been installed. It was a new steam job, developed by the British, which flung planes into the air with a force of seven G — seven times gravity. Perhaps I ought to try it just to see how it felt. The body could not stand much more, but the plane might not clear the onrushing carrier unless launched with plenty of reserve speed. It was touch and go anyway, I was told; but if I would sign a waiver to any claims for compensation in event of mishap, I could try it out for myself.

I knew that if I failed to rise to this challenge I would be washed up as a service reporter, so I put on my best grin, smiled with my good eye, and stared the Chief Petty Officer down with my glass eye; it came in very useful for staring down brass, and I used to enjoy making them wilt and glance away.

So, before long, I was strapped into a bucket seat and the CPO was instructing me about position. The engine revved up, and with a roar the catapult piston lunged, the restraining ring broke, and I felt as if I were heading for the moon. No sweat; a quiet swing around for a look at the carrier, then a terrifying approach, bumping down on deck, and another desperate yank as the plane caught the crash-wire. I have never been more thankful than when I climbed out of my harness and went below for a coffee to find myself something of a notoriety — a cross between a hero and a fool, with the accent on the latter. However, I comforted myself with the reflection that the next time I wrote about carrier operations, I would know what I was saying.

FIFTEEN

Pentagon matters were of great interest to me, but assignments I covered as a member of the White House Press Corps were of equal fascination since they gave me the opportunity to observe at first hand the character and characteristics of four United States presidents: Harry S. Truman, Dwight D. Eisenhower, and, after I joined the Canadian Broadcasting Corporation, John F. Kennedy and Lyndon Baines Johnson.

Mr. Truman inherited the White House from Franklin D. Roosevelt amid general dismay, which he shared. He was a modest little man with an overwhelming sense of the greatness of the office which had been thrust upon him. His biggest handicap was his conviction of his own inadequacy to fill it, but being a gutsy man of high courage, he soon found himself rising to the level of his high office. His attitude and outlook are conveyed by two anecdotes. He was an avid traveller and was as determined as any tourist from his native Missouri to see all that was to be seen in the world. This, and his love of history, brought him, after the termination of his presidency, to Salerno, where Allied forces had established a bridge-head during the Second World War. When Mr. Truman visited that forbidding beach, and looked up at the mountains which ringed it around, his training as an artilleryman could no longer be contained. Newsmen trailing him heard him say: "What squirrel-headed general picked *this* for a landing beach?" The words were no sooner out of his mouth than Mr. Truman realized that the "squirrel-headed general", Eisenhower, was no less than the current incumbent of the White House, and that his unthinking reaction could be taken to reflect on the great office of the presidency. He tried to rephrase his thought, but the first impression endured, and the harder he tried to erase it, the more he emphasized it; so he gave up.

Mr. Truman's next bid for lapidary immortality came as he was rambling through St. Paul's Cathedral in London reading the monumental tributes to the great departed. The inevitable reporter popped out from behind a sarcophagus, to ask: "What would you like on *your* tombstone, Mr. President?" Without a moment's hesitation, Mr. Truman replied, "Just say: He done his damndest."

Back in the United States, when he was on another safari to give "The Word to the Sticks" during his presidency, the Republicans in Congress set up a "Truth Committee". Mr. Truman was an exuberant, gossipy speaker, whose thoughts often left truth straggling far behind. The Truth Committee's job was to correct and counteract Trumanian hyperbole before it became a part of the national treasury of quotable un-facts. It tried to set up shop within an hour of Mr. Truman's departure, to catch the same crowd. At St. Paul, Minnesota, Mr. Truman gave a rousing war cry to the faithful gathered before the main hotel, while the Truth Committee hung out of a sixth-floor window, catching his every word, for immediate refutation. Mr. Truman headed back to the presidential train, to which a press coach had been attached — a convenient arrangement which gave our coverage spectacular immediacy. In the evening, Mr. Truman came back to the press car, inquiring: "Well, boys, how did I do today?"

I moved to his side: "Mr. President," I said, "did you realize that while you were talking to your crowd, the Senate Truth Committee were hanging out of a sixth-floor window just over your head?"

Mr. Truman snorted: "Truth Committee!" he laughed. "Those six are the damndest liars in the Senate, and I ought to know."

Anecdotes were bound to collect around such an earthy character as Mr. Truman. He welcomed them, and, I suspect, even launched some of his own. For instance, the Trumans had to move across the street to Blair House, while the White House underwent repairs. When these were completed, Mr. Truman took the press on an escorted tour of the White House. Pointing with his cane to the ceiling, he said: "Right there is where the leg of my bathtub came through, so we knew repairs were in order. I said to the Madam [he always referred to Mrs. Truman as 'the Madam'] I said: 'Supposing the bath had come right through with me in it, in the middle of one of your ladies' meetings!' "

"What did Mrs. Truman say to that?" we asked.

Mr. Truman assumed his naughty-boy face of innocence. "She'd have liked to slap my face," he admitted.

He greatly honoured the Washington press by accepting an invitation to lunch at the National Press Club, under house rules which permit quotable questions and answers immediately after the dessert and coffee. He must have known that he would be questioned about General Douglas MacArthur, whom he had just removed from his Korean command.

"Do you still think you did right to fire General MacArthur?" someone asked. Mr. Truman took one step back as he often did when he felt wicked. Then he shot:

"General MacArthur twice disobeyed the orders of his Commander-in-Chief, and he got what was coming to him!"

This brought the Press Club to its feet in an ovation, the like of which I never saw there before or since. One hundred and twenty seconds later Mr. Truman wiped his spectacles and sat down.

He was a strong believer in keeping people informed of his views and policies; the only way to do that, he thought, was to meet with as many small groups as possible, rather than to talk impersonally to thousands at a party rally. He put his beliefs into practice by the whistle-stop technique. This called for the campaign train to halt briefly at any crossing where a group had gathered — informed of the stop by timely notices in the local papers. Mr. Truman would appear on the back platform of the last coach; then Mrs. Truman and his daughter Margaret, to whom he was devoted, joined him, and the President would tear into a give-'em-hell speech, with plenty of fire and brimstone for the Republicans, seasoned with carefully prepared local references, and fulsome praise for his wife, Bess, and for Margaret. The rustics cheered and shouted "Give 'em hell, Harry," the engineer rang his bell, reporters scurried back to their car, the presidential train slid out of another whistle-stop, and Mr. Truman went back to his private quarters to refresh himself.

The basic technique was used with great effect when Princess Elizabeth visited the United States. Mr. Truman, an affectionate man, took a shine to her right away, and presented her to her admirers as proudly as if she had been his own daughter, instead of the future Queen of England. Mr. Truman also kept her portrait hanging in his bedroom in the White House, next to one of his favourite prairie landscapes.

There was a peril for reporters covering Mr. Truman. They became so fond of the earthy little guy that it was almost impossible to give an impartial account of his views, words, and deeds. He was Mr. Average American personified and idealized. This was vividly apparent when the Democratic Party gave thousands of its local organizers a bonus outing to Washington and a chance to meet the President. Assembled in the vast Armory were hundreds of little guys, the spitting image of Mr. Truman, as if they all came from the same mid-Western mould, which they pretty much did.

Mr. Truman's decision not to stand for a third term as President was made on the day of his inauguration in 1949, though it was not revealed at the time, of course. The search for a suitable Democratic candidate led the party's organizers to Adlai E. Stevenson, then governor of Illinois, but Stevenson, a man of high principle, was no match for the *Herald Tribune*'s White Hope, and the Republican Party's choice, General Dwight D. Eisenhower. As early as November 1946, there had been rumours, swiftly denied, that General Eisenhower would eventually run for the presidency; by late 1950, he was receiving endorsements from leading Republican politicians, including Thomas E. Dewey, a contender in the 1948 presidential campaign.

General Eisenhower had demonstrated his ability to control

the wild horses of the divergent Allies during the Second World War, and he accompanied this with a becoming mildness towards Congressional committees. He was not a political animal, however; this showed in his presidential campaign, and I shared the view of other informed Washingtonians that he never did grasp, as Mr. Truman had, the immense responsibilities of the President.

For the campaign he set up a modest, hard-to-find office in the Pentagon, to which I was expected to be able to guide the *Tribune*'s brass whenever it wanted to find out what policy, if any, was fermenting in the White Hope's mind; but this assignment was also parcelled out among the bureau staff, so I had no chance to develop the really intimate channels of information among his military staff and civilian secretaries (with the exception of his Chief of Staff) that I had enjoyed with F.D.R. and Mr. Truman. However, this did not matter much, for all business moved through the extremely capable hands of General Bedell Smith; "The Beetle" knew Ike's reluctance to make decisions — he had long personal experience to teach him — so he moved in where other lepidoptera feared to fly and gave "yes" or "no" replies to all comers. I enjoyed this association which lasted from my early days with the Canadian Broadcasting Corporation until Ike's political death, January 20, 1961, when the romantic and tragic star of John F. Kennedy all too briefly illuminated the White House.

I repeated with J.F.K. the mistake I had made with F.D.R. and Truman, that of idolizing him, so I was blind to his faults, which might have been disastrous for his great office had he lived, for he was arrogant, tyrannical, and ruthless. He ignored Congress and shook off impatiently any attempt to restrict his power. He left precedents for personal government that a succeeding president found only too convenient. However, at the time neither I nor my colleagues — not even the *Chicago Tribune* man — could resist that easy grace and body and mind which made a boomerang of every dart we flung at him.

I cherish the memory of the last time I saw him alive — a chilly afternoon in early fall when he strode out of the south gate of the

205

White House grounds, into the Oval, Jackie trotting alongside, to greet personally the pipe band of the 48th Highlanders, the Black Watch. The autumn colours tinted the leaves as the low, descending sun cast daddy-long-legs shadows across the turf. The romantic figures of Kennedy and his attractive wife combined with the nostalgic cry of the pipes to choke our throats; even the *Chicago Tribune* man wiped his lens surreptitiously with his handkerchief when he thought nobody was looking.

Within a few weeks of that parade J.F.K. had flown down to Texas, to his appointment with destiny in Dallas, and shortly afterwards I sat on the hillside at Arlington National Cemetery watching the coffin being lowered into a hole in the ground; autumn sunshine again, but in my heart a wintry conviction that I should never see his like again. The light in the White House had faded. I had no wish to cover the White House with Lyndon B. Johnson, although the first thing the 36th President and Mrs. Johnson did was to invite the White House press to go through the executive mansion to observe how carefully everything belonging to the Kennedys had been left in place; there was even a photograph in a silver frame of Jackie astride a fat piebald cob, and snapshots of the future president in baby clothes. It was a heavy-handed effort to stress continuity of tradition, personality, and policy between the old and new regimes—but to some of us it seemed like Robert Green's "upstart crow, beautified with our feathers ... with his tiger's heart wrapped in a player's hide".

Tiger's heart or not, Lyndon Johnson had to be covered, but it was a melancholy stint, for Johnson was a callous man, with a warped, sadistic spirit. The only time I saw him look really happy was during Chairman Khrushchev's visit to the United States in 1964. After a luncheon with the governor of New Jersey, Johnson and Khrushchev were to show themselves to the press. We gathered outside the Governor's Mansion; but a heavy thunderstorm came up, and we moved under a tree, seeking this dangerous refuge to avoid getting soaked. Even so, we looked like drowned rats when Johnson and Khrushchev came out onto the balcony. Seeing our pitiful condition, Khrushchev looked uncomfortable, but Johnson's face beamed with a happy smile.

It was a revealing reaction that I could never quite accept, even from the chief of state.

I became more and more reluctant to cover his White House press conferences, and to listen quietly to sneers at "the press", which he blamed for his growing unpopularity. But I bottled up my feelings and welcomed, like any other toady, a chance to visit his ranch in Texas, telling myself that it was all part of the education of a correspondent.

It was educational, sure enough. The ranch embraced thousands of acres, through which ran a small stream, dammed at one point to create a little lake. If it had been the Oxus and the Aral Sea, Mr. Johnson could not have been prouder of his puddle. The grass was overstocked with lean cattle, approximately shorthorn, which Mr. Johnson had turned to after a vain attempt to cultivate the Texas longhorn, of which a moth-eaten trophy was mounted in the mess hall.

He ranged his domain in a white Mercury convertible, followed by an obsequious range-master in a Ford pick-up. The Mercury, silent as a shadow, drew alongside me so quietly while I was walking along a narrow lane between two buildings that I nearly bumped into it. Looking down in astonishment, I found myself gazing into the knobby, brown features of the President of the United States. Neither of us showed any signs of enjoying the encounter, and the Mercury pulled silently ahead before I had quite recovered my wits. I followed it into the pasture where it drew up briefly before a wretched heifer which was limping along on an injured leg. Mr. Johnson leaned over, gave her a cursory inspection, and ordered: "She's for the butcher," then he drove on. A ranch hand culled her out.

Mr. Johnson was not a compassionate man; he made no attempt to cultivate a sentiment he rejected. He despised his subordinates as men who, somewhere or other, had failed to meet the challenge of success; he had no patience with the restrained language of diplomacy, considering that it was better to use the plainest terms to make his meaning unmistakably clear. Plain terms were understood by Johnson to be coarse language, the fouler the better.

This was illustrated by an episode which occurred in the White

House and was reported to me on unimpeachable authority by a member of the Canadian commercial staff. His chat with President Johnson took place in the Oval Room. It was nearly over when there was a knock on the door, which opened to admit a junior officer of the State Department. Seeing the President, he gazed at him for a moment like a startled rabbit, then he bolted, slamming the door behind him. Mr. Johnson shot after him, and chased him down the corridor, hurling imprecations in Johnsonian invective, leaving his visitor wondering what distinction should or could be drawn between a trigger-tempered, over-burdened executive and a psychopathic maniac. Reports of such demonstrations of instability lent a peculiarly acrid flavour to suggestions of a connection, however tenuous, between the Texan in the White House and the tragedy at Dallas. These suggestions never became concrete enough to be traced to source, for proof or disproof, but they popped up here and there for years afterwards. Even the exhaustive labours of the Warren Commission and its report, which I read carefully, did not entirely allay the ghost of a suspicion that Lee Harvey Oswald was not a loner; but, in that case, who were the other members of the conspiracy, and who protected them and covered up their trail? Was there any connection between this "conspiracy" and the Watergate mystery, years later? My guess is that both blots on the American history books will be disputed until historians, many years from now, finally remove the shrouds of each case to reveal the bare bones of what really happened.

Bitter disputes raged in the Thirties over less sinister matters. The arguments revolved around the advent of radio and the place the new medium should occupy in relation to the printed news available in the daily press; the owners of the *Herald Tribune*, along with other newspaper magnates, deplored the entry of the air waves into what had been considered a "print" field. But F.D.R.'s fireside chats, then "spot" news broadcasts, made radio a family information-and-entertainment centre that appeared to whet the public's appetite for more news. Certainly, working at the *Tribune*, I was never aware of the paper's circulation dropping.

My first experience with radio, as a performer, came early in the war when I was the *Herald Tribune*'s London correspondent. Someone from the British Broadcasting Corporation, sharing a convivial evening in the Savoy's River Room, heard me recounting my convoy trip through the Straits of Dover to illustrate my contention that there was nothing to stories, rumours, and whispered from-the-horse's-mouth non-facts. "The Straits are open," I said. "I've just steamed through them, without any significant reaction either by land or air. So the closing of the Straits is all bullshit," I roared.

The BBC man thumped me on the back until he nearly dislocated my shoulder blade. "Come on over to the radio shack and tell that story," he said, "but leave off the last word." I went with him, rattled through an interview with a competent and kindly questioner, and discovered to my amazement that my voice had good resonance and recorded well. It was a "natural" for wireless, they said. More to the point, BBC paid me three guineas for my contribution, and asked me if I had any more "Rule Britannia" items. Without knowing how or why, I was "in radio", and my little gems floated on a flood tide of public excitement and interest which presented no selling problem. You could not miss, any more than you could get off the front page, with London blitz stories.

I was avid for action, by land, sea, or air—anything to get away from London. With this new outlet for my material I could look forward to months or perhaps years of adventurous living, reasonably well-paid. When a shipment of American planes came in to be transformed into medium-range patrol bombers I was there for the trial flight. These Lockheed Vega planes were better than nothing, but they were miserable crates to fly, and had a very limited bomb-load.

The addition of a gun turret aft made an inherently unstable plane into a man-killer—addicted to "ground-spins", sluggish at controls, and virtually incapable of defence. I had read and listened to much optimistic fiction about modified planes being so stable that, even with a dead pilot at the controls, they flew around for hours, until they ran out of fuel. I did not believe these fairy tales when they were put out, and nothing I saw or heard on the medium-bomber mission undermined my scepticism. It survived unblemished by any taint of credulity, as we swung east over the North Sea to maintain a "patrol" which spotted nothing but seals, upon which we wasted a few rounds—more to reassure the crew that the weapon would fire forward than from any hostility to seals.

As we bumped along an emergency landing strip so poorly maintained that no fast fighter could have survived a touchdown, I revised my already low assessment of Britain's air defences, and resolved to reject totally all Air Force guff about the situation being "in hand". But that was not the proper material for my stories, lest they seduce the enemy into trying a landing without first achieving air mastery. Unremitting propaganda had done its work; the Germans had convinced themselves that an amphibious landing could not be successful without command of the air. From what I saw of British preparations to meet invasion, I agreed with the United States Ambassador to the court of St. James, Joseph Kennedy, who was telling anyone who would listen that the Germans would go through Britain "like shit through a goose". The British defence authorities must have shared this estimate, or they would not have made such elaborate preparations to move the government to Wales, a caper which would have given the *coup de grâce* to British resistance.

I had to tread the difficult line between assuring my listeners that the situation was such as to make continued American assistance essential to maintaining the defences of the West, without encouraging the Germans to believe that one more effort would make it desperate. I fell back on the Austrian dictum that the situation was "desperate but never grave".

I felt in my heart that this was an honest summing-up of the position, and I kept it as a guideline when I was unexpectedly asked by NBC to do a transatlantic broadcast on American assistance: Was it useful or was it just throwing good American money down the drain?

I soon received two sharp lessons. The first was: If you tell it like it is, you will offend the pooh-bahs, in the system and out of it; secondly, if you don't offend them, you will offend most of the listeners who want a vicarious David-and-Goliath duel to the death. Faced by these unacceptable alternatives, I fell back on reporting what I saw, as I saw it, and never mind whose toes I trod on.

While covering Willkie's visit to London, I was asked by the Canadian Broadcasting Corporation to supply items on that visit, and for a time after I returned to Washington, later in 1941, I was officially designated the CBC's Washington correspondent. Naturally, this post slipped from my grasp while I was with the Office of Strategic Services, but, on returning to the capital in 1946, I was excited to find that the CBC had set up shop, after a fashion, and I set about turning this to my advantage, utilizing the wealth of experience I had amassed in the years I had been reporting for the printed medium. However, while I had done enough broadcasting to know that I did not have to worry about "mike fright", that was the extent of my knowledge.

My first broadcasts to Canadian audiences gave me a feeling of re-established contact with the country in which I had spent my boyhood; as letters from listeners started to appear in my mail-box, this feeling was reinforced, and I began attempting to give a Canadian viewpoint to some of my "think pieces" which were heard on Newsroundup, a program aired daily, Monday to Friday, immediately after the six-o'clock news. Other contributions were written for Capital Report and International Commentary.

As my involvement with the Canadian Broadcasting Corporation increased, my dissatisfaction with the *Herald Tribune* mounted. Although I had been employed by the paper for nearly twenty-five years, part of the time as a foreign correspondent, my position in the Washington bureau was as low man on the totem, and there seemed no likelihood of its changing. Early in 1953 I decided that my position had become untenable. To my great joy, about the same time, the CBC made overtures to me, suggesting that I might be interested in becoming the network's Washington correspondent on a full-time basis. I leapt at the chance, left my newspaper colleagues to whatever Fate had in

211

store for them, and, on May 1, l953, began an association with the corporation which lasted until I left Washington to live in Canada in 1968.

L'ENVOI

At the time of his death, in June 1974, James M. Minifie had completed the manuscript of this book only as far as 1953. Stopping as it does at that date his story leaves unrecorded the most remarkable achievements of this most remarkable man.

Soon after he became the searching mind and interpretive voice of the Canadian Broadcasting Corporation in Washington, the words "This is James M. Minifie" became the daily signal to which most literate Canadians responded with close attention. We knew that the report on what was happening in the greatest centre of world power in human history would be accurate in substance, clear in exposition, graceful in form. Day after day for more than fifteen years his commentary on events in the United States, and the significance of those events for Canada and the world, came to us with authority, wisdom, sympathy, and humour. He stood alone among Canadians at the top of his profession.

During his Washington years Minifie gradually consolidated his views on the major questions of Canadian foreign policy — views eventually brought together in his books *Peace Maker or Powder Monkey* and *Open at the Top*, and in a myriad of articles. The influence on Canadian opinion of his words, both written and spoken, cannot be measured, but it was both deep and wide.

Even after he "retired" to Victoria seven years ago, Don Minifie maintained his active interest in national and international affairs. His occasional broadcasts were fascinating in their recollection of events past, and in the relation of those events to the recurring crises of an increasingly complex and dangerous world.

This was a man whose restless and incisive mind illumined, for us all, the weaknesses and the cruelties, the foibles and the humours, the virtues and the values, of our baffling human existence. Moved to anger by injustice and deceit, he was quick to recognize and applaud integrity. Scornful of pretension and arrogance, his compassion for those who suffered was limitless and instant.

Then his voice fell silent. And all who knew him felt the loss of his strong and wholesome influence.

For in addition to his public services, Don Minifie was a man of private excellence. Not only was he an ornament to his profession, he was a stimulant to all good men and women, a strong support to every righteous cause, a valiant opponent of all that was false or dishonourable, mean or meretricious. And beyond all this, Don was a man who, without effort, by being the person he was, quickly won and permanently held the love of all his friends.

The world was a better place because he lived, and he will be long remembered.

HUGH KEENLEYSIDE
Victoria